On the Politics of Kinship

In this book, Hannes Charen presents an alternative examination of kinship structures in political theory.

Employing a radically transdisciplinary approach, *On the Politics of Kinship* is structured in a series of six theoretical vignettes or frames. Each chapter frames a figure, aspect, or relational context of the family or kinship. Some chapters are focused on a critique of the family as a state-sanctioned institution, while others cautiously attempt to recast kinship in a way to reimagine mutual obligation through the generation of kinship practices understood as a perpetually evolving set of relational responses to finitude. In doing so, Charen considers the ways in which kinship is a plastic social response to embodied exposure, both concealed and made more evident in the bloated, feeble, and broken individualities and nationalities that seem to dominate our social and political landscape today.

On the Politics of Kinship will be of interest to political theorists, feminists, anthropologists, and social scientists in general.

Hannes Charen is an adjunct assistant professor of philosophy, aesthetics, and critical theory at Pratt Institute in Brooklyn, New York.

Routledge Innovations in Political Theory

On the Politics of Kinship

Hannes Charen

Routledge
Taylor & Francis Group

NEW YORK AND LONDON

First published 2022
by Routledge
605 Third Avenue, New York, NY 10158

and by Routledge
4 Park Square, Milton Park, Abingdon, Oxon, OX14 4RN

Routledge is an imprint of the Taylor & Francis Group, an informa business

Library of Congress Cataloging-in-Publication Data
A catalog record for this title has been requested

ISBN: 978-1-032-20670-7 (hbk)
ISBN: 978-1-032-20671-4 (pbk)
ISBN: 978-1-003-26464-4 (ebk)

DOI: 10.4324/9781003264644

Typeset in Times New Roman
by Deanta Global Publishing Services, Chennai, India

Unpolitical attempts to break out of the bourgeois family usually lead only to a deeper entanglement in it, and it sometimes seems as if the fatal germ of society, the family, were at the same time the nurturing germ-cell of uncompromising pursuit of another. With the family there passes away, while the system lasts, not only the most effective agency of the bourgeoisie, but also the resistance which, though repressing the individual, also strengthened and produced him. The end of the family paralyzes its opposition.

– Theodor W. Adorno, *Minima Moralia*[1]

Note

1 Theodor W. Adorno, *Minima Moralia* (Brooklyn: Verso, 2018) 22.

Contents

Acknowledgments

I would first and foremost like to thank Lisabeth During and Simon Critchley who both inspired the curiosity and confidence required to commit to such a project. I especially want to thank Emily Stoddart for her patience, love, and encouragement. I also want to express my deepest appreciation to both Megan Kirby for her sensitive and insightful reading and comments, and Natalja Mortensen, my editor at Routledge for her commitment to this project and for her guidance and advice. I also want to thank everyone at Routledge who worked on producing this book for their excellent work.

Finally, I want to express my gratitude to so many of my students for their insights and courageous efforts and to my supportive colleagues at Pratt Institute, especially Macarena Gomez-Barris, Dan Boscov-Ellen, Cisco Bradley, Martin Dege, Lisabeth During (again), P.J. Gorre, May Joseph, Jennifer Telesca, Cynthia Tobar, and Zhivka Valiavicharska.

Introduction

Today the family is viewed by some as the seedbed of moral responsibility, by others as the root of social and biological domination. In tragedy and melodrama the family marks a site of haunting, a cause for murder, vengeance, or war, it signifies relations enrooted in mythic genealogies, ancestral fault, and theocratic continuity. At times the family is taken as a place of refuge, resistance, and mutual aid. It's often weaponized as a determination of enmity or index of stratification based on race, ethnos, or caste, it is just as often speciously constructed as evidence for the naturalization of the division of gender and the repression of women, as well as the exclusion of non-heteronormative and non-proprietary relations. This book follows an examination of the idea of *the family* as a political category that draws from social practices of intimacy – what I understand more generally as *kinship* – irreducible to the sanctioning logic of the state and its economic algorithms. My interest here is in critically considering the most basic terms of relationality, irreducible to and generally repressed by sanctioned family structures. What, for example, is the distinction between the formalization of the family and practices of kinship – in the sense of living in common – that exceed the terms of the normal and the pathological, ones that fail nuclear models of desire or Kantian dichotomies of reason (private and public), but that also move beyond the simple desire for transgression? How to critically examine relations intractable to the logic of commodification, and those activities non-translatable, non-transferable to capitalistic or fascistic ethnographies and ontologies? In order to consider kinship as an active set of relational practices, as tactile and tactical responses to repression, trauma, exploitation, and other adversities endemic to the political formalization of intimacy, a critique of the family is necessary.

Against the traditionalist frame, which determines the family as both a natural and progressively achieved relation, one that justifies privilege and status within the state, authoritarian patriarchy substantiated by guilt, and indoctrination for civil society (competition for social power, education – and simply for survival) I would like to recast *kinship* as a set of relational practices that could just as well serve as a point of departure for rethinking a socialist *politics of hapticity*, beyond a state-based *politics of enmity*. In other words, the communal, non-commodified, and non-rationalized aspect of what we call kin – not restricted to a particular

DOI: 10.4324/9781003264644-1

configuration or the myth of blood, and certainly not determined by some fatalistic Oedipal catastrophe – emerges as a potential bond of trust demanded in the face of trauma and embodied insecurity. It is this need that is exploited by the sanctioning power of the state, its underlying economic determinations, and overarching social mores in the administered organization of care and deprivation. This relational consciousness is not in opposition to – or a rational containment of – affect or sensation, but in alignment with it. On this basis, it gives birth to a new relational self, more formidable than what we call the family – in its official garb – or what could be called the traditionalist or more precisely the *reactionary family*.

Here I follow Corey Robin's thesis that reaction is not a position which demands the reinstatement of a lost regime – to reinstitute the old aristocracy for example – but rather one which laments the loss of a specific privilege, a loss framed as a fall from a prior social attunement to naturalized stratification – the standard concept of ideology as a set of ideas that obscure actual social relations.[1] From the reactionary perspective then, the previous regime, the one which gave way to revolution or reform, failed, and therefore must be destroyed along with the revolutionaries that sought to overthrow it. Its failure is evidence enough. In other words, the reactionary is not simply atavistic but rather seeks to recapture a lost social advantage while also punishing the previous regime for failing to secure it, for succumbing to progressive forces which must also, of course, be eliminated.

This nostalgic projection follows the basic logic of repression. For this reason, the reactionary appears as a new political force or movement, distinct from the old in form, it returns unrecognized, with the goal of reinstating what the previous generation failed to maintain. "It's a bloody business, to be sure, but how else to be an aristocrat when all that's solid melts into thin air".[2] The reactionary is possessed by the drive to regain the "private life of power" as Robin puts it. It is to reassert the prior structure of disparity by repressing the vulnerability of a particular group, determined by gender, class, nation, race, desire, and so on while increasing the vulnerability of others.

If, for example, the French Revolution led to the democratization of the aristocracy – or simply the broadening of aristocratic privilege – then the "erosion of the family" becomes a threat to the reactionary demand that social power is heritable; i.e. the principle of continuity is preserved. Important here is that "the family" becomes the site of a sacred bond ruined or corrupted by progressive ideas and social practices that threaten the structural monopoly on claims of relational legitimacy endemic to a state-based polity, e.g. among other things through the structure of citizenship.

But I would also push back on the idea that we forget about kinship altogether. While I sympathize with the gesture as the most obvious and direct way to eschew the domination of a particularly repressive form of social relation, it also seems as if too much is given away to frameworks that naturalize a specific form of kinship – i.e. the family – as the only recognizable and "healthy" form of relation and trust. Is there no way to recognize degrees of solidarity and intimacy without submitting to institutional transference via forms of social exclusion and authoritarian sedimentation?

This book works beyond disciplinary boundaries in order to consider themes of ethnography, solidarity and community, authority, political and economic violence, the work of grieving, political theology, and death, as well as the possibility for a relational-commons. These themes are critically relevant today in the face of the evident limits and failures of the nation-state and the militarized neoliberalism which has come to shape not only national and global economic and ecocidal political doctrines but has also come to permeate and penetrate our most intimate anxieties by producing new forms of isolation and abstract forms of dependency. In the face of a resurgent nationalist nostalgia which responds catastrophically to this anxiety, the task here is to rethink the contradictions of intimacy, trust, and political authority in terms of a *politics of kinship*, one that remains both critical and hopeful.

A Politics of Kinship

The following set of examinations, concerning the politics of kinship, are based on the distinction – and contradiction – between *the family* understood as a formal and formalizing institution determined by, and inscribed in, an overarching political structure that on the most general level we call the state or *polis*, along with the institutions of social authority it sanctions; as opposed to *kinship*, grasped here as a pliable and spontaneous set of relations that offer a complex range of social responses to conditions necessary for the flourishing of embodied, vulnerable, and relational life. In other words, I understand kinship as an active response to and negotiation with ontological finitude, and *the family* as its denial and repression.

In one sense the distinction between the family and kinship can be likened to the distinction between formal circumscription and spontaneous resistance respectively – the former as a mechanism to contain and prevent the latter. It is this notion of kinship that I suggest is activated as a necessary tactical response to insecurity, trauma, or crisis. It is also simply a matter of survival to form bonds of trust and intimacy through the intricate webs of discursive community, which as Hannah Arendt notes, is "necessary for a biologically weak and ill-fitted organism" such as human beings.[3] On the other, it is useful to frame the family as a political theological overdetermination of kinship which is rooted in the concept of personal property, etymologically indicated in the Latin *famulus*, meaning household servant or slave.

* * *

The conflict I am interested in exploring in these pages appears in the tension between these two dimensions of relation which reaches its apex in the contradiction between the encompassing, and thus authorizing force of a state-based political configuration – particularly one rooted in settler colonialism and capitalist modes of extraction – and the demand for adequate social responses to adversity found in the cultivation of immediate, affective, and elastic relations of care. Put more simply and directly, the organic political mediation of necessity authorizes the establishment of sanctioned enclosures in determining access to the satisfaction of needs that in turn – in a circular fashion – realizes that very structure of authorization. It is the neutralization of this tautological structure which immunizes it from critique.

The variable access to the means for satisfying the demands of life, the flourishing of relations of intimacy and care – for example in grieving[4] – and the mutual sensibility those relations are predicated on are articulated in practices that persist beyond the political codification of intimacy. Insofar as *the family* becomes the legally circumscribed form of intimate relation within the state or *polis*, it also becomes, through the very force of authorization, a mechanism of exclusion. But also, potentially and hopefully, practices of kinship can indicate, produce, or enact fecund sites of resistance. This at least is what I attempt to consider in each of the chapters that follow.

In order to approach such a vast, complicated, and perhaps inexhaustible topic such as kinship, this book is organized as a series of frames. As the term implies each section casts and frames a figure, aspect, or relational context of the family or kinship. This allows for a modular approach that also presents an open-ended project that can be extended in various ways as the politics of kinship is considered beyond the pages of this book. In other words, it offers a way to open an active and synthetic discourse on kinship without pretensions to exhaustion or completion.

The Anti-Social Family

To introduce the space of inquiry I will begin with a brief but important illustration of a provocative critique of the family written in the 1980s by British philosophers and social theorists Michèle Barrett and Mary McIntosh called *The Anti-Social Family*. This allows for a direct entry point into key issues in the critique of the family, and it will also reveal some of the limits of a specific approach as we move beyond it.

Reflecting the title of their collaborative book published in 1982, Barrett and McIntosh argue that the family in Western industrialized societies is fundamentally *anti-social*. They initiate the discussion by contrasting Michael Anderson's work on family history, in which he claims there can be "no simple history of the Western family since the sixteenth century because there is not, nor has there ever been, a single-family system"[5] with Olivia Harris' question: "why then, given all we know about the variation in domestic arrangements, is it so common to find the domestic domain treated as universal, or at least a very widespread institution?"[6] This is followed by a reference to the work of Peter Laslett who contends that the idea of the extended – or non-nuclear – family in Western Europe is simply a myth.[7] He argues, it has always been the case that the nuclear family is the default configuration of kinship systems in "modern Western" societies. In other words, for Laslett, the modern family is fundamentally nuclear. The confusion, Barrett and McIntosh note, comes from the range of definitions attributed to "the family" in common parlance. A dictionary, they point out, will give you something like the following: (1) a group of people living in one household, (2) an association defined by the parent, child, sibling relation regardless of whether they share the same home, and (3) those who claim descent from the same ancestors, kindred.

Barrett and McIntosh are writing at a time and place (the United Kingdom under Thatcher) where the ideal of the family as a privileged social relation was supposedly built into economic life. An overarching normative social standard that equated the nuclear family configuration with happiness and success just seemed natural.

> Every other aspect of social life is planned on the assumption that people live in families. Those who do not are isolated and deprived .... The popular image of the family – the married couple living with their young children – is constantly projected as the image of normality and happiness.[8]

According to some (let's call this the traditionalist perspective), the nuclear familial configuration is ideal, and its failure is taken as the source of the general erosion of social hierarchy – Aristotelian, Abrahamic, or Confucian teleologies for example – necessarily transmitted by the authority of the rational-father-provider and thus a sign of social disorder and decay. It is framed as a moral dilemma that threatens the very foundations of the polis, nation, or even "civilization".[9]

On another level, what was presumably lost or threatened at that time was a social justification for a market-driven economy that preserved and regulated the division of labor between men, the relatively unconstrained father who is responsible for economic gain outside the home, and women, the administered mother within the home whose activity is limited to the increasingly narrow, increasingly commodified, and more strictly dichotomized, domestic sphere.

> Production and all paid work is organized to dovetail with a particular kind of family, one in which the wife is responsible for housekeeping and caring for family members and can be dependent on the husband's income if need be. Any housewife or parent who has had an ordinary fulltime job finds that work is planned at places and times that are incompatible with domestic responsibilities.[10]

In the modern nation-state, the nuclear family is the only legally visible social manifestation of trust and care. And this juridical determination permeates the norms governing day-to-day social life:

> The family ideal makes everything else seem pale and unsatisfactory. Those who live alone often suffer from loneliness .... Yet when we realize that this supposedly normal pattern of dependence is in fact a myth, it becomes clear that the supposedly normal pattern of women having less training, fewer job opportunities and lower pay is nothing less than a con trick made possible by the power of the family myth. The trick is given another bitter twist when it

is argued that since women now have equal rights at work, their husband no longer has the responsibility to maintain them.[11]

To stop the critique here, however, would coincide roughly with a position that regards the achievement of gender parity – in social authority and pay in the workplace – as the logical goal of feminism.[12] Here the basic structure – the dichotomous economic and familial – is kept intact with perhaps the added support required for a woman to become a mother while maintaining a fulltime job(s) and pay – in the best cases with the added "benefit" of maternity leave (and at the extreme paternity leave as well).

But Barrett and McIntosh go further. The familial knot, in which economic and social realities reinforce the family myth and vice versa, is a "house of cards" which further functions to privilege the place of care against economic reality within the family. Quoting Michael Anderson:

> The one unambiguous fact which has emerged in the last twenty years is that there can be no simple history of the western family since the sixteenth century because there is no nor has there ever been, a single-family system .... There is, except at the most trivial level, no Western family type.[13]

The problem, the authors admit, is that the definition of the family as such is contested. The failure to come up with a single systematic grasp on the concept of the family and its history is not simply a technical matter or an academic issue. It betrays an ambivalence that haunts household life, notions of sexuality, and kinship relations more broadly.[14] In a general sense then they suggest the family is simply an "ideological construct", and therefore it is necessary to understand its function in society; how it has developed historically, and in what ways it is shaped and confined by economic configurations of life, i.e. in capitalism. It is within these ideological terms that the diagnoses are constituted.[15]

Barrett and McIntosh consider two general frameworks through two statements concerning the family, the focus being on 20th-century Western Europe and North America.

1. The nuclear family is organized around the utilitarian demands of a capitalist mode of production.
2. The family has diminished, with the state replacing much of the work that used to be restricted to the domain of the family.[16]

But these two frameworks betray the limits of Barrett and McIntosh's critique. Insofar as they conflate kinship with the juridically sanctioned form of the family, they find no value whatsoever in these relations, no value other than some mitigating function in reaction to day-to-day reality, shaped in part by that ideological construct. I am interested here in understanding what kinship is as a social relation, not only distinct from other social relations, but also as a relational practice which is both necessary, and irreducible to the institutionalized form (i.e. "the family") sanctioned within the contemporary nation-state that is, in turn, structurally fundamental to its [the state's] persistence, or more precisely to its continued authorization.

My point is to develop a political theory that moves beyond the simple rejection of kinship as an oppressive institution – though it is often also that – or the romantic idealization of the family as a *haven in a heartless world* – what Michelle Barrett and Mary McIntosh call the sentiments school and Jessica Benjamin calls gender conservatism.[17] On this point, Jessica Benjamin argues that the valorization of the domestic, private sphere – even, and especially by those who might consider themselves feminists (Christopher Lasch and Jean Bethke Elshtain[18]) – is rooted in the fantasy that "celebrates the private sphere of female nurturance and criticizes social rationality while accepting this division, indeed all gender polarity, as natural and inevitable".[19] Here the problem is not only that the sanctioned family form is uncritically determined as the place in society where one can find authentic care and refuge, but also that stratification (gender and generation) within the household is overlooked, or taken for granted, implicitly accepting the claim that the private world exists as such, rather than being constituted by the social, political, and economic frameworks within which it is conceived and reconceived, produced and reproduced.

As Barrett and McIntosh understand it, the mythical family becomes the idealized domain of care instituted through the sanctioning power of the state and the normalizing force of the socius. Against the sentimentalist reading of the family, the authors suggest: "The world around the family is not a pre-existing harsh climate against which the family offers protection and warmth. It is as if the family has drawn comfort and security inside itself and left the outside world bereft. *As a bastion against a bleak society it has made that society bleak*".[20] It is insofar as the family is taken to be the monopolized site of care – countered, it might be suggested by the monopoly on violence that establishes the authorizing force of the state[21] – that Barrett and McIntosh posit the family myth as *anti-social*.

Beyond simply calling for parity in the workplace, the authors call for the dissolution of the family and the myth that sustains it – and it in turn upholds – as a social institution which functions to perform and enroot social, economic, and gender stratification. This, according to the authors, is in the interests of liberating care from its private domain, though not in order to expose it to social and economic forms of domination or exploitation. This, of course, marks the crux of the complication. In other words, the restriction of care to the nuclear form apparently functions to distribute isolation, competition, and aggression to all relations outside of the family, while maintaining a hierarchical, presumably non-commodified, and arguably non-competitive set of relations within.

But has this ever actually been the case or is it simply a fantasy meant to preserve a specific relation of social and economic life within intimate life?[22] The point for Barrett and McIntosh, as noted, is that the family as such is a myth, which, in its nuclear form, isolates and disables *practices of care*. The question here concerns how *kinship as generative association* shows up and responds in practice as opposed to its official, sanctioned form, and why, if there is such a distinction, does the sanctioned form exist at all?

At the same time, it may not be so easy, desirable, or practical to simply dispense with kinship (as an idea, as a practice, as a social construct, as a political category) altogether as Barrett and McIntosh suggest. In considering *queer kinship* Elizabeth Freeman makes the point that in "dissolving sexuality" into more capacious definitions of alliance "we risk losing site of what has enabled us to make and remake alternative social worlds over time".[23] Freeman cites Leo Bersani, who notes the incommensurability between the act of sex and conceptual meaning. For Bersani, much like Georges Bataille, to read meaning into eros is always a gesture made in bad faith, overdetermining the intransigent through the symbolic. In other words, codifying intimacy is always an act of repression.

On the other hand, Freeman suggests that

> dissident sexual acts, identities, fantasies, and orientations can certainly be the basis of all kinds of meaningful and passionate attachments on an individual level, whether or not one agrees with Bersani that it is bad faith to predicate the social upon the sexual.[24]

She adds the thought that these acts are distinct from those which are imbued with organic meaning through procreation – would it be as tempting to do so with exogenic reproduction? – even though (or despite) the fact that these acts and practices have not been situated within the *elementary structures of kinship*, as Claude Levi-Strauss famously established it.[25]

All too often, the conceptual tools available to non-familial relations are simply reduced to terms such as "community or nation", but this fails to provide modes of political, juridical, psychoanalytical, etc. acknowledgment of intensely cultivated bonds which go beyond an imagined community,[26] that in turn bind individuals through broader or deeper social claims. In other words, by eliminating non-instrumental alliance altogether we lose the ability to conceive of non-nuclear relations as anything other than "legal strangers" or even as "symbolic strangers".[27] The problem is that, on the one hand as Freeman notes: this "lack of extendability has often meant that sexual minorities are stranded between individualist notions of identity ... and on the other a romanticized notion of community as some amalgamation of individuals whose ties to smaller affective units ought to be subordinated to a more abstract collectivity, one often modelled on the liberal nation".[28] The question we come to is, how are these active relations of mutual care and love given over to dominant forms of representation, often taking a form understood as parasitical to the "natural and ideal" nuclear arrangement of kinship? Even if, along with Bersani, we reject the possibility of extracting objectified social meaning from embodied relations – e.g. from orgasmic dissolution – is there not something in between the politically sanctioned and socially recognized form of familiar relationality, and on the other side, the claim that kinship is completely relative, so to speak? On this possibility, Freeman notes:

Kinship 'matters' in the way that bodies matter: it may be produced or constructed, but it is no less urgent or tangible for that. And if kinship is anything at all – if it marks a certain terrain that cannot be fully subsumed by other institutions such as religion, politics or economics – this terrain lies in its status as a set of representational and practical strategies for accommodating all the possible ways one human being's body can be vulnerable and hence dependent upon that of another, and for mobilizing all the possible resources one body has for taking care of another.[29]

It is not that we have to come up with new terms of kinship relations, so much as we must recast our understanding of what kinship is. Following this suggestion, here I would like to consider social responses to trauma and embodied ontology at the root of a politics of precariousness. It is in these responses that I hope to glean what I would like to investigate and recast as a possibility for a politics of kinship that is neither reactionary nor one which evokes either an explicit or tacit sponsorship of neoliberal amnesia – one that inevitably maintains on a moral level that fetishized subject Marx wrote so scathingly of, the Robinsonade hero who rationalizes his own survival through the meticulous organization of space and time.

Again, it will be useful to clearly distinguish between the terms, *kinship* and *the family*. The former I use in a more capacious sense to refer to those collective practices activated in response to embodied vulnerability – rooted in what the anarchist philosopher Peter Kropotkin called mutual aid.[30] It is not restricted to a specific form and thus cannot be simply reduced to an Oedipal or any other transcendental archetype. On the other hand, *the family*, which as noted, is derived from the Latin *famulus*, indicating possession and servitude, I will use to refer to *specific*, sanctioned forms of kinship that ostensibly undergird the legitimacy of broader social, political, and economic institutions – an intimate space of confinement conditioned by the reality principle. This, however, will not always be consistent when quoting from other texts. In those cases, when it is not evident, I will try to clarify the context and meaning.

Resisting the Family

My concern is with relational bonds based on practices that substantiate communities of resistance to hypostasized forms of relation, the latter ultimately functioning to stratify society on the level of the individual through the sanctioning power of legal and professional disciplines – what Foucault called *regimes of sexuality*, ostensibly emerging with the transition from power through deduction to power through administration,[31] or as Freeman puts it, "the organization of meaning of bodily sensations".[32] Considering attempts to queer kinship seems to offer a promising entry point into alternative practices of association, solidarity, and resistance. All too often, however, what is called queering is simply a reproduction, reflection, repetition, or at best a modification of the nuclear ideal. Often it simply replaces the terms of contract while maintaining its regulating force and structure. This is Judith Butler's concern in her short essay "Is Kinship Always Already Heterosexual"?:

> The topic of gay marriage is not the same as that of gay kinship, but it seems that the two become confounded in U.S. popular opinion when we hear not only that marriage is and ought to remain a heterosexual institution and bond, but also that kinship does not work, or does not qualify as kinship, unless it assumes a recognizable family form.[33]

While the topic of family and kinship is incredibly broad, my concern here is very specific. Far from simply being a vestige of Abrahamic mores, waning in the face of modern rationalization or post-modern spectacle, kinship remains a powerful, far-reaching, and deep-seated practice, or set of practices, that functions as an unabating resource for a broad range of political techniques that circumscribe, displace, and disable practices of mutual care. I am interested here in critically considering what I call the *political theology of the family* which is grounded in the presumption that kinship is, as Carol Delaney puts it, "a natural phenomenon created by the seemingly self-evident and natural process of procreation", taken ultimately as both "nature" and a universal norm.[34] But I am also interested in modes and practices of solidarity and resistance that can be located in bonds of mutual care and intimacy, as an active social response to shared conditions of finitude. This too could be understood as kinship as a practice that actively generates fidelity, rather than a docile object involved in passive constructions of the familiar. I am also interested in ways in which these bonds can be transmitted and shared, how practices of solidarity can be extended spatially and temporally beyond the immediate locus of embodied relationality.

In reference to the reflections on domestic labor noted above, Freeman suggests that the other side of understanding kinship "in terms of dependency" which she calls "techniques of renewal" is actualized through kinship as a transformative practice. Here:

> [K]inship can also be viewed as the process by which bodies and the potential for physical and emotional attachment are created, transformed, and sustained over time. The largest and most systematized example of kinship as a technique of renewal, of course, is the domestic labor that women are expected to do to transform the raw material of a worker's wages into what he needs to labor for another day: a bed, food, clean clothes etc. This kind of bodily renewal literally reproduces the labor force. But kinship also reproduces the cultural force insofar as it also recreates and recharges bodies towards ends other than labor, such as play, love and even violence.[35]

Unlike recognition, renewal is established in practice, it is a "response to needs which makes no claims" about the identity of their bearer. "It is bodily and temporal, insofar as it simply makes people more possible, renewal grants a future".[36]

Vulnerability is already present in desire, it marks the fact that interdependency is impossible without duration, and that desire already expresses not just our exposure to others, and therefore our susceptibility to devastation, but also, our own capacity to crush, dismantle, and consume. It is for this reason that those sanctioning institutions wield so much power; the capability to shape interdependency and thus destroy it, without recompense and without mutuality, it is also why resistance can be effective and transformative.

In this sense, sanctioning institutions disable relationality through systematic reduction. Repressing ambivalence, they foreclose a necessary space for learning how to commune, and the work it takes in the face of the risks endemic to mutuality just noted. The power of such institutions is predicated on the ability to supplant and displace the need for more immediate forms of kinship, thus forming a world in their stead.

Desire also reveals the need for shelter, the root of the idea of home. Judith Butler uses the term "primary enthrallments" to describe not just the way in which we become bound to one another, but also "how such lives emerge or do not in the light of specific social organizations of sexuality".[37] This intentness and fascination are perpetually renewed in life. Insofar as a state requires the willing obedience or tacit acceptance by its polity, and in that the family is determined as the singular locus for relationality and survival, the latter furnishes a root of relation that holds fast the formal structure ostensibly securing but ultimately threatening it. Hegel, for example, thought of the family as the first ethical root of the state which acts as the organic telos of political sovereignty. He writes:

> The state is the self-conscious ethical substance, the unification of the family principle with that of civil society. The same unity, which is in the family as a feeling of love, is its essence, receiving, however, at the same time through the second principle of conscious and *spontaneous active volition the form of conscious universality*. This universal principle, with all its evolution in detail, is the absolute aim and content of the knowing subject, which thus identifies itself in its volition with the system of reasonableness.

Here, Hegel's theory of the family as the ethical root of the state is in a sense correct.[38] The state could not persist or survive without pitching itself in a profound sense – at least nominally – on the side of the family, appearing to underwrite – realized as a kind of violent indemnification – bonds which are necessary but also freeing – sometimes fleeting – that is, as a mode of relation which provides a sense of self within a familiar and fertile domain of reciprocity, one which is both spontaneous and universal, what Hegel called *Sittlichkeit* or ethical action. This, for Hegel, is the lesson of *Antigone*. But this alliance between the state and family necessarily takes the form of enclosing and diminishing the autonomy of kinship practices – essentially disabling the possibility for an active notion of kinship, as both a durable and plastic sense of relationality.

Outline and Approach

As noted above, what follows is a series of theoretical vignettes or frames, which, taken together, form a kind of conceptual collage. In each chapter I consider a way in which the family or kinship is framed in order to delimit and focus the analysis while indicating ways in which kinship persists in the absence of, or outside of the sanctioned family. Some chapters are focused on a critique of the family as a state-sanctioned institution used to channel authority through the reality principle and maintain social stratification. Others cautiously attempt to recast kinship not just in a more capacious sense, than for example the vacuous hetero-nuclear model, but in a way to reimagine mutual obligation through the generation of practices cast as a set of necessary relational responses to finitude. I consider the ways in which kinship is a social response to embodied exposure, so evident in our own bloated, feeble, and broken individualities and nationalities.

The first chapter, "Does the Family Exist? Structures and Practices of Kinship", begins with a consideration of the critical work of anthropologist David Schneider and his deconstruction of the concept of kinship as the unquestioned foundation of the discipline of anthropology. I start with the anthropological lens because it strikes me as the contemporary discipline that has established the most obstinate myth of kinship, one that claims to approach the family in a secular and presumably neutral or essential way. Here I examine the ways in which anthropology has cultivated a concept of kinship that appears to justify the modern construction of the nuclear family, despite its roots in colonial, Abrahamic, and capitalist categories. I attend to a wide range of anthropological work as well as texts by feminists, queer theorists, and philosophers as they critically respond to the ethnographic presuppositions haunting Western metaphysics. My task here is, on one hand, to critique the naturalization of specific kinship structures – as well as their imagined historical and metaphysical precedent – but also to examine the source of their authority. That is, to locate the power of kinship within the social and biological necessity of solidarity, in practices of mutual aid that respond to radical vulnerability or bodily ontology. Through this I move beyond the limits of Schneider's polemic which suggests that the notion of kinship ought to be dispensed with altogether. I turn to Judith Butler, Fred Moten, Stefano Harney, Édouard Glissant, Samuel Delany, and others in examining the *undercommons* and the *haptic* (or *hapticality*) and what Glissant calls a *poetics of relation*. This entails a shift from critique to possibility – i.e. examining potentiality within kinship practices as formidable relations conceived outside of the nuclear dyad and the Oedipal disaster it reproduces. The last pages consider Elaine Scarry's work *The Body in Pain*, to show how a system of coercion embedded within the uneven distribution of precarity is produced and reproduced through various modes of isolation, with its logical end and extreme potential expressed through practices of systematic torture – the production of *the body in pain*. Here we find the complete distillation of the state as the elimination of resistance through the control of relation.

. Chapter 2, "Patrons of the State: Division of the Public and the Private", focuses on the politico-theological division of the private and the public beginning with an examination of *De Officiis* by the Roman philosopher and statesman Cicero. The chapter outlines Cicero's concentric political philosophy of obligation, beginning with the family – *famulus* – and ending with the republic. I turn to his doctrine of the *enemy of all*, the figure of exception (the pirate) via the work of Daniel Heller-Roazen and Giorgio Agamben, the juridical mechanism at the root of radical exclusion – here reliant on the doctrine that those who to fail to commit to the patriarchal family are simply excluded from the logic of the (implied) human contract (anticipating the modern liberal subject). The state, both subtended by the regulation of intimacy and functioning as the guarantor for the legitimation of social (and extra social) relations – beginning with the family – not only underlies a politics of opposition but more deeply, determines what is excluded from the conditions for the possibility of recognition, what ultimately conditions the shape of the necropolitical. I turn to a critique of liberal enlightenment and its attendant modern subject. Specifically, I critique Kant's determination of the distinction between private and public. The chapter closes with a deeper consideration of the critique of authoritarianism via Herbert Marcuse's considerations of the underlying theological principles of political authority. This is illustrated for example in Martin Luther and John Calvin's response to Thomas Müntzer and the peasant revolts – and the socio-economic conditions leading to the systematic erosion of the commons to which they were responding. Here we can glean the roots of the force of the nation-state in its ability, or more precisely its need to authorize and thus circumscribe intimacy.

Chapter 3, "Myth of 'the Family': Biological, Social, Economic", returns to the themes developed in the first chapter. I focus on the history of family and the state in relation to capitalism. Drawing from the critical work of Kathi Weeks, Silvia Federici, Sarah Blaffer Hrdy, and others, this chapter considers how the so-called traditional family is anachronistically projected in traditionalist doctrines. In other words, its basis is implied in economic orthodoxy of perpetual growth at the expense of the commons, or any non-commodified relation (i.e. the perpetually renewing structure of original accumulation, a theme to which I return in the last chapter). Paradoxically, it is this dominant logic that militates against the conditions for the possibility of broader forms of solidarity and mutual relation. Also brought into the picture are ways in which the idea of the broken family became a mechanism of racialization and outright racist justification for poverty, surveillance, and police brutality. Included is a critique of Patrick Moynahan's reactionary polemic (in the guise of an objective study) "The Negro Family" which is sadly, still heavily cited today in traditionalist circles as well as mainstream media. I briefly consider the relationship between authoritarianism, theology, and the family via the work of Max Horkheimer. But, again, this is not just a critique, here, along with practices of squatting and urban farming, the chapter closes with an examination of the work of the socio-biologist Sarah Blaffer Hrdy, her in-depth study of *alloparenting* and the necessity of mutual aid and the catastrophic consequences of its erosion. In other words, it is not that we can ground the nuclear family in biology; in fact, it is quite the opposite, biologically the nuclear family alone is untenable if not impossible.

Occupying a central place in the book is a short deviation titled "Excursus: Memory, Relation, Death" which takes up a consideration of the politics of finitude and relations to the dead. Here, at stake is the concept of kinship as a response to ontology or finitude and therefore relation to the necropolis. Tracking this thought through the work of Jean-Paul Sartre, Robert Pogue Harrison, Martin Hägglund, and others via a critique of Martin Heidegger's privatized notion of death – i.e. death being described in his work as *the one thing no one else can do for me* – the excursus considers how the proprietary notion of death as the horizon of Being has profound political consequences, particularly vis à vis a relation to grief and memory. Here, I offer a counterargument via Jean-Paul Sartre to consider a politics of death that is relational. Insofar as we are born into the necropolis and in that death reveals ontological insecurity that not only exposes us to others – to possibility – it also allows us to grasp the ways in which projects are always a continuation of the work of the dead, always already embedded in the temporal continuities and discontinuities that inform the generative spatial and ancestral web of social life.

Chapter 4, "The Political Theology of the Family: Divine, Romantic, Algorithmic", is divided into three parts each of which approaches a different dimension of the political theology of the family. The first takes up the notion of sovereignty and the problem of continuity found in Eric Kantorowicz's classic work of political theology *The King's Two Bodies* and Eric Santner's response in *The People's Two Bodies*. Not only is the migration of the double body of the king "incorporated" into the body politic of the People, but also care and memory along with other practices associated with intimacy and trust are professionalized, often restricting and directing access to such necessities. It is the political intervention on the level of the body, the grip on substantial relations, hapticity that also determines social and political interiority and exteriority. In this sense the sacred body of the King has been transferred to the sacred body of the family. I examine the function of the sanctioned family in terms of both binational and necronational power and consider ways in which the authority of the state is ultimately predicated on the circumscription of intimacy, and so on relations ultimately cast in the face of insecurity.

The second subsection is on the *Family Romance* of the state where I work through Freud's concept of the *neurotic family romance* and Lynn Hunt's reading of the French Revolution as a political family romance. This short subsection examines the connections between intimacy, desire, and the transmission of political authority and nationalist desire, and the ways in which identity is romantically conjured between the psyche and the social order.

The third subsection is on the *algorithmic unconscious* and opens with a critique of Bernard Stiegler's anxiety concerning the corruption of the youth by the displacement of what he considers to be the traditional place of intimacy and learning in the nuclear family. Technological saturation has, for Stiegler, led to the tragic disenchantment of generational relations. Here I challenge the premise that the nuclear family – which he presupposes – really is the categorical site for intimate relations of trust and knowledge. This section moves into a different critique of technology through an examination of the algorithm, or what I call the algorithmic unconscious, with the intention of showing how technology has come to reinforce modes of stratification as well as naturalized family structures by objectifying them in the digitized world.

Chapter 5, "Extraction, Intimacy, and Kinship", critically considers the idea that material and social necessity necessitate the possibility of relations of trust and care fostered in familiar constructions that respond to, and positively acknowledge the conditions that characterize biological social life: embodied, relational, vulnerable. More specifically, by examining a key insight made by Rosa Luxemburg in her analysis of "So-Called Primitive Accumulation" – accumulation by dispossession is part of the structure of the survival of capitalism, to borrow from Freud, it is the death drive of capitalism – the text moves to an analysis of the "monstrosity of love" in the state via Hegel and alternative approaches to the ontology of kinship.

Notes

1 Corey Robin, *The Reactionary Mind: Conservatism from Edmund Burke to Donald Trump* (Oxford: Oxford University Press, 2013).
2 Ibid. 37
3 Hannah Arendt, *The Human Condition* (Chicago, IL and London: University of Chicago Press, 1998) 177.
4 The etymological root of the term from the old High German *chara* meaning lament and *charon* meaning grief, the term care, as I understand it, includes memorial and proleptic anticipation necessary for the continuity of association.
5 Michele Barrett and Mary McIntosh, *The Anti-Social Family* (New York: Verso, 2015) 81.
6 Ibid., 82.
7 However, it is clear that Laslett did not hold this to be universal outside of England and perhaps France since the 16th century. See, for example, Peter Laslett, "The Comparative History of Household and Family," *Journal of Social History* (Oxford University Press) 4, no. 1 (Autumn, 1970): 75–87.
8 McIntosh and Barrett, *The Anti-Social Family*, 77.
9 This position is distilled, for example, in the Vatican catechisms 2202 and 2207 (respectively below), under Article four on the fourth commandment: "A man and a woman united in marriage, together with their children, form a family. This institution is prior to any recognition by public authority, which has an obligation to recognize it. It should be considered the normal reference point by which the different forms of family relationship are to be evaluated." And "The family is the *original cell of social life*. It is the natural society in which husband and wife are called to give themselves in love and in the gift of life. Authority, stability, and a life of relationships within the family constitute the foundations for freedom, security, and fraternity within society. The family is the community in which, from childhood, one can learn moral values, begin to honor God, and make good use of freedom. Family life is an initiation into life in society" (http://www.vatican.va/archive/ccc_css/archive/catechism/p3s2c2a4.htm).
10 McIntosh and Barrett, *The Anti-Social Family*, 78.
11 Ibid., 79. Also, quoting the Department of Health and Social Security (UK) in 1978: "It is normal for a married woman in this country to be primarily supported by a husband, and she looks to him for support when not actually working" Ibid., 79.

12 Drawing from the autonomist Marxist tradition, Kathi Weeks critiques both the liberal feminist position that simply seeks equal access to waged work and she also scrutinizes "efforts to revalue unwaged forms of household-based labor, from housework to caring work". The problem is that neither of these positions questions the underlying mystification of the work ethic and the division of private and public it is predicated on. That is, the definition of the nuclear family. This will be discussed in more detail in Chapter 3. Kathi Weeks, *The Problem with Work: Feminism, Marxism, Antiwork Politics, and Postwork Imaginaries* (Durham, NC and London: Duke University Press, 2011) 12–13.

13 McIntosh and Barrett, *The Anti-Social Family*, 81.

14 Ibid., 84.

15 Ibid., 85.

16 Ibid., 92.

17 Jessica Benjamin, *The Bonds of Love* (New York: Random House, 1988) 198–200.

18 See Christopher Lasch, *Haven in a Heartless World: The Family Besieged* (New York: W.W. Norton, 1995) and Jean Bethke Elshtain, *Public Man, Private Woman Women in Social and Political Thought* (Princeton, NJ: Princeton University Press, 1993).

19 Jessica Benjamin, *The Bonds of Love*, 198.

20 McIntosh and Barrett, *The Anti-Social Family*, 80 (My italics).

21 On the modern nation-state, Max Weber famously wrote: "Nowadays, by contrast, we have to say that a state is that human community which (successfully) lays claim to the monopoly of legitimate physical violence within a certain territory, this 'territory' being another of the defining characteristics of the state. For the specific feature of the present is that the right to use physical violence is attributed to any and all other associations or individuals only to the extent that the state for its part permits this to happen. The state is held to be the sole source of the 'right' to use violence". Max Weber, "The Profession and Vocation of Politics," in *Political Writings*, trans. Ronald Speirs, Peter Lassman (ed.) (Cambridge: Cambridge University Press, 1994) 310–311.

22 For example, Barrett and McIntosh point out that in 1979 statistically only 31 percent of British households could be said to adhere to the nuclear form. Barret and McIntosh, *The Anti-Social Family*, 77.

23 Elizabeth Freeman, "Queer Belongings," in *A Companion to Lesbian, Gay, Bisexual, Transgender, and Queer Studies* (Oxford: Wiley Blackwell, 2015) 296.

24 Ibid., 296.

25 Ibid., 296.

26 According to Benedict Anderson, a nation, for example, is "imagined because the members of even the smallest nation will never know most of their fellow-members, meet them, or even hear of them, yet in the minds of each lives the image of their communion." Benedict Anderson, *Imagined Communities: Reflections on the Origin and Spread of Nationalism* (New York: Verso, 2006) 6.

27 Freeman, "Queer Belongings," 296.

28 Ibid., 297.

29 Ibid., 298.

30 See Peter Kropotkin, *Mutual Aid: A Factor of Evolution* (Oakland, CA: PM Press, 2021).

31 "The new procedures of power that were devised during the classical age and employed in the nineteenth century were what caused our societies to go from a *symbolics of blood* to an *analytics of sexuality.*" Michel Foucault, *The History of Sexuality, vol. 1*, trans. Robert Hurley (New York: Random House, 1998) 148. This will be discussed in more detail below.

32 Freeman, "Queer Belongings," 296.

33 Judith Butler, *Differences: A Journal of Feminist Cultural Studies*, 13, no. 1 (2002): 14.

34 Carol Delaney, "Cutting the Ties that Bind: The Sacrifice of Abraham and Patriarchal Kinship," in *Relative Values: Reconfiguring Kinship Studies*, edited by Sarah Franklin and Susan McKinnon (Durham, NC: Duke University Press, 2001) 445–467.

35 Freeman, "Queer Belongings," 298.
36 Ibid., 299.
37 Jordana Rosenberg and Judith Butler, "Serious Innovation," in *A Companion to Lesbian, Gay, Transgender and Queer Studies*, edited by George E. Haggerty and Molly McGarry (West Sussex: Blackwell Publishing, 2007) 385.
38 G.W.F. Hegel, *Philosophy of Mind, Part Three of the Philosophical Sciences* (1830), trans. William Wallace (Oxford: Clarendon Press, 1971) 535, Italics mine.

Bibliography

Theodor Adorno. *Minima Moralia*. Brooklyn, NY: Verso, 2018.

Benedict Anderson. *Imagined Communities: Reflections on the Origin and Spread of Nationalism*. New York: Verso, 2006.

Hannah Arendt. *The Human Condition*. Chicago, IL and London: University of Chicago Press, 1998.

Michele Barrett and Mary McIntosh. *The Anti-Social Family*. New York: Verso, 2015.

Jessica Benjamin. *The Bonds of Love*. New York: Random House, 1988.

Judith Butler. "Is Kinship Always Heterosexual?" *Differences: A Journal of Feminist Cultural Studies* 13, no. 1 (2002), 14–44.

Carol Delaney. "Cutting the Ties that Bind: The Sacrifice of Abraham and Patriarchal Kinship." In *Relative Values: Reconfiguring Kinship Studies*, edited by Sarah Franklin and Susan McKinnon. Durham, NC: Duke University Press, 2001.

Jean Bethke Elshtain. *Public Man, Private Woman Women in Social and Political Thought*. Princeton, NJ: Princeton University Press, 1993.

Michel Foucault. *The History of Sexuality*, vol. 1. Translated by Robert Hurley. New York: Random House, 1998.

Elizabeth Freeman. "Queer Belongings." In *A Companion to Lesbian, Gay, Bisexual, Transgender, and Queer Studies*, edited by George E. Haggerty and Molly McGarry. Oxford: Wiley Blackwell, 2015.

G.W.F. Hegel. *Philosophy of Mind, Part Three of the Philosophical Sciences (1830)*. Translated by William Wallace. Oxford: Clarendon Press, 1971.

Peter Kropotkin. *Mutual Aid: A Factor of Evolution*. Oakland, CA: PM Press, 2021.

http://www.vatican.va/archive/ccc_css/archive/catechism/p3s2c2a4.htm

Christopher Lasch. *Haven in a Heartless World: The Family Besieged*. New York: W.W. Norton, 1995.

Peter Laslett. "The Comparative History of Household and Family." *Journal of Social History* (Oxford University Press) 4, no. 1 (Autumn, 1970): 75–87.

Corey Robin. *The Reactionary Mind: Conservatism from Edmund Burke to Donald Trump*. Oxford: Oxford University Press, 2013.

Jordana Rosenberg and Judith Butler. "Serious Innovation." In *A Companion to Lesbian, Gay, Transgender and Queer Studies*, edited by George E. Haggerty and Molly McGarry. West Sussex: Blackwell Publishing, 2007.

Max Weber. "The Profession and Vocation of Politics." In *Political Writings*. trans. Ronald Speirs, Peter Lassman (ed.) Cambridge: Cambridge University Press, 1994.

Kathi Weeks. *The Problem with Work: Feminism, Marxism, Antiwork Politics, and Postwork Imaginaries*. Durham, NC and London: Duke University Press, 2011.

1 Does the Family Exist?

Structures and Practices of Kinship

It is not just substances which circulate. The Wari' body is also constituted by affects and memories. Memory, say the Wari', is located in the body, meaning the constitution of kin is based to a high degree on living alongside each other day-to-day and on reciprocally bestowed acts of affection.[1]

Humiliation is also a violent condition of the whole corporal being, which longs to surge up under the outrage but is forced, by impotence or fear, to hold itself in check.[2]

The first thought describes a metaphysics and praxis of the Wari' ("we") people, sometimes referred to by their colonial inscription as the Paaka Nova of Brazil. Here, anamnesis and affect are intertwined, resonating in some ways, I think, with Henri Bergson's considerations of bodily memory, or habit-memory in relation to pure memory.[3] According to the Wari', embodied relation is the site where kin may be manifest. Reciprocal affection – reflections of affect – produces meaning as relation. We might add that this characterizes the way affinity constitutes and sustains kin. The second quote, from the mystic and socialist revolutionary Simone Weil, tells us that the affect called humiliation offers a mainline to the flesh of the material body. It shocks and stultifies, inspiring reactive modes of concealment, expressive acts of sublimation, intrigued performances of dissimulation, forced into socially suitable expressions of bodily relations. The considerations that follow will hold on to these two ideas: (a) kinship or relationality as active and (b) the vulnerability that characterizes bodily ontology makes very specific demands on relation and therefore community. In other words, what follows is a consideration of *kinship as action* as a critique of the family, beginning with a critical examination of the conceptual foundation of anthropology as a social science.

The Anthropological Production of Kinship

David Schneider's *Critique of the Study of Kinship* marked a turning point in the discipline of anthropology.[4] By interrogating the unequivocal assumption

DOI: 10.4324/9781003264644-2

embedded in the concept of the family at the core of ethnographic research, Schneider aimed his critique at the very foundations of social science. Not only, he claimed, is there no justification for privileging the family above all other social relations, but there is no justification for assuming specific characteristics exist that accurately describe such a community across the vast plurality of human societies, practices, and histories. As the Western model of family life failed to find an analog to the social practices found in other communities, the ethnographer was forced to expand the epistemological hermeneutic indefinitely. Ethnography turned to searching for new ways to define the taboo of incest, to make sense of relations within the terms of exogamous vs. endogamous exchange, and to discern clear distinctions between consanguinity and affinity, especially when none seemed evident.

The problem, for Schneider, is that the family from this standpoint is always conceived as a privileged site of social relation defined by reproductive sexual practices. But this is clearly not always the case. By projecting this axiom onto communities that do not adhere to it, the ethnographer forces their experiences into preconceived, fixed terms of analysis. For example, Schneider points out that the 19th-century anthropologist Lewis Henry Morgan cited Tamilian society in which "my brother's sons and my cousin's sons are both my sons".[5] The terms of household relations, he noted, contradict the proprietary basis for relation in modern Western family practices. Morgan notes that in "civilized society", it would be absurd not to "privilege my own son" in considering "the inherence of my estate".[6] In other words, for Morgan, the awareness of this "most natural bond" only comes with "civilized society", where it is recognized that kindred relations "naturally" bestow a greater, more authentic degree of cohesion than other intimate associations. Thus, along with private property and monogamous marriage – which is of course required to secure the knowledge required for maintaining patriarchal societies, through the concept of generational heritability via sexual reproduction and epistemic certitude, i.e. being able to verify kin according to some axiomatic – "civilization" provides the ideal social conditions that correspond with the concept of the consanguine. The nuclear family.

It is interesting to note that it was Morgan's experience with the *Haudenosaunee*, in which kinship was matrilineal, if not matriarchal, that inspired him to send letters to missionaries across the world in order to inquire about familial relations in their respective localities.[7] While today Native Scholars rightly consider Morgan's approach to be infected with the "white savior" affliction they also, significantly point out the attributes of the *Haudenosaunee* identified by him were "personal dignity, equality, freedom and autonomy, fraternity, matriarchy, and the absence of poverty".[8] For Morgan this came down to their kinship configurations and familiar relations. Morgan thought of himself as a compassionate observer while still inherently insisting on the nuclear ideal in his work. This, of course, was predicated on an ideology of progress defined by a linear vision of history in which the idea of European civilization stood at the end. It was also based on the assumption that in not having a state form of political relation, something important is missing. It is a framework that can neither recognize nor withstand, for example as Pierre Clastres put it, the idea of a *society against the state*. Within this interpretation what would be called a *pre-state form* of society was promiscuous and, therefore, according to the so-called Bachofen thesis, necessarily matrilineal and consequently matriarchal.[9]

The tendency of matriarchy in presumably "prehistoric" or "precivilized" societies was generally accepted as an axiom in the nascent discipline of anthropology until Friedrich Engels (picking up from Marx's *Ethnological Notebooks*) took up the idea as an example of – extended it as incontrovertible proof that – non-state societies, provided examples of a thriving *ur-communismus*.[10]

The anthropological discipline – which developed around the conceptualization of kinship as *famulus*, i.e. property, that acted as a social scientific justification for specific forms of social domination within capitalism and emerged historically from and actively sustained settler colonialism – reacted to this and several studies followed that sought to dismantle that theory. "Once Engels had endorsed it, Morgan's theory was destined to become a casualty of the central conflict of the age".[11] Through a patriarchal, but also capitalist, commitment they sought to discount evidence of matrilineal, matriarchal, or gynocratic societies as outliers.[12] Matriarchy was essentially a mistake or an instance of prematurity. Matriarchy, if it even ever existed, can only be an outlier. It could never work. It is not natural. There is no evidence. And so on.

Chris Knight explains the conflict that non-Western models of kinship presented for anthropologists and the dogmatism they were met with:

> What is it to be a "son" or a "daughter", a "mother" or a "niece"? Taking careful notes among his Native American informants in 1846, Lewis Henry Morgan (1871:3) discovered to his initial surprise that an Iroquois child had several "mothers". Early in the twentieth century, Bronislaw Malinowski (1930) reacted against this idea, reshaping anthropology on the basis that it was patently absurd. No child could possibly have two mothers. Malinowski acknowledged that his Trobriand Island informants, like many other people, might systematically "distort" the true facts of kinship. Two sisters, for example, might describe themselves as "mothers" to one another's offspring, their children correspondingly addressing both as "mother". However, Malinowski insisted that such notions were ideological fictions, not to be taken seriously. Correctly analysed, the facts of kinship would always turn out to be (a) biological and (b) individual.[13]

It can be inferred from Malinowski's demands to shoehorn the informant's story into a portrait adhering to contemporary European family values – an instrumental concept for settler colonialism – that terms are always ultimately framed within the modern Enlightenment conception of the *biological* and *individual*.[14] But this also reinforces, if not justifies, a specific form of private property, familial possession (or possession of family members, i.e. division of labor), a sexual contract and moral code, and lines of inheritance.

Schneider points out the contradiction evident in the idea that on one hand there is a relation rooted in the apparently self-evident idea of blood, which imposes a stronger bond between two people – specifically the father and son – and on the other, that it took humans thousands of years to establish a society with a shared legal, psychological, and anthropological concept that matches this bond. If it is so self-evident, Schneider asks, that I would rather give my estate to my son instead of my cousin's sons, why do I require the evolution of juridical principles and social norms to grasp this natural fact? If knowledge is required, then are we trafficking in universals rooted in "nature" or have we moved on to a different domain of inquiry? Do we require an evolved reason to properly ground our sense of love and feeling of commitment? Or are we considering terms of legitimacy under the gaze of specific forms of authority? Or are we dealing with something else altogether? Part of the complication for anthropologists is that so many forms of relationality confronting them failed to fit into this schema.

A famous, and at the time scandalous, example comes from Margaret Mead's *Coming of Age in Samoa* which among other things demonstrated the idea that adolescent strife or puberty as a naturally troubled phase of youth is a myth.[15] Through comparison she showed that what is taken to be an essential stage of adolescence today attributed to chemical hormones was in fact rooted in socially structured anxieties internalized by adolescent girls. She witnessed a far more fluid understanding of kinship, such that any given member of the community may have more than one father or mother, elders were important for passing down important knowledge and ancestral stories, while divorce was a day-to-day affair, open to either party simply by exiting the household. Likewise, a child could simply exit one household and enter another and in general be met with equal acceptance. In Samoan society as opposed to the supposedly "advanced" or "developed" 1920's United States, Mead found active encourage-ment of promiscuity in young people prior to marriage. Rather than adolescence being a time of sexual repression, it was seen as a moment of sexual freedom and freedom from the responsibility of childcare in the home which was also in some ways the primary responsibility of children, not adults. All of this must have seemed stunning from the perspective of a citizen of the United States in the early twentieth century, and it was particularly scandalous as Mead turned what she learned from her ethnographic work in Samoa into a critique of the educational system in North America, while also questioning the generally prud-ish approach to sex as well as the repressive relation to death (dead bodies were for example publicly examined and at times dissected to determine the cause of illness. Children were not "protected" from this) and other restrictive and stulti-fying social structures.[16]

Two, more recent examples which can be found in Janet Carsten's collection *Cultures of Relatedness* speak to the incommensurability between concepts and practices. The "Iñupiat strongly deny that ties deriving from procreation exert any overriding moral force. Whereas claims based on different contributions to productive work are described as permanent, 'biology' does not constitute an immutable basis for relations".[17] Another instance bears out the historical mutability of practices – and therefore also concepts – of kinship. The recent traumatic upheavals in southern Sudan have changed the way in which the Nuer have understood and practiced relationality:

> the connections and disconnections of Nuer relatedness have come to be understood not only in terms of blood and cattle but also through the media of money, paper, and guns. That these media are potentially convertible into each other, and that food is convertible into blood, and blood into milk and semen, lends an extraordinary degree of transformability to Nuer idioms of relatedness. This "unboundedness" not only provides a strong contrast to the classic understandings of Nuer kinship in terms of descent groups, but has important implications for how we consider idioms of relatedness more generally.[18]

What, for example, are the consequences of considering intense relational bonds outside of their deployment for the acquisition of social power secured, for example, through proprietary relations and unidirectional transmissions of surplus value? As we will see, placing exchange at the center of the concept of relation goes far in legitimizing specific categorical determinations oriented around the circulation of authority and the distribution of vulnerability, which in turn dictates structures of relatedness and the production and reproduction of meaningful bonds. It is this conceptual dogmatism that militates against more fluid and sustainable notions of relation. It is an intricate set of assumptions that will be steadily dismantled in the following pages.

Elementary and Complex

Claude Levi-Strauss – also one of the targets of Schneider's critique – thought that the history of human societies could be divided according to kinship configurations split into two categories, *elementary* and *complex* – and in some cases also hybrids. The former described kinship structures in many ancient, indigenous, or presumably "primitive" societies. There, alliances were found to be secured between structurally defined groups through the exchange of women.[19] The rules of exogamy or endogamy in these cases are clearly circumscribed. Who one is to marry is defined exclusively by consanguinity in relation to social advantage secured through alliance. The point is that Levi-Strauss cast the incest taboo as the singular universal aspect of kinship relations, and he projected the nuclear model of the family as historically more progressive, but also more "natural", than other forms of relation. He writes:

> Here therefore is a phenomenon which has the distinctive characteristics both of nature and of its theoretical contradiction, culture. The prohibition

of incest had the universality of bent and instinct, and the coercive character of law and institution .... Inevitably extending beyond the historical and
geographical limits of culture, and co-extensive with the biological species,
the prohibition of incest, however, through social prohibition, doubles the
spontaneous action of the natural forces with which its own features contrast,
although itself identical to these forms of application.[20]

But the demand to find a hard-and-fast law to contain all familial relations reaches
a limit. Arguments over how exactly to define kinship as a universal became more
or less unintelligible as ethnographic observations revealed no such consistency
in arrangement. Schneider's question: why it is that such a community has come
to be defined around an instrumental – procreative – concept of sexual activity,
finds an answer based on one unquestioned assumption: the idea encapsulated in
the phrase "blood is thicker than water"?[21] It is only with this axiom that so much
of the work of so many anthropologists, "put so much weight on the role of kinship in the history, evolution, development of society and culture, as well as its
maintenance and functioning, whatever its form".[22]

   In other words, the idea that familial relations are prior to other kinds of bonds
because they express a "natural" rather than cultural phenomenon, or in the case of
Levi-Strauss, they function as a kind of Cartesian pineal gland between nature and
culture, paradoxically bridging the two, seems to have established the axiomatic
foundation of anthropological discourse (and an early target of the philosophical school of deconstruction).[23] Thus, the family is taken to designate a relation
that underlies all societies. If it is not readily evident in other cultures, then the
task is simply to uncover the cultural dissimulation of a given community. For
Levi-Strauss (following and modifying Marcel Mauss' work on *The Gift*[24] and
Sigmund Freud's *Totem and Taboo*[25]), this amounts to the reduction of familial
relations to exchange: "it is always a system of exchange that we find at the origin
of rules of marriage, even of those of which the apparent singularity would seem
to allow only a special and arbitrary interpretation".[26]

   At least one of Levi-Strauss' students insisted otherwise. According to Pierre
Clastres, Levi-Strauss "confuses end with means".[27] The taboo of incest, which
functions to create alliances through the exchange of women, follows a specific
function and fulfills a particular goal. But for Clastres, the exchange of women is
not undertaken for its own sake, but for the sake of waging war, or more generally
augmenting power. It is in the attempt to transform tenuous potential alliances
into kin: "from allies who are also relatives, one may hope for more constancy in
warlike solidarity, though the links of kinship are in no way a definitive guarantee
of fidelity to the alliance".[28] According to Clastres, an-archic society is one that
both strategically and tactically aims to reduce exchange as much as possible.[29]
Just as he is interested in the ways in which non-industrial societies, often categorically and actively, resist state formations he also suggests, and for the same
reasons, they are "societies against exchange";[30] in other words, association which
does not exist as such for exchange and for exchanging as much as possible as
Levi-Strauss' theory simply assumes. Instead, for Clastres, exchange specifically

functions in the interests of expanding state military power and – which is the same – for concentrating social power through the controlled accumulation of surplus that inherently confers authority via the *proprietary principle*. While it may be a symptom of a state-based political arrangement, it is not the cause of kinship.

Prioritizing sexual reproduction and exchange as the measure for the legible and legitimate familial bond also frames it as the foundation that informs everything from etiquette to linguistic structures. In her now-classic critical work *The Traffic in Women: Notes on a Political Economy of Sex*, Gayle Rubin notes that the root of inequality can be found in the organization of society around the circulation of women – through their reproductive capacity – of which we find many examples: "Women are given in marriage, taken in battle, exchanged for favors, sent as tribute, traded, bought and sold".[31] These exchanges simply become more commercialized in so-called *advanced* societies, in what Levi-Strauss called complex structures of kinship. "Men are of course trafficked too – but as slaves, hustlers, athletic stars, serfs, or as some other catastrophic social status, rather than as men. Women are transacted as slaves, serfs, prostitutes, but also simply as women".[32]

It is this last caveat – *as women* – that reveals the determination of exchange as ultimately predicated on the production of gender through a gendered division of labor. It is the achievement of this "social benefit", that explains the taboo of incest, which again functions to bind men together and "of superimposing upon the natural links of kinship the henceforth artificial links – artificial in the sense that they are removed from chance encounters or the promiscuity of family life – of alliance governed by rule".[33] This system of exchange is also a network of power, a machine in which authority flows through the rules of exploitation, commerce, and speculation. In this case, it is an expression of patriarchal domination, the foundation of the state. "It passes through women and settles upon men. The tracks which it leaves include gender identity, the division of sexes".[34] Insofar as taboo inevitably lies at the boundary between – while also motivating the production of – nature and culture, the taboo of incest, and the circulation of women lie at the root of modern society. The incest taboo then is the original social contract, and it remains at the root of the liberal social order.[35] The hierarchical arrangement of sexual difference that translates care into possession, as it is inscribed in the symbolic world, determines the coincidence of right and power, which is then associated with the right to exchange other humans.

The further problem Schneider encountered in taking the family for granted, alluded to in Rubin's critique, is that "these bonds are in principle unquestioned and unquestionable. They are *states of being not of doing, or performance* – that is, the grounds of the bonds exist or they do not".[36] Either we can identify them conceptually, pin them down, or they do not exist at all. "All of this is because kinship is a strong solidarity bond that is largely innate, a quality of human nature, biologically determined, however much social or cultural overlay may also be present".[37] But without the assumption of a generalizable rule governing the structure of kinship, Schneider suggests, it is difficult to make sense of the approach to kinship taken by anthropologists.

One of the problems is that the specificities of the bond are generalized. Kinship here is like kinship over there, it simply assumes a different configuration, but ultimately it is based on the same prohibition that controls inheritance, possession, property, exchange, and power, in that it functions to determine inclusion and exclusion – or the distinction between affinity and consanguinity. That is to say, kinship is conceived, according to the formal principles noted above, by the anthropologist as necessary: "it is not contingent or conditional and performance is presumed to follow automatically if the bond exists".[38]

Melbourne Trapper sums up Schneider's critique in this way:

> Throughout the critique we come again and again to that haunting fact that anthropologists have come home to find that their discoveries – other people's kinship – have turned out, in the end, to be nothing more than their own shadows.[39]

In other words, the ethnocentric anthropological tendency persists unconsciously in this unquestioned assumption. It is the study of a ghost which resides in the psyche of the medium who professes contact with it. But Trapper examines a notion of kinship, not simply from an ethno-epistemological perspective, i.e. whether these ethnographies are really grasping the authentic relations, of *real* practices, but rather from a perspective of political rationalities: "I am interested in promoting an understanding of 'kinship' – specifically in its representational form of the 'tribe' – in terms of governmentality".[40] Trapper's question, which begins with what is merely hinted at in Schneider, concerns the ways in which kinship is utilized in colonial constructs, shaping the social life of the colonized, as a discursive technique "at the intersection of anthropology and medicine" that corresponds with the inclinations of provincial governments that demand and require a devoted and disciplined population requisite under the imperative to achieve and maintain order.[41]

* * *

A consequence of this assumption goes far beyond simply misleading or obscuring ethnographic research that presumes to approach other societies with the intent of discovering their kinship rules. What is at stake is exactly how these assumptions inform the ways in which the discipline of anthropology functions alongside and informs colonial logic, the way it sees and fails to recognize, and thus inform and justify indigenous reeducation programs, interdictions against indigenous languages, the delegitimization of non-proprietary relations to land and water, and the projection of kinship hierarchies inscribed both theologically and epistemologically via the concept of "the family", in order to undermine the very principles of community and kinship that constitute the occupied and uprooted communities. All of this under the auspices of Enlightenment rationality.[42]

The historical conquest of Oyate treaty land is also an international phenomenon that implicates indigenous people within the colonial and imperial logics of property as they relate to the notions of dominance as expressed by both the Doctrine of Discovery and the Framework of Dominance, key concepts in international and domestic law both past and present.[43]

Describing the conceptual roots of the Oyate treaty establishing the Lake Traverse reservation, Nick Estes notes that we find an international pattern of domination of indigenous communities through the political implications of a fundamentally proprietary notion of relation. This structure informs and circumscribes relations both between humans expressed in familial-political structures (*famulus*) and relations to nature, ecosystems, or life worlds. He notes further that this can be traced back to an Abrahamic paradigm.

> Inherent within U.S. federal Indian law is the reification of the theological Christian underpinnings of the Framework of Dominance and the expressed right of sovereign Christian nations of dominion over discovered land and people, rendering both as property of their Christian discoverers. The European Old World understanding of property, for example, originates from the Latin term dominium, which means absolute ownership.[44]

The moral force of quasi-scientific expertise – ordered according to the categories "human" and "nature", subject and object – along with direct violence, shapes social relations justified by the Framework of Dominance along the political-theological commitments evident in juridical concepts of property – a thing to possess both in the sense of an object and in becoming an object.[45] At least in these cases, kinship is not discovered but produced and reproduced, to presumably bring nature into the purview of rationality and to secure "civilization" through the reification of the family, private property, and the reactive elimination of resistance.

Elizabeth Freeman points out that Schneider's critique takes kinship as a "purely social" phenomenon, by suggesting that it relies on a "modern western paradigm" insofar as it is based on a "sexualized concept of procreation".[46] It places procreation at the center of all forms of cooperation – of the ways in which "people ally with one another"[47]. This conceptual commitment can be traced back to the 19th-century German psychiatrist Richard von Krafft-Ebing who collected 238 accounts of a stunningly wide range of sexual practices by interviewing people in the countryside of Germany, inquiring about their intimacy and sex. He then proceeded to categorize these practices against the "norm" which he established as strictly procreative intercourse. In other words he placed procreation as the endpoint and cause of all erotic pleasure thereby establishing a telos as well as an etiology for sex and sexuality.[48] This first established the category of the *abnormal* in terms of eros within social scientific discourse. Schneider's commitment to inquire into the question of kinship, as simply "a modern Western paradigm", is based on the assumption that procreation is always the ultimate determining concept of alliance.[49]

Habitus and Practical Kinship

Freeman considers the work of Paul Gilroy in reflecting on the ways in which local traditions of kinship were ruptured and then erased with the transatlantic slave trade, but also how different forms of association emerged in the face of the violent cut of relational ties, and other bodily and social deprivations.[50] She writes: "Given all this, bodies have been central to conceptualizing the renewal of African American individuals and collectivities beyond the dominant kinship grid".[51] Drawing from Toni Morrison's notion of remembering that within a community, so stigmatized, for so long, by "the ideological and physical objectification" of their bodies gave rise to "new corporeal futurities"[52] she continues: "Again, it suggests an embodied but not procreative model of kinship that has powerful resonances for theorizing in a queer mode".[53] Unlike the demand for confirming a set of organizational prerequisites when searching for the family, Freeman locates necessity elsewhere, namely in biological insecurity.

This recalls Pierre Bourdieu's concept of *habitus* in relation to *practical kinship*, which is "ubiquitous … individual, private, strategic, directed towards the satisfaction of material interests", all of which is to say, quite distant from the "bio-genetic model" of kinship.[54] Bourdieu frames habitus in terms of an enduring, shared social substance arising from "systems of durable, transposable dispositions … principles of generation and structuring of practices and representations which can be objectively 'regulated' and 'regular' without in any way being the product of obedience to rules".[55] Relational practices are marked as works of improvisation and adaptation that respond to "unforeseen and ever-changing situations".[56] But this is not to be grasped in terms of motors of action and reaction taken on an individual interactive basis. For example, in the confrontation between two groups or individuals one action appears to be a response to another or is taken as caused by the other. Bourdieu points out that the actions are not produced in direct response to one another but in relation to the shared habitus and ontic framework of social intelligibility – *sensis communis*. Habitus is the embodied sensibility of the situation, which emerges in spontaneous shared interaction, in reciprocity, and commutativity. Habitus is an enduring mnemonic, if not unconscious, relation to relation. It is the condition for the possibility of social apperception and for mindreading following Sarah Blaffer Hrdy, discussed in Chapter 3.[57] But this is important: Bourdieu rejects any theses that "treat practice as a mechanical reaction, directly determined by antecedent conditions".[58] Habitus "puts itself forward with an urgency and a claim to existence excluding all deliberation".[59] It is, finally a "socially constituted system of cognitive and motivating structures"[60] Freeman considers this durability in relation to *generativity*, rather than reproduction. Here, as Freeman also notes, the Bourdieusian distinction and relation between *official* and *practical* kinship is key. Relations, in practice, are a form of "an object or intuition"; "it is the habitus, history turned into nature, i.e. denied as such, which accomplishes practically the relating of these two systems [practical and official] of relations, through the production of practice."[61] Like Schneider, Bourdieu suggests that the ethnographer diminishes the possibility of grasping *practical kinship* as soon as the inquiry is framed within official kinship terms, according to which they are: "disposed to take for gospel truth the official discourses which informants are included to present to him as long as they see themselves as spokesmen mandated to present the group's official account of itself."[62] On the one hand, it is necessary to inquire into the conditions that define a group as genealogically continuous, implying a matrix of kinship as both the necessary and sufficient condition for social cohesion.[63] But once we do this, once we inquire into the utility of kinship relations otherwise treated as self-evident, we discover that they tend to default to explanations predicated on official situations or "official representations of social structures", insofar as they function to legitimate the dominant terms of social order, social normativity that tacitly underlies structures of scarcity and violence. Bourdieu writes:

> to schematize, official kinship is opposed to practical kinship in terms of the official as opposed to the non-official (which includes the unofficial and scandalous) ... the public, explicitly codified in a magical or quasi-juridical formalism, as opposed to the private, kept in an implicit, even hidden state, collective ritual, subjectless practice, amenable to performance by agents interchangeable because collectively mandated, as opposed to strategy, directed towards the satisfaction of the practical interests of an individual or group of individuals.[64]

For Bourdieu practical kinship is actively constructed; it is something people generate "and with which they do something".[65] Practical kinship is tactical rather than strategic. In principle this goes in direct opposition to the legal-normative structure of sanctioned relational frameworks. The political technique of translation and the consequent erasure of these practices underlie the conditions for the diminishment and invisibility of relations either simply not recognized or cast as inherently illicit, and so failing to adhere to the ideal form of relation (which again is paradoxically framed both as the most natural condition and as a progressive achievement).

The Family as Political Territory

On the level of the nation-state, this tension clearly underlies the justification of family separation, resulting from restricted immigration policies in various parts of the world. The official language defending those policies in the United States, for example, has been typically reactive. In response to criticisms of forced family separations at the US-Mexico border, the United States Department of Health and Human Service (HHS) claims:

> The assertion that unaccompanied alien children (UAC) are "lost" is completely false. This is a classic example of the adage "No good deed goes unpunished". The Office of Refugee Resettlement (ORR), which is part of the Department of Health and Human Services, began voluntarily making

calls in 2016 as a 30-day follow-up on the release of UAC to make sure that UAC and their sponsors did not require additional services. This additional step, which is not required and was not done previously, is now being used to confuse and spread misinformation.[66]

The statement goes on to declare that even though the children deemed "lost" cannot be contacted by HHS, it is probably due to the fact that the parents are "illegal anyway", implying that legal status justifies the putative actions of the state. The point is that from the perspective of the state,[67] the contradiction between the sacred status of the family, as an institution protected at all costs by sovereign political authority, and the violation of the integrity of certain families, must somehow be resolved. That is to say, the sacred foundation of the family – and "family values" – as such is allegedly being protected by (and therefore used to justify, hence "good deed") the increasingly restrictive immigration policies[68] also paradoxically functions to break apart other families, to make families of others (i.e. their intimate relations), impossible as foundations of social agency and "healthy social development". These families become a profanation of the nation-state which functions, as Hannah Arendt so perspicaciously pointed out, to protect "citizens", on the specious but foundational category "human", the precondition for the process of dehumanization endemic to the nation-state. Those who do not belong are transferred from the status of the sacred to that of the accursed. They are deprived of visibility and relation through the political technique of concentration (a fundamentally police action), the second of the so-called solutions to the "Jewish problem" in Hitler's Reich.[69]

In this case, those families which are sanctioned as legal – protected by the category of citizenship – are pitted against those who are unauthorized. Loyalty to a family requires loyalty to the protective state, whereas loyalty to an extended or constructed kinship, a commune or gang, presents a competitive threat to the state because it undermines the moral presumptions underlying economic and biological productivity and the political authority that unifies them. Like the logic of incarceration, the detention camps that have been established and persist to divide and contain families of refugees along the border directly target the conditions for the possibility for necessary, affective, haptic, and otherwise entangled relations, replacing them with controlled isolation. The fundamental harm done through the alienation of relations of care, particularly for the most vulnerable, occurs via the attack on association at its very core. This, again, marks the limit and horizon of the logical foundation of the authority of the state, that is, the guarantor for the conditions for the possibility of survival both social and biological. In the following pages, I will deepen my considerations of marginal and at times invisible practices of kinship as a response to vulnerability and crisis and at the end of this chapter return to the question of the body, relation, and the state.

Undercommons and Haptic Contagion

Judith Butler's expansive approach to kinship in her considerations of gay marriage begins with the following thought:

If we understand kinship as a set of practices that institutes relationships of various kinds which negotiate the reproduction of life and the demands of death, then kinship practices will be those that emerge to address fundamental forms of human dependency, which may include birth, child-rearing, relations of emotional dependency and support, generational ties, illness, dying, and death (to name a few).[70]

Butler bypasses the either/or structure upon which Schneider's critique is based. Instead she claims that kinship cannot simply be reduced to a "fully autonomous sphere" of relation that is unconnected to friendship or other forms of community, or even official forms of sanctioning, but at the same time is not "'over' or 'dead'" simply for the reason that it resists formalization and thereby escapes the methods of tracking according to the conventions of ethnographers, other social scientists, corporate advertisers, social media, or the state.[71] While Butler agrees with Schneider's critique of reified categories of relation and the idealized projection of formal systems of kinship, she takes up his challenge to understand kinship as an *activity* or *practice* rather than as an *existent* or *being*. Butler writes:

This would help us, I believe, move away from the situation in which a hypostatized structure of relations lurks behind any actual social arrangement and permit us to consider how modes of patterned and performative doing bring kinship categories into operation and become the means by which they undergo transformation and displacement.[72]

Illustrating the decoupling of marriage and kinship, Butler cites Carol Stacks' study of the resilience and organization in urban black communities.[73]

Carol Stacks' work, for example, reflects upon her investigative experiences in some of the poorest black communities in the Midwest. She found evidence contradicting the stereotypical characterization of minority communities as suffering from the proliferation of "dysfunction" in family life. What she found instead was incredible resilience and complexity in their kinship networks.[74] Stacks writes:

In the Flats the responsibility for providing food, care, clothing, shelter and for socializing children within domestic networks may be spread over several households. Which household a given individual belongs to is not a particularly meaningful question, as we have seen that daily domestic organization depends on several things: where people sleep. Where they eat, and where they offer their time and money. Although those who eat together and contribute toward the rent are generally considered by Flat's residents to form minimal domestic units, household changes rarely affect the exchanges and daily dependencies of those who take part in common activity.[75]

She continues by describing the ways in which those who are evicted are taken in by those considered kin; a relation determined through the generation of networks of bonds of trust sustained through these shared practices. It is the expression of an active form of resilience based on common space, fluid resources, and the plasticity of relationality, in what counts as familiar and what *feels like home*: "Households expand and contract with the loss of a job, a death in the family, the beginning and end of a sexual partnership, or the end of a friendship".[76] There exists a strong but flexible material, aesthetic, and cultural support in these incredibly precarious communities. It is only through the active mobilization of these domestic *kin-constructs* that not only function as a necessity for survival but also become veritable "workshops of social reproduction" that flourish in the face of economic and political adversity.[77]

A second instance can be gleaned in the work of Fred Moten and Stephano Harney, in what they describe as the *undercommons* – of which there are as many examples as there are institutions that dictate the terms of coming together, that foreclose communing outside of these terms, e.g. the university. One case cited is the extreme displacement and bodily violence endured by those exiled from the African continent through the slave trade. In view of the traumatic displacement – the rupture from ancestry and kin, from a past and a future – that was experienced in bowels of vessels traversing the middle passage, in considering the response to rupture that the transatlantic holds actualized, Harney and Moten refer to a sense of radical homelessness which, in turn, founds a condition upon which an embodied familiarity of a crushed people emerges. Torn from their kin and land, packed into the dank hulls of ships, a kind of kinship was disseminated via a conditional and *haptic contagion*:

> To have been shipped is to have been moved by others, with others. It is to feel at home with the homeless, at ease with the fugitive, at peace with the pursued, at rest with the ones who consent not to be one. Outlawed, interdicted, intimate things of the hold, containerized contagion, logistics externalises logic itself to reach you, but this is not enough to get at the social logics, the social *poiesis*, running through logisticality.[78]

Even within the perverse and brutalizing conditions produced by the austere algorithmic slave ship logistics, a sense of home, a social *poiesis*, must be constructed. It is this that hints at what the authors call the *undercommons*, described as:

> a feel, a sentiment with its own interiority, there on skin, soul no longer inside but there for all to hear, for all to move. Soul music is a medium of this interiority on the skin, its regret the lament for Fantasy in the Hold broken hapticality, its self-regulatory powers the invitation to build sentimentality together again, feeling each other again.[79]

But this *hapticality*, described as a *capacity* and also *love*: "to feel through others, for them to feel through you", is at the very least not a matter of regulation – not successfully anyhow – not a matter of state, religion, economy, territory, empire, not even a people, name, or totem. That is, in the face of being denied precisely those things that are meant to "produce sentiment" in addition to the list above, including the family: "Though forced to touch and be touched, to sense and be sensed in that space of no space, though refused sentiment, history and home, we feel (for) each other".[80] And in feeling – a feeling-with and for – relation becomes a way of making a world within the worldless, itself conceived within the world destroying entrails of human atrocity.

Édouard Glissant also imagines the experience of abysmal exile realized in these Stygian crossings, but only as the first moment in a long series of forced dislocations and foreclosed agencies. In the same sense that this initial uprooting did not meet with rebellion, there was no pride in being chosen, "no vanity" in the "prescience and actual experience of Relation". It was not a coordinated movement. Everywhere *tactical hapticality* supplanted strategic understanding. "They did not believe they were giving birth to any modern force", Glissant writes, "they live Relation and cleared the way for it, to the extent that the oblivion of the abyss comes to them, and that consequently their memory intensifies".[81] Eventually this gives rise to new forms and methods of relating, of building *in common*. Strategy returned through a built-up reserve and the increased resilience produced through the repetition of relational practices: fragmented and creolized language, music (blues), and a new poetry, a set of expressive responses of a marooned people. Glissant phrases it a *poetics of relation*, which is meant not as a connection between, or synthesis of, two or more points, but rather in terms of that association which dispenses with the teleological orientation of center and periphery, insofar as it is immediate and total with "its always approximate truth … given in a narrative."[82] For the subjects of colonization, this project is not yet at the level of self-expression. It is not a humanist project in that sense, that is, in the sense that it is only available to those who are not already radically separated from themselves, open only to those possessed by the luxury of self-expression.[83] Glissant's point here is that when "caught in that multiple echo, you are in fact divided, you cannot understand yourself or be yourself."[84]

These texts, outlining the extremities of humanly constructed inhumanity, in different ways actively resist the assumption that impoverished, marginalized, devastated communities are inordinately afflicted by a family life – or suffer due to the presumed fact – that is "disorganized", "broken", or tragically matriarchal, in failing to adhere to projected or manufactured necessity: for example in order to create a "healthy home environment", to bring up "well-adjusted" children.

The well-marked path to reproducing productive and obedient citizens, the either/or of delinquency and ambition, of pathology and normativity, drains all relations of other more responsive and spontaneous makings.[85] While it is of course true that the history of racist-, gender-, and class-based brutality in the United States has been foundational as a politically institutionalized techne – beginning with the settler-colonial project and its attendant slave, apartheid, and genocidal politics, it has systematically employed violence with precision at the level of kinship (e.g. miscegenation laws, red lining, systematic incarceration, concentration camps, child abduction – indigenous "boarding schools" for example, ghettoization, expulsion, police brutality, gentrification, forced sterilization, and poverty) what is often ignored in these judgments of "disorganization" is the significance that forms of improvised solidarity, through trust and shared resources, has occupied in communities terrorized by state policies and the attendant "economic realities" that appear to justify them. In other words, the plasticity of kinship understood as a set of practices and capacities as opposed to a static, juridical, theological, or quasi-scientific determination shows how the bonds of care can be both spontaneous and establish a foundational set of interconnections that act as a resilient and fecund site of political solidarity, even and especially in conditions of the radically "exiled and errant" as Glissant puts it. Moreover, they affirm the importance of practical bonds as acts of resistance, as Butler notes, citing how women in ghettoized black communities create networks of kinship – not simply determined by genealogical ties – that function to resist the "pathologization and intense surveillance" inordinately affecting those localities or populations. On the continuity of struggle seeded in those crossings, the relatively recent events in Ferguson sparked an unprecedented movement of solidarity across the United States culminating in the birth of Black Lives Matter and the subsequent Movement for Black Lives, which is often explicitly described as built on and through the force of kinship solidarity. Keeanga–Yamahtta Taylor writes:

> In the name of Michael Brown a beautiful black storm against state violence is brewing so dense that it has created a gravity of its own .... It looks explicitly not only to St. Louis city and county police and other municipal law enforcement, but also the imperial wars in the Middle East as sites of murder and trauma .... this growing youth movement has all the ancestral sweetness of kinship. In the words of a local hip-hop artist, "Our grandparents would be proud of us." [86]

Butler cites similar examples, in terms of queer relations, that until recently were completely excluded from recognition in the eyes of sanctioning authorities; rendered aberrant or primitive in psychoanalytic[87] or anthropological discourse, respectively.[88] Communities whose vulnerability is exacerbated by their pathologization came together precisely in the face of the demand to create bonds of trust. In the face of intense vulnerability, it is an act of resistance and survival, an activity of communing that opens potentialities of persistent solidarity in the face of threatened erasure. Similarly, in *A Dying Colonialism*, Frantz Fanon describes the ways in which the Algerian family was radically transformed through revolt. The transformations, he notes, are performed in a two-fold movement. The first occurred with the repressive violence implemented by the occupying French forces: "a father taken into custody in the street in the company of his children, stripped along with them, tortured before their eyes ... the women left to find ways of keeping the children from starving to death".[89] The most profound effect on the family, according to Fanon, was in the breakup and dissolution of crystallized and concretized traditional ideas, as those customs not only lost practical relevance but also became an obstacle to liberation. This led to obvious conflicts within the social fabric of everyday life and required the adjustment if not uprooting of authority within the knots of kin relations, namely the old patriarchal father figure had to relinquish his traditional role in relation to all members of the family. The second aspect of transformation occurred in the mobilization of the Algerian people beginning with the most intimate relations. That is, the traditional family structure gave way to a resilient plasticity that responded directly to the needs of liberation, the necessity of political visibility. Fanon recounts these changes for each customary position within the family. For example, for *the daughter*, the veil was weaponized and these new values at once realized the necessity of liberation for Algerian women, who were traditionally kept illiterate, expected to succumb to arranged marriages in blind obedience to the patriarch-father, "the unveiled Algerian woman, who assumed an increasingly important place in revolutionary action, developed her personality, discovered the exalting realm of responsibility .... The woman-for-marriage disappeared and gradually gave way to the woman-for-action".[90] For Fanon this signified a development of social consciousness alongside a restructuring of social rules necessary for resistance to settler occupation.

Generating Threads of Relation

Seeking legitimation in the eyes of authority is also a demand for recognition. However, this carries with it the implication of successively, and uncritically, recognizing those sanctioning institutions as governing acts of enclosure. The desire to be blessed by the scepter of legitimacy also implicitly authorizes its force of exclusion. It leads to the deeper assumption that the sanctioned and unsanctioned are exhaustive of all relations; that there is a line to draw through intimacy and commitment, a division that is fully cognized by a governing rationality. In other words, in producing these two categories, the sanctioning institution divides relations of intimacy and trust, or "fundamental forms of human dependency", into two domains.[91] Thus, the sanctioning of gay marriage has the further consequence of stratifying queer – or really all – intimacies into the same Manichean logic, the legitimate and illegitimate based on the gently expanding nuclear model of the family. Along with the same formal contraction, it broadly assumes the demands imposed by the tensions between the logic of universal fungibility at the root of commodification, and the force of stratified space and time of the nation-state. Here we are faced with a conflict. On the one hand the demand for legitimacy is also the demand for thinkability and recognition (epistemology and ontology, respectively) while on the other we might find value in that which lies outside of normativity – the not-yet legitimate or the now illegitimate – as that which is not appropriated by convention and standardization. Something unthinkable in conventional discourse also carries with it the possibility for radical practices irreducible to preconceived terms of accomplishment, social or mental health, or other established terms of stratification. Butler puts it this way:

> There is, however, a more fundamental occlusion at work here .... There is, thus, outside the struggle between the legitimate and the illegitimate – which is one that has as its goal the conversion of the illegitimate into the legitimate

– a field that is less thinkable, one not figured in light of its ultimate convertibility into legitimacy".[92]

While it is critical to recognize that which is determined as outside the framework of legitimacy – the "unthinkable" in order to grasp that which is excluded from rationality – there is also the desire to "savor the status of unthinkability" as a "site of pure resistance" as the engagement in figures of practices or relations.[93] How then can we think politics from such a "site of unrepresentability" and moreover how to think politics without precisely considering these sites that persist outside of visibility?[94]

* * *

This recalls Samuel Delany's key work on architectures of desire: "urban renewal" as the sanitization of city neighborhoods, as well as areas that lend themselves to spontaneous social interactions, generating a veritable *undercommons*, to again borrow a term from Moten and Harney. His focus is on the infamous destruction of Times Square.[95] These spaces, prior to their economic-moralistic reorganization, at least momentarily according to Delany, offer chance interactions that move beyond the typical routines implicitly reinforced in more formalized urban areas, in this case, through erotic impulse. Although he is not concerned here with kinship per se, he focuses on spaces in the city in which "interclass contact and communication in a mode of good will" provide the most "rewarding and protective solace" in the face of the brutally flattened relations of a failing capitalist society:

> The class war raging constantly and often silently in the comparatively stabilized societies of the developed world perpetually works for the erosion of the social practices through which interclass communication takes place and of the institutions holding those practices stable, so that new institutions must always be conceived and set in place to take over the jobs of those that are battered again and again till they are destroyed.[96]

The drive to "sanitize" city neighborhoods comes under the auspices of the safety and health of its citizens, thoroughly substantiated by expertise, departmental authorities, anthropologists, and other professionals – the enumeration of new pathologies that functioned to sever the "cleanup" mission from the rants of a Travis Bickle as he psychotically observes the dregs of city life, envisioning one fine day when he can flush it all down the fucking toilet for the coming *tabula rasa* recalls the same attempt at political distancing performed by officials whose political policies are in fact complimentary to the reactionary groups engaged in street fighting and attacks on marginalized communities and movements for social change under the claim of securing private property and "taking back" the country.[97] Delany writes:

> Over the last decade and a half, however, a notion of safety has arisen, a notion that runs from safe sex (once … it becomes anything more than

making sure your partner uses a condom when you are anally penetrated by males of unknown HIV status, whether you are male or female) to safe neighborhoods, safe cities, and committed (i.e. safe) relationships, a notion that currently functions much the way the notion of "security" and "conformity" did in the fifties.[98]

And just as in the 50s, unconquered spaces of spontaneous interaction are pulled to pieces in order to make way for a cultural and economic blank slate. Slated for destruction: "unsafe sex, neighborhoods filled with un-desirables (read 'unsafe characters'), promiscuity". And just as in the 50s, the "safe" institutions center on the monogamous household, the "white" suburban bourgeois non-community. Those "unsafe relations" will be eliminated, those "psychologically 'dangerous' relations, though the danger is rarely specified in any way other than to suggest its failure to conform to the ideal bourgeois marriage" acts as an ostensibly progressive response to the New York City of the late 1970s. That place and time stood out as a veritable attack on the bourgeois family. It was a seedbed of experimental relationality that threatened the very fabric of bourgeois life and it inspired some of the most interesting and critical science fiction of the late 20th century.[99]

* * *

To return to the crisis in criticality discussed above, the dilemma comes with the temptation to simply reject the institution as such: "here is where the critical spirit, the one that operates at the limit of the intelligible, also risks being regarded as apolitical".[100] However, the very distinction which arises between criticality and the political situates the former as a place of refuge from politics. Criticality is not a static position or an objectively circumscribed, finally determined place; rather it designates a tension between the demand for political apprehension and a query into the very basis for the legitimation of authorizing institutions, that space and language that counts as political – the terms to which thinkability is reduced in order to appear.

When Jordana Rosenberg asks Butler about her commitment to the politics of *unreality* – what is at stake in living in a domain of unreality? – that is, to finding language to consider those social bonds that dwell beyond thinkability, the not-yet licit or illicit, i.e. "the kinds of social bonds that can be wrought by those who live in suspended or shadow ontologies", Butler remarks:

> This needful attachment is fully stupid, fully dependent on others who are ordered by a social world we never chose. And yet we need this domain of unfreedom in order to live and to survive. I am wondering how much of this predicament remains with us as we attach to identity categories and political self-understandings.[101]

In the case of so-called chosen families, it is often misleading to frame these relationships – a response to the demand and need for a familiar context or care – simply as a choice, like a consumer browsing a mall, or swiping through the available possibilities of prospective affines on a dating app. That frame simply ignores the necessity of securing a foundation of relationality, that mutual generation of the familiar, i.e. one of trust, minimally in some form of feeling, some kind of immediate communication, some *undercommon*, in relation to adversity, erasure, and precarity that is not chosen – as a response to the facticity of the situation. The difference between friendship and kinship then is one between choice and necessity. The latter is a response to both chance and need, and it is the recognition that possibility is always consigned to obligation, just as obligation conditions possibility.[102] It is in becoming conscious of this rupture of the self, and the prerequisite for the intimacy of others to express the bond of kinship, which ultimately underwrites the ego, rather than, conversely, being underwritten by a choice, which can unravel as readily as it was assembled. Instead, one then must work with what is at hand, and in this sense, it is not a matter of whim, but a situation we are precariously cast into – in this sense, much like a family one is physically born into, which is often distinguished from other social relations precisely because it is never chosen and as Freud realized, rarely forgotten.

Vulnerability and Solidarity

Judith Butler's book *Frames of War* was written in response to global war in the 21st century "focusing on cultural modes of regulating affective and ethical dispositions through a selective and differential framing of violence".[103] The terms frame, frames, or framing refer to epistemological rather than hermeneutic frameworks – that which appears according to a given delimitation of the world that inspires various responses. Framing itself is an authorizing gesture, it circumscribes the range of inquiry. It is through such framing that we acknowledge or recognize – or fail to acknowledge or recognize – "the lives of others lost or injured".[104] In this way, the issue of framing is at once concerned with knowledge and ontology, insofar as that which is known often determines what constitutes a life and just as often determines the conditions for its flourishing, or not. Butler writes:

> The precarity of life imposes an obligation upon us. We have to ask about the conditions under which it becomes possible to apprehend a life or set of lives as precarious, and those that make it less possible, or indeed impossible.[105]

But how can we understand this obligation in relation to embodied vulnerability? Departing from the common intuition that evidence of vulnerability leads to "a heightening of violence" through a direct instigation to destroy those implicated, Judith Butler much like Audre Lorde, suggests that we need to rethink our relation to precariousness and the injurious; our fundamental dependency on one another not as something to recoil from, disable, or react to, but something which allows us to make "broader political claims about rights of protection and entitlements to persistence and flourishing".[106] However, this can only occur with a rethinking of the ways that a body is always entrusted to another. It is not that I have a body and then it is introduced to social order, into a given reality, or world.

The very constitution of my body is predicated on its exposure to sensibility and intelligibility through the social, in the fundamentally precarious disposition of embodiment and it is through this condition that the social is produced. Much like Bourdieu's notion of habitus discussed above, the social in this sense is not what you and I make when we interact, but that which we respond to when responding to one another. We might say that relationality precedes rationality, or as Butler puts it, apprehension precedes recognition.[107] In other words, it is through my vulnerability as an embodied being that I am open, or "given over", to communing with others. It is in this synthetic relational context that I become a self. Much like Kierkegaard's notion of the self as synthesis, as an ongoing negotiation between necessity and freedom, finitude and the infinite, and resignation and faith. For Kierkegaard the self is not an individual but a relating to a relation.[108] The political implications in this are profound:

> The being of the body to which this ontology refers is one that is always given over to others, to norms, to social and political organizations that have developed historically in order to maximize precariousness for some and minimiz[ing] it for others.[109]

But Butler poses the question more specifically: in what sense does life then extend beyond the sanctioned conditions of recognition and invisibility?[110] This claim does not mean that life as such is always resistant to the confines of normativity, but rather that "each and every construction of life requires time to do its job, and that no job it does can overcome time itself".[111] And so these terms are always extended and modified, we open up new ways to relate, or respond, and spontaneously develop ligatures of association and disassociation. If the corporeal is the basis for obligation, it is also because exposure already implies the social. My task here is to rethink kinship beyond its instrumentalization as a site of exposure to – and social/psychological reinforcement of – this differential allocation, in effect providing a register of relation in response to the uneven distribution of social power. And while the apprehension of vulnerability can provide a substantial and trusted perspective, one that underwrites solidarity and therefore precedes recognition, it can also augment or motivate the expression of violence, or more generally be utilized to justify accretions of institutional power concentrated by and, therefore, constituting the anxiety-driven nation-state. To paraphrase Butler, precariousness is managed by concepts of life and death but is never resolved by them, or any discourse (alone) for that matter.[112] Instead, bodies must be attended to, must interact with, and physically support one another. It is this radical exposure and concomitant obligation that most directly expresses the synthetic practice of kinship.

Corporeal Isolation and the Logic of the State

For a counter illustration – through a bit of a deviation – in which a state activates – or accumulates the potential to determine, ratify, administer – extreme vulnerability, I will close this frame by briefly considering the *politics of deprivation* and the logic of governance (in terms of embodied relation) via two points from Elaine Scarry's intense examination of political corporeality in *The Body in Pain*,[113] specifically from the section on the "Structure of Torture".

On the one hand, the use of torture from this standpoint does not simply function to magnify the experience of pain in the subject in order to extract information, but rather, the real aim is to demonstrate the incontestability of sovereign power through the act of inflicting pain. It is exactly because the reality of the authorizing force is at risk of appearing arbitrary, and therefore unstable, that it resorts to torture, which for Scarry is the ultimate world-diminishing relation, or perhaps non-relation is the better term.[114] Within the torture room the "conversion of pain into the fiction of absolute power" is most intimately performed.[115] In the experience of being "beaten on the soles of the feet", simulated drowning, hanging by the wrists, needles slipped under the fingernails, burning of the skin and hair, electric shock, sexual humiliation, or bone breaking, at once every object in the room becomes transformed into an implement of pain as all other relations, values, or meanings dissipate. Consciousness becomes pain, pain becomes world. This is perhaps most effectively realized in lengthy stints in solitary confinement, a gradual and perhaps more enduring form of torture, in which sense and social deprivation may permanently change the body's sensual response to stimuli.[116] If we transfer this to the expression of the power of a nation-state today – its force of partitioning and extraction, its economic determinism ultimately reinforced by violence – we find that its reality makes itself felt through the immiseration it produces. And this misery is accentuated and increased as the system nears its own crisis, in other words, as it reveals its own failure which can no longer be adequately repressed.

The brutality of poverty, for example, is denied as multifarious points of social translation fix deprivation within the authorizing rationale of the system, as evidence that it functions – normative concepts such as failure, inferiority, stupidity, laziness, lack of motivation, lack of confidence, insanity, criminality, and ultimately failed marriages and "broken homes" among other things are all objectified in poverty and education – correctly allowing those who cannot adhere to its demands, naturally enough, to toil or perish. If "intense pain is world destroying",[117] then intense poverty is world decaying, which is to say it expresses a prolonged, deliberate, and rationalized destruction. Impoverishment is slow torture through which the world diminishes as the laser focus on the means for escaping hunger and want, whether through labor, crime, or perhaps most profoundly narcosis – *self*-destruction. This can only end in the exhaustion of the relational self. It is against this structural conditioning of the means of satisfying need that both expresses and augments the authorizing force of the state. The anemic nuclear family as the only legally recognized relation of intimacy, around which society and economy is, to a great degree, oriented and organized, diminishes the ability for communities to sustain themselves and frustrates the flourishing of undercommons to become sustainable against the constant threat of debt and poverty. The commodification of childcare and healthcare are just two examples of this structural diminishment.

The second but related point concerns the body as a site for communication, the corporeal condition which underwrites language. Scarry writes: "The nature of confession is falsified by an idiom built on the word 'betrayal': in confession, one betrays oneself and all those aspects of the world–friend, family, country, cause – that the self is made up of it".[118] As noted, extreme physical pain occludes the world, one is "in the grip of pain", we sometimes say. The body is conceived as a sight of direct communication, and communicability is foreclosed most swiftly through pain.[119] Our bodies in relation substantiate our ability to grasp a world as an extension into language and gesture broadly understood. Much like Butler's notes on precarity, Scarry's observations on torture show us that a body must be taken care of, must meet certain criteria in order to become and maintain a self. It must feel and sense others and things, warmth, and nourishment, for example, as part of the shared habitus of care. The body becomes the most fecund site for orienting the grip of adversity. It must seek out relations to attend to its haunting dependency.

"World, self, and voice are lost, or nearly lost, through the intense pain of torture".[120] Scarry makes the further point that the very juxtaposition of two radically different situations: one body in absolute pain, deprived of world, self, and language, relating to another body devoid of pain, without deprivation, as the director and distributor of precariousness: "the larger the prisoner"s pain, the larger the torturer's world".[121] Evident precisely in the contrast between "annihilating negation" and pure affirmation, we find the translation of pain into the power of authorization as the extreme end of the logic of the state. It is the isolated body at war with the world that justifies the relinquishment of liberty in the name of natural law (i.e. survival) according to Hobbes in the *Leviathan*.[122] Destroyed is the possibility for relation that implicitly extends to the "overwhelming characteristic of the domestic, that its protective, narrowing act in the location of the human being's most expansive potential".[123]

The *unmaking of the world*, the world-destroying act, is one which mutilates the domestic, domicile, or domus, by isolating the body through pain. Scarry writes: "the protective, healing, expansive acts implicit in 'host' and 'hostel' and 'hospitable' and 'hospital' all converge back into 'hospes', which in turn moves back to the root 'hos' meaning house, shelter, or refuge".[124] This she contrasts with *hostis* and hostility, the "'host' deprived of all ground of his power in acts of reciprocity and equality but the 'host' deprived of all ground, the host of the eucharist, the sacrificial victim".[125] A similar ambivalence is identified in Butler's work where she notes that the promise of security attributed to the nation-state is also the exposure to violence which it wields: "so to rely on the nation-state for protection from violence is precisely to exchange one potential violence for another."[126] This grip on necessity works to secure authority both from a standpoint internal to the state and as a mechanism that is reactively determinative of its boundaries in modern warfare which bypasses the old rules of war by extending the range of tactics beyond purely militaristic strategy.

* * *

To close I will briefly illustrate one last example of the systematic destruction of kinship bonds that has become an instrumental strategy in modern warfare. Persuading Winston Churchill to undertake a massive campaign deliberately targeting civilian populations ..., bodies ..., families ..., kin – which in general was accomplished with unprecedented efficiency in the Second World War – Sir Arthur Harris, "commander-in-chief of the bombing command", resorted to the following logic: "that those who have loosed these horrors upon mankind will now in their homes and persons feel the shattering strokes of just retribution".[127] That is, the ultimate target is not, in fact, the perpetrators, the decision-makers, beneficiaries, and architects of genocide or imperial expansion of the *lebensraum*, not even the grunts in the field were the target, nor was the *Schutzstaffel*. It is the principle of life, relation itself, the necessity that underlies the (no doubt) dubiously claimed purpose and function of the militarized state that here reproduces in form the logic of extermination. W.G. Sebald comments that for Harris, the retribution matched his sympathy for destruction for its own sake, clearly echoing the logic of acceleration at the core of the Futurism that spawned Mussolini's fascism. It was certainly effective in transforming cities into veritable *necropolei*, the lone survivors among the ruins akin to those in Hiroshima or Nagasaki often bereft of the will to live. The ultimate logic of contemporary warfare defined by the nation-state is in the strategic foresight and tactical ability to radically diminish, if not entirely excise, the capacity to sustain or create community out of intense and intimate bonds of relation. The goal of warfare today is to transform a polity, a community, or a people into a wasteland of apparitions. Its ultimate task is to destabilize relations of trust established and reestablished as the *habitus* of the community. It is, finally, to disable practical kinship.

Notes

1 Aparecida Vilaça, "Chronically Unstable Bodies: Reflections an Amazonian Corporalities," *Journal of the Royal Anthropological Institute*, September 1 (2005): 449.

2 Simone Weil, "The Love of God and Affliction," *Waiting for God* (New York: G. P. Putnam's Sons, 1951) 118.

3 In *Matter and Memory*, Bergson for example writes: "The bodily memory, made up of the sum of the sensori-motor systems organized by habit, is then a quasi-instantaneous memory to which true memory of the past serves as a base" And "the sensori-motor apparatus furnish to ineffective, that is unconscious, memories, the means of taking on a body, of materializing themselves, in short of becoming present." Henri Bergson, *Matter and Memory*, trans. N.M. Paul and W.S. Palmer (New York: Zone Books, 1988) 152–153.

4 David Schneider, *Critique of the Study of Kinship* (Ann Arbor, MI: University of Michigan Press, 1984).

5 Ibid., 168.

6 Ibid., 168.

7 This led to the publication of *Systems of Consanguinity and Affinity* in 1871 describing 139 kinship systems. See, Helen Gardner, "The Origin of Kinship in Oceania: Lewis Henry Morgan and Lorimer Fison," *Oceania*, 78, no. 2 (July, 2008): 137. Of course, the questions and answers were filtered through missionaries and the Catholic lens that shaped their mission.

8   Bordertown Violence Working Group: Nick Estes, Melanie K. Yazzie, Jennifer Nez Denetdale, and David Correia, *Red Nation Rising: From Bordertown Violence to Native Liberation* (New York: PM Press, 2021) 117.

9   J.J. Bachofen, *Das Mutterrecht. Eine Untersuchung über die Gynaikokratie der alten Welt nach ihrer religiosen und rechtlichen Natur*, (Basel: B. Schwabe 1897).

10   "As Marx and Engels read all this, they excitedly concluded that Iroquois women must traditionally have possessed what modern trade unionists could only dream of – collective ownership and control over their own productive lives." C. Knight, "Early Human Kinship Was Matrilineal," in *Early Human Kinship*, edited by N.J. Allen, H. Callan, R. Dunbar and W. James (Oxford: Blackwell, 2008) 68.

11   Knight continues by citing Robert Lowies' reflections on Morgan's work: "attracted the notice of Marx and Engels, who accepted and popularised its evolutionary doctrines as being in harmony with their own philosophy. As a result it was promptly translated into various European tongues, and German workingmen would sometimes reveal an uncanny familiarity with the Hawaiian and Iroquois mode of designating kin, matters not obviously connected with a proletarian revolution." Ibid., 69.

12   For a fascinating account of the history of the ideological underpinnings of the anthropological presumptions, see: C. Knight, "Early Human Kinship Was Matrilineal" cited above. We might also add that conceptually, a society that has no way of regulating reproduction via the concept of blood and ownership (monogamous marriage) cannot secure a political concept of patriarchy based on reproduction and possession unless monogamous marriage is instituted. Without this, there is no political mechanism to guarantee or determine fatherhood, i.e. who the father is. Arguably Hobbes saw this clearly in the *Leviathan* where he writes: "If there be no contract the dominion is in the mother." Thomas Hobbes, *Leviathan* (Boston, MA: Hackett, 1994) Chapter XX para. 5.

13   C. Knight, "Early Human Kinship Was Matrilineal," 61.

14   Robin Fox suggests: "It is because anthropologists have consistently looked at the problem from the egofocus that they have been baffled by it. They have placed ego at the centre of his kinship network and tried to work the system out in terms of his personal relationships." Robin Fox, *Kinship and Marriage: An Anthropological Perspective* (Harmondsworth: Penguin, 1967) 84.

15   Margaret Mead, *Coming of Age in Samoa* (New York: Harper Collins, 2001).

16   Ibid. See especially the last two chapters: "Our Educational Problems in Light of Samoan Contrasts" and "Education for Choice".

17   Janet Carsten, *Cultures of Relatedness: New Approaches to the Study of Kinship* (Cambridge: Cambridge University Press, 2000) 1. See also, "Identity and Substance: The broadening bases of relatedness among the Nuer of southern Sudan" by Sharon Elaine Hutchinson.

18   Ibid., 2. See also "'He used to be my relative': exploring the bases of relatedness among Inupiat of northern Alaska" by Barbara Bodenhorn in the same collection.

19   "It is not so much, then, whether some groups allow marriage that others prohibit, but whether there are any groups in which no type of marriage whatever is prohibited. The answer must be completely in the negative." Claude Levi-Stauss, *Elementary Structures of Kinship*, trans. James Harle Bell and John Richard von Sturmer (Boston, MA: Beacon Press, 1969) 9.

20   Ibid., 10

21   Schneider, *Critique*, 165.

22   Ibid., 165.

23   Which is precisely why Jacques Derrida opens with this point with his deconstruction of the dichotomy nature/culture produced by the Social Sciences in *'Structure, Sign and Play in the Discourse of the Human Sciences'*. Derrida writes: "By commencing his work with the *factum* of the incest prohibition, Levi-Strauss thus places himself at the very point at which this difference, which has always been assumed to be self-evident, finds itself erased or questioned." (283) Still, the old concepts are conserved but

their limits are pointed out. They are critiqued but they are held on to so long as they remain useful. Jacques Derrida, *Writing and Difference*, trans. Alan Bass (Chicago, IL: University of Chicago Press, 1978) 278–294.

24 The primary question which Mauss seeks to answer in this study is the following: "What rule of legality and self-interest ... compels the gift that has been received to be obligatorily reciprocated? What power resides in the object given that causes its recipient to pay it back?" Marcel Mauss, *The Gift*, trans. W. D. Hollis (London: Routledge, 2002) 4.

25 This is where Freud, drawing from the work of Sir Thomas Fraser's *Golden Bough*, as well as the research of Wilhelm Wundt, Charles Darwin, and a wide range of ethnographers and anthropologists, joins anthropological insights to his research into psychoanalysis – namely the way in which taboo shows up in modern society (obsessional neurosis). Freud speculates about the original event as rooted in tribal solidarity, exchange and taboo – in which the sons murder their father, consume him and ostensibly replace him with a totem. It is in the lasting vestiges of shame and guilt, signified by taboo that the brothers exchange the sisters, rather than keeping them for themselves. However, the horror of insecurity at the vacuum of authority and an instinct driven world led them to reinstate the law and build a totem to the father, to the lost authority, imbuing it with the power of taboo. Transgression of taboo then opens the door for the horrific chaos that is associated with the dissolution of authority, the loss of the father, the reality principle or the master signifier as Jacques Lacan understood it. Freud writes: "The violent primal father had doubtless been the feared and envied model of each one of the company of brothers: and in the act of devouring him they accomplished their identification with him, and each one of them acquired a portion of his strength. The totem meal, which is perhaps mankind's earliest festival, would thus be a repetition and a commemoration of this memorable and criminal deed, which was the beginning of so many things-of social organization, of moral restrictions and of religion." Sigmund Freud, *Totem and Taboo* (London: Routledge, 1999) 142. In his short essay 'Our Attitudes towards Death' in *Timely Reflections on War and Death*, Freud writes: "If God's son has to sacrifice his life to free humanity from original sin, then according to the law of *talion* ... that sin must have been a killing or murder .... And if original sin was an offense against God the father, then humanity's oldest crime must have been patricide", see 'Timely Reflections on War and Death' in *Murder, Mourning and Melancholia* (New York and London: Penguin, 2005) 187.

26 Claude Levi-Strauss, *Elementary Structures*, 478.

27 Pierre Clastres, *Archaeology of Violence*, trans. Jeanine Herman (Los Angeles, CA: semiotext(e), 2010) 268.

28 Ibid., 169.

29 Ibid., 170.

30 Ibid., 269. For Clastres' theory concerning an-archic society, see Pierre Clastres, *Society against the State* (New York: Zone Books 1989). There Clastres writes: "The term subsistence economy, is acceptable for describing the economic organization of those societies, provided it is taken to mean *not* the necessity that derives from a *lack*, an incapacity inherent in that type of society and its technology; but on the contrary: the refusal of a useless *excess*, the determination to make productive activity agree with the satisfaction of needs. And nothing more." (195) and "When in primitive society, the economic dynamic lends itself to definition as a distinct and autonomous domain, when the activity of production becomes alienated, accountable labor, levied by men who enjoy the fruits of that labor, what has come to pass is that society has been divided between rulers and ruled, masters and subjects – it has ceased to exorcise the thing that will be its ruin: power and respect for power." (198) One of his obvious presuppositions is that the state form of political organization necessarily precludes egalitarianism and necessarily includes alienation, particularly alienated labor. That is, surplus production is the condition for the possibility of

surplus power, i.e. a ruling class. Potlach is one way that surplus is destroyed. The division of labor is predicated on the state form and vice versa, they imply each other. A similar line of thought can be found in Marshall Sahlins' *Stone Age Economics* (London and New York: Routledge, 1974) which posits hunter gatherer societies as the original affluent society, based not just on subsistence and the reduction of needs but also the absence of the demand to produce for production sake – or the equation of production as meaning. More recently James C. Scott makes the argument that such a surplus, and therefore for him the state, only emerges from intensive grain based agricultural societies. Grain is one of the few high nutrient crops that can be stored for long periods of time. It is, according to Scott the first time a real sustainable system of taxation could be implemented.

31 Gayle Rubin, "The Traffic in Women: Notes on a Political Economy of Sex," in *Toward an Anthropology of Women*, edited by Rayna R. Reiter (Monthly Review Press, 1975) 157–210, p. 175.
32 Ibid., 175.
33 Levi-Strauss, *Elementary Structures*, 480.
34 Rubin, "Traffic," 47.
35 See note on Freud above.
36 Schneider, *Critique of Kinship*, 165 (my emphasis).
37 Ibid., 165–166.
38 Ibid., 166.
39 Melbourne Trapper, "Blood/Kinship, Governmentality, and Cultures of Order in Colonial Africa," in *Relative Values*, edited by Sarah Franklin and Susan McKinnon (Durham, NC: Duke University Press, 2001) 330.
40 Ibid., 331.
41 Ibid., 331.
42 "For enlightenment, anything which does not conform
    to the standard of calculability and utility must be viewed with suspicion.
    Once the movement is able to develop unhampered by external
    oppression, there is no holding it back. Its own ideas of human rights then
    fare no better than the older universals. Any intellectual resistance it encounters
    merely increases its strength. The reason is that enlightenment
    also recognizes itself in the old myths. No matter which myths are invoked against
    it, by being used as arguments they are made to acknowledge the
    very principle of corrosive rationality of which enlightenment stands accused.
    Enlightenment is totalitarian."

    Max Horkheimer and Theodor W. Adorno, *Dialectic of Enlightenment: Philosophical Fragments,* trans. Edmund Jephcott (Stanford, CA: Stanford University Press, 2002) 4–5.
43 Nick Estes, "Wounded Knee: Settler Colonial Property Regimes and Indigenous Liberation." Capitalism Nature Socialism, 2013 Vol. 24, No. 3, 190–202
44 Ibid.
45 Ibid., 332.
46 Freeman, "Queer Belongings," 301.
47 Ibid., 301.
48 Richard von Krafft-Ebing, *Psychopathia Sexualis*, edited by John LoPicolo (New York: Arcade Books, 2011)
49 Freeman, "Queer Belongings," 300–301.
50 See, Paul Gilroy, *The Black Atlantic: Modernity and Double Consciousness* (Cambridge, MA: Harvard University Press, 1993). On the technics by which nationalisms are built through "the symbolism of ethnic and national reproduction" through the production of myth, securing a gendered division of labor in the collective imagination, Gilroy notes: "The unholy forces of nationalist biopolitics intersect on the bodies of women charged with the reproduction of absolute ethnic difference

and the continuity of bloodlines. The integrity of the nation becomes the integrity of its masculinity. In fact, it can be a nation only if the correct versions of gender hierarchy has been established and reproduced." Paul Gilroy, *Against Race: Imagining Political Culture Beyond the Color Line* (Cambridge, MA: Harvard University Press, 2000) 127.

51 Freeman, "Queer Belongings," 303.
52 Ibid., 303. In her extremely compelling essay 'The Site of Memory' Toni Morrison notes: "Like Simone de Beauvoir, he [James Baldwin] moves from the event to the image that it left. My route is the reverse: The image comes first and tells me what the 'memory' is about." Toni Morrison, "The Site of Memory," in *Inventing the Truth: The Art and Craft of Memoir*, edited by William Zinsser (Boston, MA and New York: Houghton Mifflin, 1995) 83–102 (94–95).
53 Freeman, "Queer Belongings," 303.
54 Ibid., 305.
55 Pierre Bourdieu, *Outline of a Theory of Practice*, trans. Richard Nice (Cambridge: Cambridge University Press, 1977) 72.
56 Ibid., 72.
57 On the development of mindreading in *homo sapien sapiens* as key in the survival of the species see: Michael Tomasello, Malinda Carpenter, Josep Call, Tanya Behne, and Henrike Moll, "Understanding and Sharing Intentions: The Origins of Cultural Cognition," *Behavioral and Brain Sciences*, 28 (2005): 675–735. Max Planck Institute for Evolutionary Anthropology, D-04103 Leipzig, Germany.
58 Bourdieu, *Outline of a Theory of Practice*, 72–73.
59 Ibid., 76.
60 Ibid., 76.
61 Ibid., 35–36.
62 Ibid., 37.
63 Ibid., 31–32.
64 Ibid., 33–34.
65 Ibid., 34–35.
66 See *Statement by HHS Deputy Secretary on Unaccompanied Alien Children Program* (https://www.hhs.gov/about/news/2018/05/28/statement-hhs-deputy-secretary-unaccompanied-alien-children-program.html) (accessed 15 July 2018).
67 Again, I understand the state simply as a political entity constituted by the monopoly on violence as well as the institutional distribution of precariousness (and therefore spaces of care) and territorial sovereignty.
68 "to put an end to dangerous loopholes in US immigration laws like the practice of 'catch and release', in which federal authorities release illegal immigrants to await hearings for which few show up. In the worst cases, these loopholes are being exploited by human traffickers and violent gangs like MS-13." See *Statement by HHS Deputy Secretary on Unaccompanied Alien Children Program* (https://www.hhs.gov/about/news/2018/05/28/statement-hhs-deputy-secretary-unaccompanied-alien-children-program.html) (accessed 15 July 2018).
69 Hannah Arendt, *The Origins of Totalitarianism* (Cleveland, OH: Meridian Books, 1962) 290–304.
70 Judith Butler, "Is Kinship Always Heterosexual?" *Differences: A Journal of Feminist Cultural Studies*, 13, no. 1 (2002): 14–15.
71 Ibid., 15.
72 Ibid., 34.
73 Ibid., 15. Carol Stacks, *All Our Kin: Strategies for Survival in a Black Community* (New York: Basic Books, 1983).
74 Carol Stack, *All Our Kin*, 22.
75 Ibid., 90.
76 Ibid., 91.

77 Ibid., 93.
78 Stephano Harney and Fred Moten, *The Undercommons: Fugitive Planning & Black Study* (Minor Compositions, Wivenhoe/New York/Port Watson, 2013) 97.
79 Ibid., 98.
80 Ibid., 98–99.
81 Eduard Glissant, *Poetics of Relation*, trans. Betsy Wing (Ann Arbor, MI: University of Michigan Press, 1997) 7–8.
82 Glissant, *Poetics of Relation*, 27.
83 Édouard Glissant. *Caribbean Discourses* (Charlottesville: University Press of Virginia, 1996). 171.
84 Ibid., 169.
85 For a critique of some of the mainstream currents in French psychoanalysis arguing for these very reasons against queer or otherwise configured families see Judith Butler, "Secular Politics, Torture and Secular Time," in *Frames of War, When Is Life Grievable?* (New York: Verso, 2016) 101–136.
86 Quoted in: Keeanga–Yamahtta Taylor, *From #Black Lives Matter to Black Liberation* (Chicago, IL: Haymarket Books, 2016) 158.
87 On contemporary psychoanalytic doctrines concerning the healthy family, Butler cites psychoanalyst Michael Schneider's work on psychopathology and politics: "who in offering his opinions on cultural affairs has publicly maintained that the state must step in to take the place of the absent father, not through welfare benefits (itself conceived as a maternal deformation of the state), but through the imposition of law, discipline, and uncompromising modes of punishment and imprisonment. In his view, this is the only way to secure the cultural foundations of citizenship, that is, the cultural foundations that are required for the exercise of a certain conception of freedom. Thus, the state policies that create extreme class differentials, pervasive racism in employment practices, efforts to separate families in order to save children from Islamic formations, and efforts to sequester the *banlieues* as intensified sites of racialized poverty, are exonerated and effaced through such explanations." Butler, *Frames of War*, 115.
88 This was, of course, exacerbated with the AIDS crisis in the 1980s which informs Butler's critique. "In the initial years of the AIDS crisis in the US the public vigils, and the Names Project broke through the public shame associated with dying from AIDS, a shame associated sometimes with homosexuality, and especially anal sex, and sometimes with drugs and promiscuity." Butler, *Frames*, 39.
89 Frantz Fanon, *A Dying Colonialism*, trans. Haakon Chevalier (New York: Grove Press, 1959) 100.
90 Ibid., 107–108.
91 Butler, *Frames of War*, 15.
92 Ibid., 17.
93 Ibid., 17–18.
94 Ibid., 18.
95 Samuel Delany, *Times Square Red, Times Square Blue* (New York: New York University Press, 1999).
96 Ibid., 121.
97 Travis Bickle, played of course by Robert De Niro, in Martin Scorsese's 1977 *Taxi Driver*.
98 Ibid., 121–122.
99 For an excellent exploration in prose into various labyrinthine constructions of relations of mutual aid in the face of catastrophe, isolation and decay see Samuel Delany's magnum opus *Dhalgren* (New York: Random House, 1996).
100 Butler, "Is Kinship Always Heterosexual?," 19.
101 Jordana Rosenberg and Judith Butler, "Serious Innovation," in *A Companion to Lesbian, Gay, Transgender and Queer Studies*, edited by George E. Haggerty and Molly McGarry (Hoboken, NJ: Blackwell Publishing, 2007) 384.

102 "But if possibility outruns necessity so that the self runs away from itself in possibility, it has no necessity to which it is to return; this is possibility's despair. This self becomes an abstract possibility; it flounders in possibility until exhausted but neither moves from the place where it is nor arrives any-where, for necessity is literally that place; to become one-self is literally a movement in that place. To become is a movement away from that place, but to become oneself is a movement in that place." Søren Kierkegaard, *The Sickness unto Death*, trans. Hong and Hong (Princeton, NJ: Princeton University Press, 1980) 35–36.

103 Ibid., 1.

104 Ibid., 2.

105 Ibid., 2.

106 Ibid., 2.

107 Recognition in the Hegelian sense requires mutual or "reciprocal action". Butler seeks to grasp *apprehension* as well as *intelligibility* in light of the notion of recognition. The first she sees as a "mode of knowing that is not yet recognition." While intelligibility for Butler is "understood as the general historical schema/schemas that establish domains of the knowable" – "cognition" for Hegel. Ibid., 6.

108 "The self is a relation that relates itself to itself or is the relation's relating itself to itself in the relation; the self is not the relation but is the relation's relating itself to itself. A human being is a synthesis of the infinite and the finite, of the temporal and the eternal, of freedom and necessity, in short, a synthesis." See Søren Kierkegaard, *The Sickness unto Death*, trans. Hong and Hong (Princeton, NJ: Princeton University Press, 1983) 13. Also, see footnote 103 above.

109 Butler, *Frames of War*, 2–3.

110 Ibid. 4. "I do not think that precariousness is a function of effect of recognition, nor that recognition is the only or best way to register precariousness. To say a life is injurable, for instance, or that it can be lost, destroyed or systematically neglected to the point of death, is to underscore not only the finitude of a life (that death is certain) but also its precariousness (that life requires various social and economic conditions to be met in order to be sustained as life". Ibid., 35.

111 Ibid., 4.

112 Ibid., 18.

113 Elaine Scarry, *The Body in Pain: The Making and Unmaking of the World* (Oxford: Oxford University Press, 1985).

114 Ibid., 27.

115 Ibid., 27.

116 This is well documented but for more information, see for example, the recent Vera Institute of Justice study published in April 2021: https://www.vera.org/downloads/publications/the-impacts-of-solitary-confinement.pdf

117 Ibid., 31.

118 Ibid., 29.

119 Hannah Arendt writes: "Indeed, the most intense feeling we know of, intense to the point of blotting out all other experiences, namely, the experience of great bodily pain, is at the same time the most private and least communicable of all." Hannah Arendt, *The Human Condition* (Chicago, IL: University of Chicago Press, 1958) 50.

120 Ibid., 35. Scarry notes in regard to extreme pain: "What is meant by 'seeing stars' is that the contents of consciousness are, during those moments, obliterated, that the name of one's child, the memory of a friend's face, are all absent." Ibid., 30.

121 Ibid., 36.

122 Thomas Hobbes, *Leviathan or the Matter, Forme, & Power of a Common-Wealth Ecclesiasticall and Civill* (London: Andrew Crooke, at the Green Dragon in St. Pauls Church-yard, 1651) 79–80.

123 Ibid., 40.

124 Ibid., 40.

125 Ibid., 45.

126 Ibid., 26.
127 W.G. Sebald, *On the Natural History of Destruction*, trans. Anthea Bell (New York: Random House, 2004) 19.

Bibliography

Hannah Arendt. *The Human Condition*. Chicago, IL: University of Chicago Press, 1958.

Hannah Arendt. *The Origins of Totalitarianism*. Cleveland, OH: Meridian Books, 1962.

J.J. Bachofen. *Das Mutterrecht. Eine Untersuchung über die Gynaikokratie der alten Welt nach ihrer religiosen und rechtlichen Natur*. Basel: B. Schwabe 1897.

Henri Bergson. *Matter and Memory*. Translated by N.M. Paul and W.S. Palmer. New York: Zone Books, 1988.

Bordertown Violence Working Group, Nick Estes, Melanie K. Yazzie, Jennifer Nez Denetdale and David Correia. *Red Nation Rising: From Bordertown Violence to Native Liberation*. New York: PM Press, 2021.

Pierre Bourdieu. *Outline of a Theory of Practice*. Translated by Richard Nice. Cambridge: Cambridge University Press, 1977.

Judith Butler. "Is Kinship Always Heterosexual?" *Differences: A Journal of Feminist Cultural Studies*, 13, no. 1 (2002): 101–136.

Judith Butler. "Secular Politics, Torture and Secular Time." In *Frames of War, When Is Life Grievable?* New York: Verso, 2016.

Janet Carsten. *Cultures of Relatedness: New Approaches to the Study of Kinship*. Cambridge: Cambridge University Press, 2000.

Pierre Clastres. *Archaeology of Violence*. Translated by Jeanine Herman. Los Angeles, CA: Semiotext(e), 2010.

Samuel Delany. *Dhalgren*. New York: Random House, 1996.

Samuel Delany. *Times Square Red, Times Square Blue*. New York: New York University Press, 1999.

Jacques Derrida. *Writing and Difference*. Translated by Alan Bass. Chicago, IL: University of Chicago Press, 1978.

Nick Estes. "Wounded Knee: Settler Colonial Property Regimes and Indigenous Liberation." *Capitalism Nature Socialism*, 24, no. 3 (2013): 190–202.

Frantz Fanon. *A Dying Colonialism*. Translated by Haakon Chevalier. New York: Grove Press, 1959.

Robin Fox. *Kinship and Marriage: An Anthropological Perspective*. Harmondsworth: Penguin, 1967.

Elizabeth Freeman. "Queer Belongings." In *A Companion to Lesbian, Gay, Bisexual, Transgender, and Queer Studies*, edited by George E. Haggerty and Molly McGarry. Oxford: Wiley Blackwell, 2015.

Sigmund Freud. "Timely Reflections on War and Death." In *Murder, Mourning and Melancholia*. New York and London: Penguin, 2005.

Sigmund Freud. *Totem and Taboo*. London: Routledge, 1999.

Paul Gilroy. *The Black Atlantic: Modernity and Double Consciousness*. Cambridge, MA: Harvard University Press, 1993.

Édouard Glissant. *Caribbean Discourses*. Charlottesville: University Press of Virginia, 1996.

Édouard Glissant. *Poetics of Relation*. Translated by Betsy Wing. Ann Arbor, MI: University of Michigan Press, 1997.

Stephano Harney and Fred Moten. *The Undercommons: Fugitive Planning & Black Study*. Wivenhoe/New York/Port Watson: Minor Compositions, 2013.

Thomas Hobbes. *Leviathan*. Boston, MA: Hackett, 1994.

Max Horkheimer and Theodor W. Adorno. *Dialectic of Enlightenment: Philosophical Fragments*. Stanford, CA: Stanford University Press, 2002.

Søren Kierkegaard. *The Sickness unto Death*. Translated by Hong and Hong. Princeton, NJ: Princeton University Press, 1980.

C. Knight "Early Human Kinship Was Matrilineal." In *Early Human Kinship*, edited by N.J. Allen, H. Callan, R. Dunbar and W. James. Oxford: Blackwell, 2008.

Richard von Krafft-Ebing. *Psychopathia Sexualis*, edited by John LoPicolo. New York: Arcade Books, 2011.

Claude Levi-Stauss. *Elementary Structures of Kinship*. Translated by James Harle Bell and John Richard von Sturmer. Boston, MA: Beacon Press, 1969.

Marcel Mauss. *The Gift*. Translated by W. D. Hollis. London: Routledge, 2002.

Margaret Mead. *Coming of Age in Samoa*. New York: Harper Collins, 2001.

Toni Morrison. "The Site of Memory." In *Inventing the Truth: The Art and Craft of Memoir*, edited by William Zinsser. Boston, MA/New York: Houghton Mifflin, 1995.

Jordana Rosenberg and Judith Butler. "Serious Innovation." In *A Companion to Lesbian, Gay, Bisexual, Transgender and Queer Studies*, edited by George E. Haggerty and Molly McGarry. Hoboken, NJ: Blackwell Publishing, 2007.

Gayle Rubin. "The Traffic in Women: Notes on a Political Economy of Sex." In *Toward an Anthropology of Women*, edited by Rayna R. Reiter. New York: Monthly Review Press.

Marshall Sahlins. *Stone Age Economics*. London and New York: Routledge, 1974.

Elaine Scarry. *The Body in Pain: The Making and Unmaking of the World*. Oxford: Oxford University Press, 1985.

David Schneider. *Critique of the Study of Kinship*. Ann Arbor, MI: University of Michigan Press, 1984.

W.G. Sebald. *On the Natural History of Destruction*. Translated by Anthea Bell. New York: Random House, 2004.

Carol Stacks. *All Our Kin: Strategies for Survival in a Black Community*. New York: Basic Books, 1983.

Keeanga Yamahtta Taylor. *From #Black Lives Matter to Black Liberation*. Chicago, IL: Haymarket Books, 2016.

Michael Tomasello, Malinda Carpenter, Josep Call, Tanya Behne and Henrike Moll. "Understanding and Sharing Intentions: The Origins of Cultural Cognition." *Behavioral and Brain Sciences*, 28 (2005): 675–735. Max Planck Institute for Evolutionary Anthropology, D-04103 Leipzig, Germany.

Melbourne Trapper. "Blood/Kinship, Governmentality, and Cultures of Order in Colonial Africa." In *Relative Values*, edited by Sarah Franklin and Susan McKinnon. Durham, NC: Duke University Press, 2001.

Aparecida Vilaça. "Chronically Unstable Bodies: Reflections an Amazonian Corporalities." *Journal of the Royal Anthropological Institute*, September 1 (2005).

Simone Weil. "The Love of God and Affliction." In *Waiting for God*. New York: G. P. Putnam's Sons, 1951.

2 Patrons of the State

Division of the Public and the Private

Here I will turn to a consideration of kinship in the family form as it relates to broader ideas of sanctioned authority and the state, and the associated socio-material consequences. Specifically, I want to consider the relationship between authority and the dichotomization of society into the public and private spheres – the latter diminished in favor of the former. I will briefly consider the structure and function of the family as presented in *De officiis* (usually translated as *On Duties* or *On Obligations*), by the Roman statesman and philosopher, Marcus Tullius Cicero. From there I will consider the public and private as it appears in Kant's short article *The answer to the question: What is Enlightenment?* I will then turn to Herbert Marcuse's consideration of authority as it is expressed through the social reforms of Martin Luther and John Calvin.

The point of this chapter is to show how the necessity of intimate care which implies biological demands for survival and the acquisition of meaningful relations, constitutes an irreducible and reliable set of relational practices which are contained and controlled for the justification or rationalization of a world required by a state or empire. This authority can be understood, following the discussion of Pierre Clastres in Chapter 1, as the accumulation of surplus power, in that it is always secured at the expense of the demands of the familiar; the immediate bonds, skills, and knowledges that sustain it. This is achieved in two ways. The first, as expressed in the work of Cicero, by conceiving of the family as the key principle and locus of duty which radiates outward to the borders of the republic or empire. The second is through the strict division of the private and public; the former diminished, in favor of the latter which takes on the quality of the universal. The universal in turn is borrowed from the Catholic tradition, now liberated from the transnational church and enrooted in the national consciousness as the divine justification for authority. Consequently, national *ekstasis* is supported by apparent universals (freedom, liberty, justice, property, and so on) from which it derives its force of persuasion and marks the truth of violence unleashed against the tenacious demands from marginal communities to dismantle its authority.[1]

DOI: 10.4324/9781003264644-3

Cicero's Family

In his political treatise, *De officiis* (*On Obligation*) Cicero situates the foundation of political community within the principle of duty, the "seedbed" of which can be found in the family. He places mutual obligation between spousal partners at the center of the circle of familial obligations, as the most intense and tightest bond, followed by commitment to ones' children, and then to the broader household "in which everything is shared".[2] Following this, obligation to siblings provides the next layer and then comes the extended family,[3] including cousins, aunts, uncles, and so on. This duty moves outward concentrically from the matrimonial couple until it encompasses the city-state and finally the "fellowship of human species". The bond is diluted as it expands.

Ultimately, it is through the proliferation of bonds that arise from matrimony, that the political community emerges according to the Roman philosopher, writing at the time to his son – in the wake of the murder of Julius Caesar no less.[4] In fact, Cicero produces this work as part of the fulfillment of his pedagogical task as a father to educate his son in the principles of duty.[5] The treatise is the performance of the principle it develops. Cicero cites goodwill and love as the essence of relation constituted by the familial bond: "for it is a great thing to have the same ancestral memorials, to practice the same religious rites, and to share common ancestral tombs".[6] Of all fellowships, Cicero continues, it is those in which people are bound "by familiarity" that are the most formidable. But here he adds, the most "serious" and most "dear" of all fellowships is the one between each person and the republic.

> Parents are dear, and children, relatives and acquaintances are dear, but our country has on its own embraced all the affections of all of us. What good man would hesitate to face death on her behalf, if it would do her a service?[7]

This seems to undermine the general principle of relational diffusion initiating these considerations. Cicero places the republic as the guardian of affective bonds, emplaced by the virtue of honor, in this way conditioning the possibility of familial security. Here his thought is very much shaped by the Stoics. In particular, he was inspired by Penaetius[8] who held that while the virtuous and the beneficial could be considered apart, at the end "nothing was ... good and beneficial unless it was virtuous ... if an action appears to be both beneficial and dishonorable, one appearance must be misleading".[9]

Cicero is not concerned with establishing the nature of ethical truth or moral judgment, rather he is simply interested in the contradictions that appear in the governance of society between three kinds of deliberation: "honorable and the reverse, beneficial and the reverse, and how to resolve apparent clashes between the two".[10] Like Aristotle, Cicero considers *eudaemonia*, to be the proper aim of life, and therefore also the primary task of governance. In order to accomplish this, political order must be attuned to the coincidence of the honorable and the beneficial, an achievement Cicero takes to be based on a natural comportment of human being, which if properly approximated will lead to a form of rule that fulfills both – the virtuous and good. Cicero writes:

> The man who defines the highest good in such a way that it has no connection with virtue, measuring it by his own advantages rather than by honorableness, cannot (if he is in agreement with himself and is not occasionally overcome by the goodness of his own nature) cultivate either friendship or justice or liberality. There can certainly be no brave man who judges that pain is the greatest evil, nor a man of restraint who defines pleasures as the highest good.[11]

After claiming that obligations are synonymous with ethical or moral goodness – "on the discharge of obligations depends all that is right, and in their neglect, all that is wrong"[12] – Cicero notes that even those who commit crimes adhere to such obligations, and therefore punishment must recognize its limits. Even enemies who surrender in battle must in turn be treated with the proper dignity afforded to *the enemy* as a reflexive structure. The establishment of a polis or state implies the tacit respect of other like entities. It prefers symmetrical warfare because it recognizes itself in it. It is here that respect for the outer circle of the family of humans, again, "the immense fellowship of human species" is substantiated.[13] Despite its principle of exemplarity, the republic, or city-state, or nation-state, cannot exist in a vacuum. Naturally, it is here that Tully makes an exception. There are those who, despite being creatures of language have given up any obligation to others, and against those creatures, no restraint in punishment shall be made. In other words, the enactment of violence shall not hesitate to aim at extermination. This is the figure of the pirate, a figure of absolute enmity.

In his remarkable book *The Enemy of All*, Daniel Heller-Roazen writes:

> That "there ought not to be any pledged word nor any oath mutually binding" with a pirate means no more and no less than this: no obligation should be owed the pirate – not even that to be shown to the rightful antagonist. The pirate escapes not one but all circles of responsibility drawn in the Roman work, "The common enemy of all" (*communis hostis omnium*), he cannot be considered criminal, because he does not belong to the city-state; yet he also cannot be counted among the foreign opponents of war, since he cannot be "included in the number of lawful enemies".[14]

Heller-Roazen notes that the existence of such a person or group of people, does not undermine the "set of responsibilities to which he does not belong" but rather stands as an exception that proves the rule.[15] And still there is something deeply ambiguous about the determination of this being that takes part in language – and presumably community of sorts – but somehow maintains the status of exclusion from the ambit of discursive species. Heller-Roazen speculates, this may be for one of two reasons – or perhaps both. The first is that the pirate on the sea is not grounded territorially. All other communities known to the Romans would have had some relation to sedentary life within a "clearly delimited territory", if nothing else they can be located, can be held to their word, and most importantly, something could be taken from them. The terms of retribution are clear and symmetrical. The terms of conflict are mutually territorial and thus they recognize the same right of possession, they share a world bound by the potential of contractual promise that those who travel on *liquid paths* eschew. This marks the second possible reason given by Heller-Roazen, the assumption that the *enemy of all* does not partake in "good faith, that is constancy and fidelity to what is said and agreed" the very principles for the possibility of justice for Cicero.[16] This is why the enemy has dignity, while the *enemy of all* does not. Though he doesn't mention it, it seems as though this second speculation falls apart at its very basis. A creature that cannot rely on consistency in anything, one who does not have the capacity to promise at all – rather than simply promising in other, unfamiliar ways – cannot be a discursive creature and therefore cannot be inscribed in the legal order of the state. That is, there are no common grounds that establish and sustain the very terms of the language of agreement.

Several things should be noted. For Cicero, the figure of the pirate is always expressed in the singular. But it is clear that a pirate cannot exist in a social vacuum, and Cicero surely knew this. A seafaring ship of any worth requires a significant, highly coordinated, and reliably communicable crew. To perform their buccaneering tasks, they must rely on language, and therefore agreement, fidelity, and community. This is proven simply by the coordination required to accomplish the formidable act of robbing a potentially well-armed vessel on the high seas. The question is, if, in order to be successful, the crew is to act as one – and if they weren't, Cicero would have no reason to include them in his treatise, particularly as a category of the creature whose threatening existence inspires the demand of genocide – then they must have some semblance of obligation to one another. Clearly, degrees of obligation are discussed and decided, satisfying at least one of the conditions for the possibility of a polity according to Aristotle, and it seems Cicero as well. The pirate must have the capacity to promise. But if we return to the first reason, perhaps we can go a bit deeper.

One perennial way of marking territory is through the work of memorial and burial insofar as they offer a social process by which the past is signified, and meaning is inscribed on the earth. It is a fundamental practice that contributes to making a social world. We engrave the ground with those who came before us, memorializing the territory in which we dwell. We live in cities and nations built by those who have perished, and we take up projects that define our lives at the place where we are abandoned by the living. Put another way, we take up residency with the dead in the projects we pursue. But this idea also seems to presuppose a sedentary relation to the material earth. Never mind the fact that people do not always "bury" their dead, we can see how this would be an important aspect of "civilization" from the perspective of a Roman, or any other strictly arboreal society, where borders, property laws, houses, the division of civic space are constitutive of empire.

In his remarkable study on the sway of the dead, Robert Pogue Harrison writes:

> In the eschatological imagination where such visions are born, the earth and sea belong to different, even opposing orders. In its solidity and stability the earth is inscribable, we can build upon its ground, while the sea offers no such foothold for human worldhood.[17]

While the dead haunt the soil of the republic from which the force of retribution can be drawn, there is an unfathomability associated with the sea. It is abysmal, it swallows time and space in its itinerant rhythms, and leaves no foothold for ancestral claims. The pirate, or we could say the transient community of pirates – but maybe also the squatter, the migrant worker, the tramp, the terrorist, the wanderer, the junky, the queer, the prostitute, the animal, the magician, the xenos – fail to recognize legitimate possession, property as conceived by empire, which finds its roots reaffirmed in marriage, social and biological reproduction, and the household. "Erasure does not mean disappearance only; it means that the site of disappearance remains unmarkable. There are no gravestones on the sea".[18] Nor are their homes, at least as Cicero would have conceived them. Like Aristotle's barbarians, Cicero's pirates are monstrosities, offending the very basis of humanity as they dwell upon the uninscribable, timeless, and thus inhuman chaos of liquidity.

> Whereas the earth sympathizes with human virtue, in the sense that it rewards backbreaking labor with generous harvests, or gives us the ground on which to build our destinies, commemorate our achievements, and honor our dead, the sea is dumb to human petition[19]

We might recognize something about these piratical strangers as practitioners of tactical resistance, conjured in the face of a more or less hostile economic, political, social, or juridical authority rooted in the state. And we might recognize Cicero's principles of solidarity unto death in the association of *official kinship*, as the soil required for the cultivation of "good citizens", obedient to the proper order of obligation spanning the distance from immediate affective obligations to the violent mediations of national identity. Cicero is infecting his son with a definitive sense of duty through this text, a veritable categorical imperative oriented toward a state rooted in blood-soaked soil. He is training him in lifelong fidelity to Rome. But implied in the family for Cicero – and really any state-sanctioned form of the family – we find the demand for recognizing inequality, or put a different way, the training is one that directly produces and justifies dominance, from the most intimate circle to the broadest, from the empty center of the law to the borders of its suspension. One's relation to oneself, one's recollection of the self, is already then bound up with how the self is authorized in such a relation. It is here that we find the coincidence of the national and the familiar, or fidelity to the community as it relates to the familial, and hostility to that which is evicted, or included through the concept of membership and its attendant institutions and exclusions.

Enlightenment Division of the Public and Private

Is it not under a similar doctrine that the duty to cultivate a "healthy family life", is used to thinly conceal the social and political imperative to assure the proper transmission of authority within the household such that the following generations guarantee the continuity of the polis, empire, or nation-state? What disappears within this lens are the myriad and heterogeneous practices of cooperation activated within marginalized, outsider, and otherwise configured communities, whose primary orientation to the association is neither national nor patriotic, and which do not seem to fit within the sanctioned forms of relation or commodified forms of non-relation. The real threat is not from the monstrous brutality of the pirates, so much as the menace to the very structure of political authority embedded in the possibility that human communities that fail to uphold the "natural order", may not only exist but may even flourish without it. There they stand as incontrovertible evidence, as a striking and dangerous contradiction to the police state and its abstract justifications. If possession is cultivated within the family, then it is this form of domination that must be guarded at all costs; to flagrantly forgo the rules of "nature" presents a spectral threat to those specious justifications of proprietary kinship.

If we cast this lens on today's dominant social-political order we find communities crippled by policies that reward social performance, such that any failure to realize a "happy life", and especially a life without poverty, rests entirely on the failure of the individual. But this goes back not just to capitalist logic strictly understood – which demands the translation of all quality to quantity, all activity into a calculation of expansive influence or social prestige – but a logic that can be found at the very heart of enlightenment thought.[20] The exclusion of relationality from political discourse inherent in the stratification of reason – categorized as private and public – has the effect of translating, or really reducing all political agency to the categories of individual and state. And perhaps we can use this insight, this demand for territoriality that marks and mars the very concept of the political – as Carl Schmitt understood it as a state of external opposition – with claims of possession.[21] According to the classical logic of the state, the family is a projection of the "natural" (primitive) community within the "artificial" (civilized) community: the private (particular) and the public (universal), respectively. If we go back to Kant's understanding of the enlightened state, we find a very similar formal structure. For Kant, in his brief article "Answer to the Question: What is Enlightenment?"[22] "the private use of reason" also includes the institutions that make up civil society. His examples are "a book, a pastor and a physician' and elsewhere, the "police officer", the "tax collector" and the "cleric",[23] but we can extend this to include: the market, religious institutions, the factory or workplace, medical facilities and schools, the military, courts, and other bureaucratic institutions.

Reason within the enlightened state is dichotomous and all social activity is divided between the private and public spheres. Accordingly, when one occupies a position or otherwise participates as a member within the enclosures that function according to the logic of economy, religion or government, one is not free to critique the logic upon which the structures of those establishments and their obligations are conditioned. In other words, an institution that is legitimated by the state – as the above examples must be – ought not to be examined from within. The enlightenment thought here claims that within institutions one must obey, but outside of them one ought to rely on reason to determine whether these institutions should be reformed or dismantled, and if so in what way. Considered as the *private use of reason* the former does not qualify as the proper place for free discourse. For one, it would threaten the fabric of the community – that is, it would risk undermining the structures that facilitate the day-to-day functioning of society, and such erosion could lead to the breakdown of lawfulness. "Perhaps a fall of personal despotism or of avaricious or tyrannical oppression may be accomplished by revolution, but never a true reform in ways of thinking. Rather, new prejudices will serve as well as old ones to harness the great unthinking mass".[24] Reform occurs via the free use of public reason, which Kant character-izes in the following way: "By the public use of one's reason I understand the use which a person makes of it as a scholar before the reading public".[25]

Not only is insurgency, oppositional violence – or even, presumably, resistance either from within enclosures or in the public sphere – excluded from the possibil-ity of ushering in the enlightenment, it is unclear when or how the public use of reason can be exercised, and upon what grounds it ought to convince. Moreover, people who are not used to relying on reason, those who just crept out from under the rock of superstition where rote obedience reigns, must become acclimated to this new guiding principle. They must get used to the light so to speak.

> Statutes, formulas, those mechanical tools of the rational employment of his natural gifts, are the fetters of an everlasting tutelage. Whoever throws them off makes only an uncertain leap over the narrowest ditch because he is not accustomed to that free motion. Therefore, there are few who have succeeded by their own exercise of mind both in freeing themselves from incompetence and in achieving a steady pace.[26]

The nagging question throughout these pages concerns those few who somehow lift themselves out of the cave of superstition, which I will get to shortly.

The free use of reason, Kant continues, is something which most people fear, and he singles out women ("the entire fair sex") as being particularly susceptible to such anxiety. He likens this bondage to a work animal strapped to a cart by the bondsman. Furthermore, he critiques private reason – which he claims can only be instrumental – as a failed deployment of reason, that altogether misses the proper goal which is of course freedom, or autonomy for the rational being, for all rational beings as individuals in a universal order. The place of public discourse then can be found in the free press, the town square, public debates, and so on.

As a good philosopher, Kant attributes freedom to enlightenment and enlight-enment, in turn, to freedom. In other words, much like the symbiosis found between the virtuous and beneficial in Cicero, only a positive outcome can be accomplished by the public use of reason. However, "paradoxically", he suggests, with the admission of "too much freedom", the freedom of society as a whole becomes restrained. To be clear, at this point there are two exceptions to Kant's generalized notion of universal enlightenment. One is that too much freedom, which presumably means too much reason, leads to bondage, and the other, as mentioned above, is that a select few are able to reach enlightenment presumably without the help of others. They somehow pass from the private use of reason to the public use, allowing them to overcome the stultification of sloth and cowardice. Again, freedom of reason is fine so long as one obeys in their everyday duties,[27] as long as the institutions that authorize the private use of reason are maintained. As Michel Foucault puts it, for Kant: "autonomy is not opposed to obeying the sovereign", or more clearly as Rainer Werner Fassbinder's mother astonishingly remarks in the film *Deutschland Im Herbst*:[28] "The best thing would be some kind of authoritarian ruler who is good, kind and orderly".[29]

At the outset, Kant states that *Menschheit* is responsible for the persistence of the general condition of immaturity. That is, that the authorities positioned outside the potentially autonomous rational being: the clergyman, the General, the book, the doctor, all decide for us. It is not that we cannot or do not realize that we could decide for ourselves, it is that we are "too lazy" and we "lack the confidence" (Kant uses the more heroic term *des Mutes* or "of courage"). He repeats this idea in the final lines of the text.

Foucault writes:

> Governing people, in the broad meaning of the word [as they spoke of it in the 16th century, of governing children, or governing family, or governing souls] is not a way to force people to do what the governor wants; it is always a versatile equilibrium, with complementarity and conflicts between techniques which impose coercion and processes through which the self is constructed or modified by himself.[30]

On this very point Kant writes: "The touchstone of everything that can be concluded as a law for a people lies in the question whether the people could have imposed such a law on itself".[31] The task of the benevolent leader then is to institute the conditions which accord with the will of the individual, whose self-conception is, in turn, one which must coincide with the universal. Internal life matches external reality, capricious desire coincides with universal truth or at least the truth of the economy and state. If this is the case, then the question of the very function of private institutions comes under scrutiny. Why maintain the private sphere at all when it is presumably always instrumental and therefore irrational? How then, from the perspective of the not yet enlightened is the status of an enlightened leader to be understood? How do they know when their obedience is to the universal embodied by a presumably enlightened and thus benevolent leader, or to the arbitrary will of a despot who claims to stand for the universal? As Hannah Arendt observed, all Adolf Eichmann had to do to claim he was a Kantian was to substitute the term "reason" in the Categorical Imperative with *the*

Third Reich.[32] These queries remain unanswered in Kant. What we can do, however, is examine this peculiar structure in an attempt to understand the purpose of establishing this apparently dichotomous political distinction and the role it has in determining the state as universal.

The Reason of the State and the Paradox of Sovereignty

The distinction between family (private enclosure) and society (public discourse) then is one which is conceived as that of irrational and rational, and therefore as nature and artifice respectively. But at the same time, for Kant, this situates civic institutions – the standpoint from within those institutions – as private, and in that sense, they carry the same status as the family (i.e. irrational or instrumental). The private use of reason, therefore, can be determined as a distributive function of the enlightened state, while *the family* is situated as one among a plurality of private institutions (i.e. society) circumscribed by instrumental reason and the requisite condition of obedience. Acts of sanctioning, authorized solely by the state, function to divide activity by establishing this distinction. State-sanctioned churches, businesses, and families are essentially enclosures that are predicated on the authority of the governing apparatus of the state, which itself, in terms of its own inner workings – both governmental and legislative – is also technically a private space – strangely – sanctioned by the public reason of the presumably enlightened leader; which of course must be taken with faith, as those who are not yet enlightened have an underdeveloped faculty of knowledge and therefore lack the maturity for discerning whether the source of authority is reasonable or not. And yet, "the public use of one's reason must always be free".[33] Clearly, the implication of freedom, in relation to its limits, constitutes the horizon of the universal at the level of the state, which confers onto it the status of sovereign institution.

The state in this sense is *autopoietic*. It requires no justification in that it is assumed to guarantee rational freedom within its borders. But here we come to a paradox, recalling what Giorgio Agamben describes as the *paradox of sovereignty*. Following Carl Schmitt's definition of sovereignty – based on *the power to decide the state of exception*, or, what is the same, judging when an emergency calls for the suspension of the rule of law[34] – Agamben identifies the sovereign as both outside and inside the law. In other words: "the law is outside itself" or: "I, the sovereign who am outside the law, declare that there is nothing outside the law'."[35] Sovereignty, in other words, marks a fundamental, aporetic limit, it is both source – or principle – and end of the juridical order.

Giorgio Agamben notes: "The exception appears in its absolute form when it is a question of creating a situation in which juridical rules can be valid".[36] He continues by quoting Schmitt at length: "'Every general rule demands a regular, everyday frame of life to which it can be factually applied and which is submitted to its regulations. The rule requires a homogenous medium'."[37] In other words, the rule requires a stable reference of reality – the total state – within which it is activated, a rule "cannot exist in chaos". This normative background gives the rule validity: "All law is 'situational law'."[38] It is this decision that, according to Schmitt, demonstrates "the nature of state sovereignty". The "homogenous medium" or general backdrop of normativity, we could say – now following Kant's narrative – is rooted in the institutions which cannot be questioned from within, but only externally, in the sphere of activity determined and circumscribed by the state as universal, which underpins the reason of the state.

For Kant, the difference between an "enlightened age" and an "age of enlightenment" which, significantly, is also the "age of Frederick", is that the latter paves the way for the former. It is the difference between potentiality and actuality. Kant writes: "after nature has long since discharged them [mankind] from external direction (*naturaliter maiorennes*), nevertheless remains under lifelong tutelage, and why it is so easy for others to set themselves up as their guardians. It is so easy not to be of age".[39] And yet, while maturity has not yet been accomplished, dependency on a *patron* like Frederick – much like the Christian shepherd attending his flock – is required. In other words, there is no public use of reason that could challenge authority deemed rational and thus autonomous. Again, in the enlightened state, the imperative: "do your duty don't ask questions", is supplanted by the demand: "Obey, and you will be able to reason as much as you like".[40] The implication here is that while private freedom always remains submissive, that is, instrumental – in that it serves a particular rather than universal cause – it is public reason that ought to be free.[41]

Accordingly, the function of governance is to direct the demands of the private realm to public ends ("or at least prevent them from destroying public ends"[42]). Michel Foucault, like Max Horkheimer, suggests that this is an explicit reversal of the old Christian idea of private consciousness.[43] Herbert Marcuse in a similar vein suggests that this "'external' sphere of social existence" the universal law functions as the ground not simply for authorizing existing governing institutions,

> but also authority in general as a social necessity; universal voluntary self-limitation of individual freedom in a general system of the subordination of some and the domination of others is necessary for the peremptory securing of bourgeois society, which is built on relations of private property.[44]

In other words, the ban on internal critique places public reason in the position of the sovereign in relation to – and at the same time constituting – internal spaces of social relation. However, the broader enclosure called *the state* functions in two senses on the level of private reason, as Kant defines it, which is exceptionally authorized to sanction those public spaces as such, ultimately restricting reason to the limits of the nation-state as the horizon of the universal. This reflects the first way in which the state always falls short of its aim (presuming its aim is universal as defined on the level of species rather than nations), as *the right to have rights* as a rational being are already curtailed, in that it limits its purview to that of citizens or residents of the nation-state and not for "rational beings", much less "human beings" and certainly not sentient life as such. The instrumentality of the state is simply concealed under the specious category of the universal over which it has the sole defining authority. On the other hand, the private reason of the state sovereign, the benevolent enlightened leader – or political representatives – who supposedly channels rationality, is authorized to direct the state to fulfill its maturation. Put another way, while the exception in Kant's analysis is unstated, we can glean its presence in the very concept of the *enlightened, benevolent ruler*.

Patrons of the State and Family

Here we discover the will of the sovereign, which coincides with the universal, which is thereby *the neutral*, becomes in a sense sanctioned to manage the transition to enlightenment. In other words, the particular returns as an authority in becoming the universal. In the 19th-century German constitutional monarchy, the bridge that connected this dualistic structure was of course the constitution and the parliament, the legislative aspect of the state. This presupposes but also performs the strict distinction between society and the state, which as Schmitt shows in his analysis of the total state, dissolves with the 19th-century "transition to the economic state".[45] Particularly in the United States, where the liberal state becomes increasingly "non-invasive" in economic matters – that is, in augmenting and sanctioning the authority of a liberal economic logic thereby imbued with the force of the universal – and limited in curtailing the so-called individual economic freedoms, in this way recasting the Hobbesian *state of nature* under the police control of the nation-state, ostensibly returning liberty to the individual. However, the assumption that the state ought to play the role of *the neutral*, formal authority meant to protect the dominant economic rationale as well as the constitution, and the prevailing social norms is a mark of totalization. Nevertheless, the opposition remains in the background as an antagonist to the "free market", the consequence realized in the coincidence of the state and society, that is, the total state. Still, in Kant's account, which is our concern here, the enlightened sovereign Prussian King becomes a figure much like a specialist or technocrat who administers reasonable authority to those who are disqualified from governing themselves i.e. those whose interests are partial or local and fail to coincide with the logic of the "rational state".

The sovereign ushers the polity into enlightenment by anticipating the destiny to be fulfilled with the actualization of reason. Put another way, the sovereign is the private use of reason that becomes the form of governance, not just equivalent to the public use of reason, but to the correct or rational aim of enlightened reason which is categorically cleansed of particularity. In this way, the task is to govern public reason – which in liberalism, again, ultimately means the protection of the logic of the national (universal) interests within a transnational market – taken to its logical end describes authoritarian liberalism, marked by, as discussed via Wolfgang Streeck "capitalism as a way of life".[46] As Streeck notes, "The depoliticized condition of a liberal economy is itself the outcome of politics, in the sense of a specific use of the authority of the state of specific political purposes".[47]

In an article titled "Heller, Schmitt and the Euro" Streeck looks to Carl Schmitt's considerations, in the early 1930s, of the total state and the authoritarian state as it exposes the "deep tensions between capitalism and democracy".[48] For Schmitt the "total state" which characterized Weimer Germany (a supposedly pluralistic parliamentary democracy) at the time and maybe said to roughly characterize the current liberal nation-state, is a "weak state", even in its "appearance of omnipresence". It is weak because its authority is in contention between various forces, various interest groups, "including the organized working class", all vying to bend the commitment of the state to their ostensibly particular goals.[49] From the standpoint of the economy this approximately democratic state introduced "the ever present danger of a 'distortion' of market outcomes in the name of democratic-popular ... concepts of 'social justice', detracting from efficiency as well as curtailing basic rights of property".[50] Schmitt was worried at the time about national cohesion, insisting that on the equivalence of the concept of a healthy political state and absolute sovereignty (characterized by the total permeation of society and the state). Singular authority (authoritarianism) is the proper antidote to the potential strife introduced by dissensus. It is the absolute actualization of the concept of the political. The threat of *stasis* dissolved with the actualization of the real authoritarian state in 1933, in which political unity was forced through the development of – or sacrifice to – a war economy. Here the Leviathan, Streeck notes, maintains a liberal economic order and a "free market", basically introducing a model of liberal authoritarianism. For Hobbes, of course, the *Leviathan* can only be initiated by the simultaneous renunciation of liberty by what then is constituted as the polity. This is done voluntarily, but in the interests of natural law (the survival drive) and is possible because of natural right (my right to freely give up my liberty). The state then is both weak and strong. It simply negates the conditions for the possibility of contentious interests (pluralistic democratic interests, organized labor, social justice movements, but also "greedy interests", etc.) from appearing, while maintaining national interests under a homogenous economic order.

The strong state intervenes when the market, or its own sovereignty, is under threat. "Before Hitler sent the leaders of the Left to the camps, the total state still bore the risk that it might become democratic".[51] This, for Streeck, sets the stage for the adoption of the post-1945 ordoliberalism in which the primary role of the state is to police and protect economic growth which allegedly led to the *Wirtschaftswunder* of the 1950s in the *Bundesrepublik*. In a way, economic expansion replaced territorial expansion. Streeck continues with a compelling analysis of the bridge between neoliberalism (where the economy precedes the Leviathan) and ordoliberalism (in which the Leviathan precedes the economic order) that followed, but the point here is more general. For Streeck, the three primary types of economic and political governance emerging from the early- to mid-twentieth century, namely New Deal democracy, authoritarian state communism, and National Socialism (fascism), all share the characteristics of the total state described by Schmitt. In all the cases, we find the increased coincidence of society and state tending toward "a new politics carving out a space for free markets sustained and guarded by state authority while protected from egalitarian democratic infringement".[52] Keynsian mediation supplanted by Hayekian principles of competition, – i.e. "growth through stronger incentives for the winners and more severe punishments for the losers" – the market, objectified by "scientific economic laws" and data (market corrections, employment statistics, GDP, and so on) eventually immunized from the actual and potential demands emerging from democratic and egalitarian forces. Again, to go back to Schmitt, the strong state protects the economic order, the weak state withdraws from protecting the polity from the cannibalistic logic of accumulation and extraction. Streeck goes on to show how this leads to the structure of the tripartite governance of the European Union (*European Council, European Commission, European Court of Justice*) as a transnational fulfillment of the total state.

This, however, swings too wide of the concerns at hand. What is so interesting and apt here is the persistent demand for traditional values, from those mostly hegemonic constituents committed to ordo or neoliberal politics on a nationalist basis, including the state itself. A "successful family" must also be defined in correspondence with the ruling economic logic. But neither the principle of the nuclear family nor the sacred status of the economy submits to critique. Both lie outside of the contentious tides of discourse and political collision; immunized by scientific, theological, and nationalistic axioms, i.e., the braided authority of the reality principle. The family here provides a frame of reference for the sphere of competition. It becomes the kingdom for which one is fighting tooth and nail, the flesh of the body politic. Its failure always relegated to the failure of the individual. Continuing with the theme of the family and political authority, I will follow a slightly different thread in order to analyze some of the theological underpinnings of this structure of authorization.

Politico-Theological Structures of Authorization

To get to the roots of this politico-theological logic, it would behoove us to go a bit deeper into the history of the idea of modern authority, defined by the horizon of the state. In a short book titled *On Authority*, Herbert Marcuse analyzes what he takes to be a quintessentially protestant notion of authority – implying its logic is endemic to the liberal state – through a short pamphlet authored by Martin Luther, titled, *The Freedom of a Christian (Von der Freiheit eines Christenmenschen)*. He summarizes the spirit of the brochure with the following salient formulation:

> freedom was assigned to the "inner" sphere of the person, to the "inner" man, and at the same time the "outer" person was subjected to a system of worldly powers; the system of earthly authorities was transcended through private autonomy and reason; person and work were separated (person and office) with the resultant "double morality"; actual unfreedom and inequality were justified as a consequence of inner freedom and equality.[53]

Marcuse claims that the reformation reaches its apex in the demand for unquestioned obedience to authority, when Luther famously reprimanded a group of Christians who demanded freedom after being enslaved by the Turks at the time, warning them to eschew resistance. Luther quips: "You must bear in mind that you have lost your freedom and become someone else's property, and that without the will and knowledge of your master you cannot get out of this without sin or disobedience".[54] It is precisely on these grounds, Marcuse recalls, that the revolutionary Thomas Müntzer, in turn, rebuked Martin Luther for his capriciousness, on the one hand critiquing – on biblical grounds – the powerful aristocracy for stealing what is not theirs, while on the other, failing to get to the root of the logic of theft already embedded in the conception of private property. Müntzer wrote for example: "[Luther] conceals the real origin of all robbery .... For see, our lords and princes are the basis for all profiteering, theft and robbery; they make all creatures their property."[55] Much like Cicero's absolute disdain for pirates discussed above, Luther saw the political rebellion as radically evil, calling it a "flood of wickedness". Even those who rob and steal, he held "leave the head that can punish them intact" but rebellion "*attacks punishment itself*".[56]

It is this separation of the bodily (material) and spiritual, which leads to the institutionalization of authority according to Marcuse. This prepared the soil for a "modern" understanding of authority that is: "the condition of absolute isolation and atomization into which the individual is thrown after the dissolution of the medieval universe appears here ... in the terrible truthful image of the isolation of the prisoner in his cell" after all, Marcuse then quotes Luther,

> For God has fully ordained that the under-person shall be alone unto himself and has taken the sword from him and put him into prison. If he rebels against this and combines with others and breaks out and takes the sword, then before God he deserves condemnation and death.[57]

This formalization of authority is attendant to any metaphysical or tautological justification of reality – in particular when its ends no longer seem relevant or practically valuable, that is to say, the point when freedom becomes a theological matter, one that, after the reformation, coincides with the nation-state.

It is this structure that Marx in turn associates directly with the naturalization of domination within the family. Along with Engels, he writes:

> Out of this very contradiction between the particular and the common interests, the common interest assumes an independent form as the *state*, which is divorced from the real individual and collective interests, and at the same time as an *illusory community*, always based, however, on the real ties existing in every family conglomeration and tribal conglomeration – such as flesh and blood, language, division of labor.[58]

It is the categorical stratification of society into "over and under' that corresponds to the separation of office and persons, based on the concepts of dignity and obedience within concrete family life, which in turn corresponds to a world ordained by God. One implication is that resistance, or more likely evasion or repression, only occurs on a spiritual level. In dark times, one maintains spiritual freedom, a mainline to the eternal divine.

The "real ties existing in every family conglomeration" allows the nation-state to achieve the status of necessity, shedding evidence of capriciousness that mostly characterizes an otherwise illusory community. This was of course Luther's way of backtracking after he witnessed the peasant revolts, themselves inspired by his early calls for "unconditional freedom".[59] Marcuse points out, it was the very objectification of authority that the claim of Christian freedom and the accompanying notion of a "'natural realm' of love, equality and justice" became an even more destructive threat to the "completely formalized social order".[60]

These ideas acted as the energizing force behind the 16th-century German Peasants' War, the emergence of the Anabaptists and other revolutionary sects from the massive ranks of the poor, captured in Thomas Müntzer's communist principle: *omnia sunt communia*. His aim was to foment revolt against the elite, those whose position he claimed Luther to be unjustifiably supporting. In his remarkable study on millenarianism, Norman Cohn reflects on the event: "the peasants showed themselves not at all eschatologically minded but politically minded in the sense that they thought in terms of real situations and realizable possibilities".[61] And this, Marcuse asserts, is where Calvin enters by eliminating the contradiction between the earthly order and the spiritual one. Yes, "the earth is evil", as Justine from Lars von Trier's *Melancholia* surmises on the eve of its destruction,[62] however, it is through the idea of predestination that what is given as *sacred* and *true*, and in that sense *nature* in that it is already given with birth, that immunizes the individual from responsibility to this world, thus saving them from the contradictions inherent in the commitment to freedom. The apocalypse takes the place of politics.

For Calvin, there is no contradiction between "Christian freedom" and the organic earth. Echoing Weber's *Spirit of Capitalism and the Protestant Ethic*, Marcuse writes:

> Christians must live their life to the honor and glory of the divine majesty, and in it the success of their praxis is the *ratio cognoscendi* (reason of knowing) their selection. The *ratio essendi* (reason of existence) of this selection belongs to God and is eternally hidden from men.[63]

The true cause of existence is hermetically sealed within the opaque shell of divine fate. On this view it is not, as in the Roman Catholic conception, that one must perform good works in order to clear a path to redemption, rather, it is evidence of a blessed life – here, in the chthonic realm – which indicates proof that one is chosen. For Calvin, original sin is simply transferred to the concept of *disobedience*. Obedience then functions to secure order through "a system, emanating from the family, of *subjectio* and *superioritas*, to which God had given his name for protection."[64] Obedience and suffering supplant freedom, as the "'religious moral law' becomes equated with 'natural law'" and becomes the compulsory norm for the practical configuration of the Church.[65]

Calvin, of course, goes further than Luther. He defines the task of the family as one of bending and breaking the will of the child in order to internalize their own social and political subjection.[66] In both protestant trajectories, the family was subject to a "programmatic reorganization" that Marcuse suggests was key in toppling the authority of the Catholic Church. And onto the head of household – not so different than Cicero here – was conferred divine authority.

> The subordination of the individual to the temporal ruler appears just as natural, obvious, and "eternal" as subordination to the authority of the father is meant to be …. Max Weber emphasizes the entry of "calculation into the traditional organizations of brotherhood" as a decisive feature of the transformation of the family through the penetration of the "capitalist spirit".[67]

As authority becomes increasingly subject to rationalization, the communal aspect of the family atrophies, while at the same time the family as such becomes progressively subject to calculated administration.[68]

Here he notes that Luther reads, "obedience to over-persons" who have to "give orders or rules" into the fourth commandment. That is, anyone with authority legitimated in the family of the Christian community or state, becomes a kind of father. "Good governance" is equated with the cultivation of obedience within the family – faithfully producing what Nietzsche would later call promising beasts. In other words, parental authority becomes the foundation upon which Luther's idea of a good society is founded. Again, quoting Luther: "'where the rule of parents is absent, this would mean the end of the whole world, for without governance it could not survive', 'there is no greater dominion on the earth than the dominion of the parents'" and so on.[69] But it is not parents alone that ought to be obeyed. In order to mature into effective authorities themselves, the children must be indoctrinated into becoming integrated into the authority-system, i.e. becoming versed in the rules of respect and obedience, knowing when to comply and when to demand complicity. For Luther, the family was simply the "first rule", the origin of all other forms of authority. This anticipates the blueprint for the constitution of the sovereign nation-state which requires familial training to thoroughly enroot national identity, social obedience, and linguistic obligation.

It is not just the threat of violence that substantiates the sovereignty of the nation-state, it is the unified identity of theology, language, history, and cultural identity, all of which is captured by what Johann Gottlieb Fichte would call the *Innen Grenzen* of the nation.[70] Calvin, of course, goes further than Luther. In his work *Institutes*, he implies that the source of resistance to obedience can be attributed to the "perverse" affliction of arrogance. Along with the key tactic of producing a supple and malleable polity, trained in the habits of submission:

"The social function of the family" and the bourgeois family (authority-system) find their coincidence here.

If we return to Kant's division of the private and public, we see here too that obedience is required in the former. It is presumably only when one is adequately trained – "matured" – within the family and other privative institutions, that one is ready to employ rational discourse in the public domain. But if the public use of reason is distinct from the private, in that the former is universal while the latter instrumental, how can a presumably irrational relation (family) prepare individuals for rationality (actualized by the state)? And how would this translate to political critique, radical change, or even progressive reform if the ruler, the representative, the despot, or dictator, is already enlightened and therefore embodies universal authority? At what point is transmission accomplished and thus autonomy achieved? Woefully the answer is never. That is because the training which is performed within the family and pedagogical institutions comes down inevitably to the rationalization and reproduction of existing society (the divide between the governing and governed, the enlightened and ignorant) in the practical obedience to the authority-system that constitutes the reality principle.

As we can see from the reflections above on Kant, although we find a kind of reversal from the idea of inner freedom found in Luther (and Augustine before him) ultimately the system of obedience is simply secularized as it is supplanted by duty. The divine world is brought down to the level of the politically sanctioned public realm, founded upon the enlightenment "universal", and the technocrats that can identify its presence and make the necessary adjustments to uphold the normative relations sustaining it. But this idea of duty, like that found in Cicero, is predicated on a naturalization of social order, a coercive structure within which freedom is circumscribed within a space of supposedly free public discourse. So long as the dichotomization of public and private is maintained, that which is designated as public is simply the suspension of one kind of language game over all others.

Cicero, Luther, Calvin, and Kant seem to share a profound anxiety concerning the possibility of losing the father as law and authority, as the founding principle upon which stratification – based, for example, on property relations which require epistemic verification and juridical authority – is threatened. Who after all is your father? How do you know? Why do you know?[71] A father who transmits obedience and obligation not to another patriarch but to the state, ultimately signified in the *patron*, or benevolent leader, or today the nationalist leader who evokes interest in and embodies identification with the nation-state as exemplary – signifying the sovereign individual, and demonstrating a model for authentic membership based on the projection of values deemed fundamental. In this case, the nation-state, like the Christian community discussed above, is not just the guarantor for preserving the sanctity of family life, but also determines the identity of the encompassing nation-family that presumably allows the nuclear household to flourish. As noted above, nostalgia here is projected. It is simply the fantasy of conditions that satisfy relational necessity, authorizing the existence of the nation-state and its economic order. It transmits, transfers, generalizes, the immediate demand for mutual obligation, trust, and the force of Hobbesian *natural law* to the national territorial dimension. Insofar as it extends beyond the immediacy of care, it requires a degree of cohesion that is at once reflective of territorial claims (exteriority) and a common "inner essence" (interiority) that defines the substance of a nation.[72]

* * *

For Luther and Cicero, the threat to the very structure of punishment and obedience must be met with the force of extermination.[73] At that point, it is no longer humans – or anything dignified for that matter – that are being addressed, but an offending material tantamount to an infection or epidemic, an affliction of "nature" to be overcome – a category that signifies that which is irrational, cowardly, and without dignity. As with Kant, Luther simply secularizes this structure, thus order and truth coincide as does obedience, courage, and rationality. What is banned from political visibility is that which is determined by it to be private – solipsistic – and thus deprived of rational discourse. Immediate relations of care, the development of empathy, and the expression of dignity, respect, and obligation – qualities that might characterize Hegel's *immediate substantiality of Spirit* – are redirected within the structure of the *enlightened state* – as guarantor of value – and the brutalizing economic order it ordains with that borrowed category honored as the unique achievement of secularist ingenuity, the universal.

If caring for the dead and all that it implies in the lives of the living, is necessary for the flourishing and sustenance of an intimate, non-instrumental foundation of community, then the grip on the narrative of death also becomes key in securing the apparent necessity of the state, which always ultimately requires the intimate and must go beyond the instrumental. The mechanism for this, within the presumably secular authorization of access to fundamental resources for sustaining life, can be found in the demand for and distribution of vulnerability within the division of the private and public. It is on this premise that the state justifies the civil order society (for Hegel, the second ethical root of the state discussed in Chapter 5) that it is charged with protecting. What remains is only the most austere and anemic proprietary community that we call the *nuclear family*. And, it is because the necessity of substantial relationality cannot be eliminated altogether – it cannot be exhausted by pecuniary logic – without complete collapse, that we cannot finally get rid of it. It is for this reason that nationalist discourses hijack feeling (*Empfindung*) in the services of formal authorization (rationalization) of a people to "fight for their homes". This claim means very little without a state to sanctify it in law, evident in the violent protection of its border and the legal determination of who belongs where along with the affective appeal to the security of familiarity. And it is impossible to think of this status of belonging without adhering to differentials of social power that justify parameters of success, authority, and dignity within the boundaries of that state. Together, this constitutes the concept of political theology in that the concept of nation and the structure conferred onto it by the state remains unquestioned by those who adore it. It is the sacred that is affirmed and reaffirmed by extreme disparity and extreme violence. And it is the family that signifies this sacrifice most intimately.

Notes

1 For Freud, group psychology which characterizes nationalism is compared to love or hypnosis. Its primary quality is evident in the diminishment of difference within the group and the corresponding augmented difference defining those considered outsiders or strangers. See, Sigmund Freud, *Mass Psychology and Other Writings*, trans. J.A. Underwood (New York: Penguin, 2004) 95–99.

2 Marcus Tullius Cicero, *On Duties* (Cambridge: Cambridge University Press, 1991) 22–23.

3 However, this does not imply that the nuclear family as it is conceived today was understood as the core or essential family unit. As Paul Veyne in his fascinating work on private life, rightly points out: "The 'voice of blood' spoke very little in Rome. What mattered more than blood was family name. Bastards took their mother's name, and legitimation or recognition of paternity did not exist …. The ruling oligarchy replenished its ranks with its own legitimate children and with the sons of former slaves. Freed slaves adopted the family name of the master who set them free …. Adoptions and the social advancement of freed slaves compensated for the low rate of natural reproduction, for the Romans made no fetish of natural kinship." Paul Veyne, *A History of Private Life: From Pagan Rome to Byzantium*, trans. Arthur Goldhammer (Cambridge, MA: Harvard University Press, 1987) 12.

4 Cicero, *On Duties*, 23.

5 Ibid., 24–25.

6 Ibid., 25.

7 Ibid., 23.

8 M.T. Griffin and E.M. Atkins, "Introduction," in Cicero, *On Duties* (Cambridge: Cambridge University Press, 1991), xxi–xxii, also see Cicero, *On Duties*, 4–5.

9 Ibid., xxxvi.

10 Ibid., xxi.

11 Ibid., 3.

12 Marcus Tullius Cicero, *De Officiis*, Loeb Classical Library (Cambridge, MA: Harvard University Press, 1913) 7.

13 Cicero, *On Duties*, 22–23.

14 Daniel Heller-Roazen, *The Enemy of All: Piracy and the Law of Nation* (New York: Zone Books, 2009) 16.

15 Much like the figure of the sovereign exception analyzed in Giorgio Agamben's *Homo Sacer*, which he formulates as follows: "'the law is outside itself' or: 'I, the sovereign who am outside the law, declare that there is nothing outside the law.'" Which I will discuss in a slightly different context below. Giorgio Agamben, *Homo Sacer: Sovereign Power and Bare Life*, trans. Daniel Heller-Roazen (Stanford, CA: Stanford University Press, 1998) 14.

16 Heller-Roazen, *The Enemy of All*, 17.

17 Robert Pogue Harrison, *The Dominion of the Dead*, Chicago, IL: University of Chicago Press, 2003. 4.

18 Ibid., 12.

19 Ibid., 12.

20 Just to be clear, I take these to be two doctrines that reinforce one another rather than an either/or. The concept of the private as exclusion is also required for the life blood of capitalism to flow.

21 "According to modern linguistic usage, the state is the political status of an organized people in an enclosed territorial unit"; "Let us assume that in the realm of morality the final distinctions are between good and evil, in aesthetics beautiful and ugly, in economics profitable and unprofitable …. The specific political distinction to which political actions and motives can be reduced is that between friend and enemy". Carl Schmitt, *The Concept of the Political*, trans. George Schwab (Chicago, IL: University of Chicago Press, 2007) 19, 26.

22 Immanuel Kant, *Was ist Aufklärung?* in *The Politics of Truth* (Los Angeles, CA: semiotext(e), 2007).
23 Ibid., 31–33.
24 Ibid., 31.
25 Ibid., 31.
26 Ibid., 30.
27 It is tempting to draw a parallel here between the structure of the limits of pure reason that Kant establishes in the first critique, but that is another matter altogether.
28 This occurs just after the broadcast on the radio reporting about the Lufthansa flight 181 hijacked in Mogadishu by the PFLP – which was used as a bargaining tool to free members of the RAF from prison, and the subsequent alleged suicides of Andreas Baader, Gudrun Ensslin and Jan-Carl Raspe in Stammheim maximum-security prison. The RAF was formed in part as a response to the persistence of fascist politicians in post-war governmental positions as well as the "Americanization" or neoliberalization of Germany.
29 *Deutschland Im Herbst*, dir. Rainer Werner Fassbinder et al. (1978).
30 Michel Foucault, *The Politics of Truth* (Los Angeles, CA: Semiotext(e), 2007) 154.
31 Immanuel Kant, *Was ist Aufklärung?* in *The Politics of Truth*, 34.
32 Instead of universalizing one's act he asked the question whether he was acting in such a way "that the Führer, if he knew your action would approve it." Hannah Arendt, *Eichmann in Jerusalem: A Report on the Banality of Evil* (New York: Penguin, 2006) 136.
33 Ibid., 31.
34 Schmitt gets this from Kierkegaard, specifically the *teleological suspension of the ethical and the exception* explored in *Fear and Trembling* and *Repetition* respectively. Basically, this is Abraham who is willing to kill his son on faith. This is rewarded with the divine promise of future nations, thus we could say this is the nature of an Abrahamic state. Søren Kierkegaard, *Fear and Trembling/Repetition*, vol. 6, Trans. Howard V. Hong and Edna H. Hong (Princeton: Princeton University Press, 1983).
35 Giorgio Agamben, *Homo Sacer: Sovereign Power and Bare Life*, trans. Daniel-Heller Roazen (Stanford, CA: University of Stanford Press, 1998) 15.
36 Ibid., 16.
37 Ibid., 16.
38 Ibid., 16–17.
39 Quoted from "Was ist Aufklarung?" 29.
40 Kant characterizes this as expression of only "one prince in the world", namely Fredrick. Ibid. 31, and "this is the age of enlightenment, or the century of Fredrick". Ibid., 35.
41 Foucault describes it this way: "The question ... is that of knowing how the use of reason can take the public form that it requires .... Kant in conclusion, proposes to Fredrick II, in scarcely veiled terms, a sort of contract – what might be called the contract of *rational despotism with free reason: the public and free use of autonomous reason will be the best guarantee of obedience*, on condition, however, that *the political principle that must be obeyed and itself be in conformity with universal reason*". Michel Foucault, "What is Enlightenment?", *Politics of Truth*, 103 (my emphasis).
42 Ibid., 31.
43 Ibid., 104.
44 Herbert Marcuse, *On Authority* (New York: Verso, 2008) 50.
45 Carl Schmitt, "The Way to the Total State", in *Four Articles: 1931–1938*, trans. Simona Draghici (Washington, DC: Plutarch Press, 1999) 12.
46 Wolfgang Streeck, *How Will Capitalism End? Essays on a Failing System* (New York: Verso Books, 2017), 216.
47 Ibid., 151.
48 Ibid., 151–163.

49 Ibid., 152. See also Schmitt, "The Way to the Total State", 14–17.
50 *Streeck, How Will Capitalism End?*, 151.
51 Ibid., 152.
52 Ibid., 155.
53 Herbert Marcuse, *On Authority*, 12. Luther's salient and seemingly contradictory summary of Saint Paul defines the Christian as both master of all and slave of all, both free (spiritual life) and in bondage (earthly life):

> *"Damit wir gründlich können erkennen, was ein Christenmensch sei und was es sei um die Freiheit, die ihm Christus erworben und gegeben hat, davon Sankt Paulus viel schreibt, will ich diese zwei Sätze aufstellen:*
>
> 1. *Ein Christenmensch ist ein freier Herr über alle Ding und niemand Untertan.*
> 2. *Ein Christenmensch ist ein dienstbarer Knecht aller Ding und jedermann Unter tan."*

See, Martin Luther, *Von der Freiheit eines Christenmenschen* (Stuttgart: Philipp Reclam GmbH & Co., 1962) 125.
54 Quoted in Marcuse, *On Authority*, 19–20.
55 Ibid., 20 (fn. 19).
56 Ibid., 20 (my emphasis).
57 Ibid., 20–21.
58 Karl Marx and Friedrich Engels, *The German Ideology* (Amherst: Prometheus Books, 1998) 52.
59 Marcuse, *On Authority*, 21.
60 Ibid., 22.
61 Norman Cohn, *The Pursuit of the Millennium* (New York: Oxford University Press, 1970) 245.
62 Justine played by Kirsten Dunst in Lars von Trier's *Melancholia* calmly explains: "the earth is evil, we don't need to grieve for it, nobody will miss it". The difference of course is that for Justine there is no spiritual freedom, there is only a nihilistic freedom evident in the construction of a cave of annihilation, an inversion of Plato's cave, in the face of radical finitude. Then again, perhaps that is the extent of spiritual freedom, hence Justine's melancholia in the face of false consciousness of bourgeois freedom presented in the film in the grand wedding at her sister Claire's (Charlotte Gainsbourg) house. The second half of the film presents a transformation from melancholia to mourning in Justine. Her energized response to the impending sight of immanent destruction is evidence of relief that she can finally mourn that which has been dying all along. Lars von Trier (Dir.), *Melancholia*, Zentropa, 2011.
63 Marcuse, *On Authority*, 23.
64 Here Marcuse quotes Calvin, "The titles of Father, God and Lord, all meet in him alone, and hence, whenever any one of them is mentioned our mind should be impressed with the same feeling of reverence". Marcuse, *On Authority*, 24.
65 Ibid., 24.
66 This of course goes hand in hand with the internalization of freedom, the atomization of post medieval society and the justification of a fully authoritarian system. Ibid., 18–21.
67 Ibid., 29.
68 Ibid., 30.
69 Ibid., 32, See *Luther als Pädagog*, edited by E. Wagner (Klassiker der Pädigogik, vol. II) (Langensalza: Schulbuchhandlung, 1887) 70.
70 We find the roots of such a nationalism anticipated in Fichte's *Addresses to the German Nation*, in which he identifies the "present age" as one which is suffering from a prevalence of capriciousness (selfishness or *Wilkür*). The antidote he notes is

to understand and establish territorial continuity along the lines of what he called the *Innen Grenzen*, or inner borders of the natural nation. In his famous thirteenth address Fichte notes:

> "To begin with, and above all else, the first, original and truly natural frontiers of states are undoubtedly their inner frontiers. Those who speak the same language are already, before all human art, joined together by mere nature with a multitude of invisible ties; they understand one another and are able to communicate ever more clearly; they belong together and are naturally one, an indivisible whole.... The external limits of territories only follow as a consequence of this inner frontier, drawn by man's spiritual nature itself."

See Johann Gottlieb Fichte, *Addresses to the German Nation* (Cambridge: Cambridge University Press, 2008) 166–167.

71 We could add Thomas Hobbes to this list, who claims that patriarchy, and therefore for him sovereignty, cannot exist without the marriage contract. He writes in the *Leviathan*, "If there be no contract the dominion is in the mother". Thomas Hobbes, *Leviathan* (Boston, MA: Hackett, 1994) Chapter XX para. 5.

72 See note on Fichte, above.

73 It should be noted that Hitler too shared this position and explicitly praises Protestantism as a properly German religion (except for its apparently stubborn attitude towards Jewish people, which is too generous for Hitler's taste, despite I suppose Luther's own severe and well-known antisemitism). In *Mein Kampf*, he writes: "Therefore Protestantism will always take its part in promoting German ideals as far as concerns moral integrity or national education, when the German spiritual being or language or spiritual freedom are to be defended: because these represent the principles on which Protestantism itself is grounded". Later, he also identifies three foundations for the state. The first is "popular support", the second is the need to "consolidate the foundations of that authority by the creation of force", and finally perhaps the most important for Hitler is what he calls *authority of tradition*: "If popular support and power are united together and can endure for a certain time, then an authority may arise which is based on a still stronger foundation, namely, the authority of tradition. And, finally, if popular support, power, and tradition are united together, then the authority based on them may be looked upon as invincible". It is this presumable invincibility that guarantees the extermination of threat. Adolf Hitler, *Mein Kampf* (London: Hurst and Blackett Ltd., 1939) 398.

Bibliography

Theodor Adorno. "Freudian Theory and the Pattern of Fascist Propaganda." In *The Essential Frankfurt School Reader*, edited by Andrew Arato and Eike Gephardt. New York: Continuum, 1982.

Hannah Arendt. *Eichmann in Jerusalem: A Report on the Banality of Evil*. New York: Penguin, 2006.

Giorgio Agamben. *Homo Sacer: Sovereign Power and Bare Life*. Translated by Daniel-Heller Roazen. Stanford, CA: University of Stanford Press, 1998.

Etienne Balibar. "Fichte and the Internal Border: On *Addresses to the German Nation*." In *Masses, Classes and Ideas: Studies on Politics and Philosophy before and after Marx*. Translated by James Swenson. New York: Routledge, 1994.

Marcus Tullius Cicero. *On Duties*. Cambridge: Cambridge University Press, 1991.

Norman Cohn. *The Pursuit of the Millennium*. New York: Oxford University Press, 1970.

Rainer Werner Fassbinder et al. (Dir.). *Deutschland Im Herbst*. (Prod. Theo Heinz and Eberhard Junkersdorf) Studio Canal, 1978.

J.G. Fichte. *Addresses to the German Nation*. Cambridge: Cambridge University Press, 2009.

Michel Foucault. *The Politics of Truth*. Los Angeles, CA: Semiotext(e), 2007.

Sigmund Freud. *Mass Psychology and Other Writings*. Translated by J.A. Underwood. New York: Penguin, 2004.

Robert Pogue Harrison. *The Dominion of the Dead*. Chicago, IL: University of Chicago Press, 2003.

Daniel Heller-Roazen. *The Enemy of All: Piracy and the Law of Nation*. New York: Zone Books, 2009.

Adolf Hitler. *Mein Kampf*. London: Hurst and Blackett Ltd., 1939.

Thomas Hobbes. *Leviathan*. Boston, MA: Hackett, 1994.

Immanuel Kant. "Was ist Auflklärung?" In *The Politics of Truth*, edited by Sylvère Lotringer. Los Angeles, CA: semiotext(e), 2007.

Søren Kierkegaard. *Fear and Trembling/Repetition*, vol. 6. Translated by Howard V. Hong and Edna H. Hong. Princeton: Princeton University Press, 1983.

Martin Luther. *Von der Freiheit eines Christenmenschen*. Stuttgart: Philipp Reclam GmbH & Co., 1962.

Herbert Marcuse. *On Authority*. New York: Verso, 2008.

Karl Marx and Friedrich Engels. *The German Ideology*. Amherst: Prometheus Books, 1998.

Carl Schmitt. "The Way to the Total State." In *Four Articles: 1931–1938*, translated by Simona Draghici. Washington, DC: Plutarch Press, 1999.

Carl Schmitt. *The Concept of the Political*. Translated by George Schwab, Chicago, IL: University of Chicago Press, 2007.

Wolfgang Streeck. *How Will Capitalism End? Essays on a Failing System*. New York: Verso Books, 2017.

Lars von Trier (Dir.). *Melancholia*. Zentropa, 2011.

Paul Veyne. *A History of Private Life: From Pagan Rome to Byzantium*. Translated by Arthur Goldhammer. Cambridge: Harvard University Press, 1987.

E. Wagner (ed.). *Luther als Pädagog (Klassiker der Pädigogik, vol. II)*. Langensalza: F.G.L. Gressler, 1892.

3 Myth of "the Family"

Biological, Social, Economic

This chapter opens with a brief consideration of the political theology of authority that relates directly to Chapter 2 and moves on to frame the persistence of the myth of the family both in the mainstream media and within juridical discourse. From there I consider the work of socio-biologist Sarah Blaffer Hrdy who counters the idea that the nuclear patriarchal family has precedent in deep biological history. Instead, all evidence points to communities relying on collective alloparenting and intensive practices of mutual aid.

Following these considerations and forming the primary aim of this chapter, I focus on the coincidence of the juridical-economic determination of *the family* and myths of human nature, as well as the systematic exclusions of the social from kinship through the legal category of the sanctioned family. While Chapter 2 focuses on the political division of the public and private, here I will turn to the economic division of the public and private. The term economy is understood both broadly and narrowly. General economy refers to practical activity meant to secure the needs of a community – *oikonomeia*. In a more restricted sense the economic refers to specific historical systems of production which often have more to do with systematizing distribution and naturalizing stratification than creating a generally eudaemonic society.

Authority and Economic Obedience

Much of the early Frankfurt School research focused on the family as a training ground for producing authoritarian psychic structures in children;[1] that is, in training young people to adhere to the conforming principles of an authoritarian society and its concomitant terms of value – including xenophobia and nationalism. In his study on "Authority and the Family", Max Horkheimer claimed that the protestant conception of God introduces the "most direct expression" of "the reification of authority".[2] According to the doctrine, it is not because God adheres to qualities such as wisdom and moral goodness that he deserves reverence and obedience. In those cases, Horkheimer points out, obedience would be "based on good reason", one could partake in goodness and wisdom by obeying that which best adheres to those qualities. Obedience in that case is the common orientation

DOI: 10.4324/9781003264644-4

around agreed-upon principles (virtues) according to which activity is directed. Instead, the protestant precept establishes the authority of God as synonymous with the good – morality is simply that which adheres to the will of God.

This goes back to fascinating debates in the Church concerning the ontological coincidence – or not – of the Good and the Divine that reached their peak of intensity just prior to the Lutheran reformation.[3] Again, for Luther and many other theologians who broke with the Catholic Church, God was prior to and thus the condition for benevolence rather than the perfect manifestation of it. "In the consciousness of the present age authority is not even a relationship but an inalienable property of the superior being, a qualitative difference".[4] But what exactly is transmitted in the authoritarian family? How is the property of authority conferred onto the individual? Horkheimer writes: "the authority-promoting function of the family affects the family itself in two ways: the economic structure of society, for which the family is one condition, makes the father the master and directly creates in his offspring the disposition to start their own household in turn".[5] Even in the case of "women's emancipation" let's say from the official household strictly understood, according to Horkheimer, it is too late in that unemployment has become a "structural part of the present society".[6]

Here, Horkheimer asserts that the patriarchal authority structure persists long after its material basis has dissolved, which again resonates with the divine command theory of transcendent morality in that divine authority has no relation to practical life. He further attributes the specific form the family takes to the cultural forces that intervene between kinship and economic structures noting: "The idealization of paternal authority, the pretense that it comes from a divine decision or the nature of things or reason proves on closer examination to be the glorification of an economically conditioned institution".[7] Here authority, reality, and pragmatics coincide and subtend the force of reason establishing traditionalist claims of "social health" through the normative family structure.

This is precisely the underlying reasoning behind the recent op-ed in the *Los Angeles Times* written by the right-wing pundit Jonah Goldberg, daftly titled "Why family matters, and why traditional families are still best".[8] Goldberg cites a number of recent "studies" maintaining that children "especially boys" do best in a "traditional household", which he suggests is ideally restricted in practice to the monogamous hetero-patriarchal – or at least paternal – nuclear family, i.e., the family as a moral-machine for the proper reproduction of bodies and attendant transmissions of authority. He even goes so far as to cite a quote from the highly questionable – not to mention blatantly racist and misogynistic – reports authored by Daniel Patrick Moynihan, titled *The Negro Family*, which warns against the chaos that will infect a society that implements policies that ultimately encourage the erosion of the integrity of the sacred nuclear family.[9]

In a more recent book by American conservative columnist George Will – which argues that the social conservatism of the past has been woefully abandoned, defeated by progressives in the last three decades – Will claims that persistence of economic stratification in the United States, in poor Black communities, in particular, ought to be blamed entirely on the dissolution of the family. As supposedly incontrovertible evidence, he too cites the specious reports by Moynihan (and little else) as proof of this supposed fact.[10] Directly implicating those families led by women as particularly damaging for young generations, both Will and Goldberg's primary axiom is not just that the most important source of meaning in a person's life comes from their family, but that in order to fully develop a healthy self – an economically productive-moral subject – in this respect, a strong patriarchal source of authority is required. Goldberg suggests that these studies found that adoptive families produce less "well-adjusted individuals" which makes sense because "well adjusted" here means docile, conforming to the moral principles of productive technocratic capitalism. While Goldberg offers that they also show a child brought up in, for example, an impoverished or abusive nuclear family would "of course be better off" living with "adopted" parents and "of course" a child growing up in a "Chinese or Russian orphanage" would clearly perform more effectively with an American wealthy gay couple, this only exacerbates the willful naiveté that marks most claims in support of "traditional" frameworks of kinship – which, again, as discussed in Chapter 1, are not so clear and not even so "traditional".

The logic of the argument ends with the ideological normative framework of "American" society – as the exemplary juridico-economic-political system apparently taken to best approximate nature, moral, and social health – and could be applied to any dominant form of sanctioned or structurally normalized relation. It is no different than the Panglossian logic that in any given community, those who adhere to the authorized form of domination tend to adjust more effectively to the demands of that society. The conclusion, naturally enough is that obedience and conformism appear as the superior social comportment rather than, for example, criticism, resistance, revolt, non-conformity, or any other bases for otherwise constructed communities.

It is clear that the anxiety fueling this specific overdetermination is located in the fear that the authority of the father – ostensibly required to properly indoctrinate children in reverence to paternal power, national identity, and therefore the symbolic law, both determining and determined by the state, as it persists in society outside the family – has irreversibly diminished. It is in the coincidence of the father with truth and the good (to recall the arguments concerning theological metaethics above) that renders his position sacred. The "broken family" is that group in which the proper "natural" order of authority – the embodiment of the good and the true – is ruptured – i.e. evil. The disadvantages brought about by this situation can be blamed on the failure of the individual to uphold the proper form of relation.

This is no longer always explicitly couched in Abrahamic language – though often enough it still is – but instead relies on the claimed expertise demonstrated in ethnographies, psychological studies, behavior and performance at school, statistics, and other algorithms, i.e. those authorities that justify the policing of communities and the demands constituting the sanctioned family. Prominent Catholic theologians such as Robert P. George and Cardinal Rigali claim that justification for the nuclear family is inherently rational (rationality understood as a gift from the most rational God). In this case, of course, it is the other side of the divine command theory where we find God cast as the most excellent adherence to rationality. In fact, George claims his entire argument stands or falls with the rational argument for the justification of the traditional family.[11] But that rationality – to return to a point made in Chapter 1 citing Krafft-Ebing – is predicated on a strictly instrumental reproductive imperative as the telos of intimacy, one which essentializes patriarchal authority.

Both positions fail to account for the aggravating circumstances endemic to the neutralization of the status quo – of the constructed social, economic, and political reality that instituted social divisions require. The nuclear family appears eternal and pure, rooted in a (specious) notion of "tradition" rather than the more contingent construction that it is.[12] In this case, *the family* is a charade that justifies and authorizes the systematic withdrawal or transfer of access to modes of necessity – nourishment and community – among the millions of identically organized (monocultural) micro-social systems. Far from simply expressing a trite, personal, or religious quip, Goldberg's column and Will's book point to a larger, structural, and deeply embedded set of assumptions concerning the "healthy family". While the nuclear family is expressed in Abrahamic doctrine as the ideal (Edenic) form of human community, it is well known that this projection is often found as an unquestioned underpinning within the social sciences and juridical norms. The concern, here as noted above, has to do with the political, legal, and theoretical consequences of accepting the myth of the nuclear family and the sexual contract it implies, as "natural", while simultaneously an achievement of progress, and thus psychologically, socially, and politically ideal.

Alloparenting and the Evolutionary Origins of Mutuality

There are plenty of examples of this narrative entering secular legal discourse, I will just mention one for now. In 2005 the US Supreme Court upheld a ruling by the 11th US Circuit Court of Appeals that ruled in favor of the law banning gay couples from adopting children noting: "'The accumulated wisdom of several millennia of Human Experience' has demonstrated 'that the optimal family structure in which to raise children was one with a mother and father married to each other'".[13] This is quoted in Sarah Blaffer Hrdy's key work on the evolutionary origins of mutuality, which takes up this question from a socio-biological perspective. She demonstrates that precisely the opposite is the case. If we can make any assumptions about the form of kinship proliferating throughout human sociality for "millennia", it would be that caretaking and upbringing is necessarily a broadly collective practice. Rather than the burden of raising children being cast onto a mythical monogamous couple, various practices of *alloparenting* prevailed in preindustrial and "prehistorical" societies. Hrdy suggests that "novel rearing conditions among a line of early hominins meant that youngsters grew up depending on a wider range of caretakers than just their mothers, and this dependence produced selection pressures that favored individuals who were better at decoding the mental states of others" that is the ability to develop complex intersubjective affective bonds and to distinguish friend from foe.[14]

Humans are far from unique in possessing the capability for imitation, compassion (the possession of mirror neurons) giving a range of abilities to identify with others. But according to Hrdy, what she calls "emotionally modern humans" developed far prior to anatomically modern humans over 200,000 years ago. (For context, our last common ape ancestor existed presumably around 1.5 million years ago). What Hrdy's thesis amounts to is that humans evolved from an exclusively mother-centered structure of infant care, evident in the four non-human great apes where mothers categorically refuse to allow anyone near their baby, to more nomadic hunter-gathering, forage-horticultural, and transhumant agricultural economies that not only include but require the broad sharing of caretaking tasks. Hrdy does not question the fact that mothers are in most cases unquestionably the primary caregiver but that infant sharing is something that emerges as biologically necessary, an affective practice of survival in pre-historical human societies: "what hunter-gatherer mothers do not do postpartum is refuse to let anyone else come near and hold the baby".[15] One remarkable observation made by primatologists is that non-human primates categorically accept their offspring even in the case of extreme malformations, whereas for humans "a newborn perceived as defective may be drowned, buried alive, or simply wrapped in leaves and left in the bush within hours of birth"[16] as was the case we are told with Moses and Oedipus.

At the beginning of a chapter titled *Will the Real Pleistocene Family Please Step Forward?*, Hrdy considers the typical museum diorama depicting an early hominid family – think of the Museum of Natural History in Manhattan. Perhaps we see "beetle browed caveman" just back from the hunt, dragging some bloodied beast toward the communal fire where in flickering light a woman is holding a child. We tend to assume, Hrdy suggests, that the woman is the biological mother of the child. But the idea that "by nature" the man or head of household is the "provider" and that women are domestic caretakers is undermined not only by evidence that human diets in most of the communities we have evidential access to, were made up of far more vegetables than meat, thus gathering, forage-horticultural, or semi-nomadic farming was the more reliable source of vitality, but also that in societies that live in similar hunter-gatherer circumstances today rely far more on gathering, which proves to be a much more reliable method of securing nutrition than hunting which usually occurs in a form of "bonanzas".[17] In other words, even with sophisticated weapons today, hunting rarely produces sufficient calories and nutrition for the sustenance of a community.[18] Hrdy's conclusion is that the influence of "variable paternal commitments" on upbringing (and whatever might be understood as the child's mental or social health) is predicated on the local conditions within which they are living. "In some environments, presence of the father has no detectable impact on child survival".[19]

The purpose of considering this material here is to show not only that there is no biological-evolutionary, natural, or pragmatic basis for the nuclear family in terms of ideal configurations of care, but that even in communities which rely on fathers for survival, either in densely populated societies where the main threat to life is intraspecific aggression, as well as communities that rely on meat more than other substances for nutrition, the nuclear family ideal never functions to provide a flourishing social environment without cooperation, outsourcing or professionalization. If anything, the insufficiency of the nuclear arrangement makes it the most ideal form of regulated intimate relation for maximizing the commodification of care.

Even in the case where a community relies heavily on hunting,[20] it is categorically the case that the "meat is shared according to strict 'from each according to his means' ethic of 'cooperate frequently and share fully'".[21] Often in societies in which resources are unpredictable multiple fathers are lined up as additional means of support.

> Even in times and places renowned for patriarchal family structures, such as the Qing dynasty in China or in traditional India, desperately poor parents sometimes made ends meet by incorporating an extra man (usually some kind of wage earner) into the marital unit.[22]

This is also often the situation today Hrdy notes, in an increasingly crowded globalized world in which resources have become more uncertain. Depleted by manufactured scarcity, war, economic bondage, and ecological catastrophe, mothers in "Africa, the Caribbean to the *banilieues* of Europe and US inner cities routinely enter into sequential polyanderous ... relationships to make do, hedge bets, or improve their lot".[23] Hrdy continues, citing forage-horticultural communities in Amazonia such as

> the Bari of Venezuela, the Ache of Paraguay, Wayano of French Guiana, Matis of Peru, Takana of Bolivia, or the Arawete, Kulina, Kuikuru, Mehinaku, or Canela of Brazil, it is socially acceptable, even expected, for the husband to permit real or fictive ceremonial "brothers" to sleep with his wife.[24,25]

Hrdy's thesis is that recent discoveries have shown that cooperation rather than competition is the attribute that most closely characterizes the social disposition required for survival, and it is only through developing intricate techniques and complex, affective networks of association in which the principle of mutual aid prevailed, that human beings have even survived. But to respond directly to the traditionalist line, there is little evidence that the specific social role of the father is ever a necessity. Anthropologist David. L. Lancy notes: "Of all the cast of characters in this melodrama, the role of father is the most subject to creative script variation". And often "far from being the dominant influence in their children's lives, the biological parents were just two of a large cast of potential child-minders".[26]

Opposing the Hobbesian state of nature as a war of all against all based on the principle of selfishness, Hrdy suggests that researchers are coming around to the idea that it would be far more accurate to take seriously Spinoza's idea that "the Endeavor to live in a shared, peaceful agreement with others is an extension of the endeavor to preserve oneself".[27,28] With regard to those hunter-gatherer, for-age-horticultural, nomadic, and semi-nomadic communities, Hrdy notes it simply makes no sense to "project onto such people the within-group wealth differentials typical of more stratified societies today".[29]

If we are going to resort to evidence from deep history, what we find is a generalized principle of cooperation supported by

> new findings of how irrational, how emotional, how caring, and even how selfless human decisions can be are transforming disciplines long grounded in the premise that the world is a competitive place where to be a rational actor means being a selfish one.[30]

The plasticity required by communities that rely on mutual aid for survival ought to lead to the conclusion that *alloparenting* was both a general and necessary practice not just for persistence but for achieving general material affluence. In other words, the idea that humans are by nature sociopaths that require policing, surveillance, and authoritarian order (rooted and reproduced in patriarchal upbringing) is being displaced in the social sciences by another narrative, one that recognizes that "human beings are born predisposed" through "hypersocial attributes that allow us to monitor the mental states and feelings of others", "to care how they relate to others".[31]

Not only the fact that human children are born biologically premature, but simply the fact that they rely so much on nourishment secured by others ought to lead us to the idea that sharing and mutuality, and a bio-social sensitivity akin to *mind reading* is the foundation upon which community thrives. Here the social sciences are coming around to the idea that a socialist political disposition that eschews the failed meritocracy based on the fantasy of war of all against all, more accurately coincides with a sustainable social and biological arrangement, which has precedent in deep history. A broad-based, flexible pattern of care more accurately describes an attunement common to embodied discursive hominids – conditioned no doubt by tens or hundreds of thousands of years of nomadic or semi-nomadic subsistence of foraging, horticulture, and simple farming – than the individualized, atomized competitive stance that to our peril we are trained to adhere to today.

Intimate Enclosures: Genesis of the Sanctioned Family

The general atrophy of the "official family" in the recent history of the nation-state can be observed simply by comparing the definitions of the family established by the United States Census Bureau between 1870 and 2010. We see the most extreme shift happening in 1930 when the definition of "the household" was explicitly separated from the concept of "the family":

In 1860, in the United States, the legal family was defined as:

> By the term "family" is meant either one person living separately and alone in a house, or a part of a house, and providing for him or herself, or several

persons living together in a house, or part of a house, upon one common means of support and separately from others in similar circumstances. A widow living alone and separately providing for herself, or 200 individuals living together and provided for by a common head, should each be numbered as one family.

The 1870 definition adds the activity of eating together:

Under whatever circumstances, and in whatever numbers, people live together under one roof, and are provided for at a common table, there is a family in the meaning of the law.

By comparison, the 1930 version states:

Persons related in any way to the head of the family by blood, marriage or adoption are counted as members of the family.

And the 2010 version remains quite similar:

A family consists of a householder and one or more other people living in the same household who are related to the householder by birth, marriage or adoption.[32]

One hundred and fifty years separate the earliest and latest definitions above, in which we quickly discover the progressively constricted definition of the family from a juridical standpoint. This provides some grasp of the plasticity of recognized forms of kinship, as well as practices, even within the legal framework of a state. In other words, even the legal precedent of the formal nuclear doesn't seem to have very deep roots.

In the 1860 definition we glean two key principles: first, the community lives "upon one common means of support" or are "provided by a common head", whether the association consists of one person or 200, and finally that they dwell together in a house, apartment, or other forms of habitat. Essentially, it is a group of people who share a home. The 1870 definition, as noted above, adds the qualification of being "provided for at the common table". The phrase "under whatever circumstances", applied to place, number of people, so long as they share a roof and table, indicates a markedly unrestrictive notion of the legal family at that time, theoretically encompassing crime families, religious cults, communes, orphanages, homesteaders, squats, and so on. It is defined by the necessities of shared shelter and shared food. That is, the communal relation between members is defined by non-commodified relations, i.e. it is predicated at least in part on resources held in common. In other words, the relation is neither one of employment, nor citizenship, nor even friendship but rather one of mutual obligation, living in common, in "a home". There is nothing in these definitions that explicitly consider family relations to be proprietary as it is by contrast expressed, for example, in Roman law (Cicero, *On Duties*). But the definitions all seem to exclude nomadic, vagrant, wandering, or otherwise itinerant communities from the category. Otherwise, the key point is that the community has some degree of economic self-sufficiency "in common". One implication is that the more restrictive and nuanced familial norms – including ownership – were determined by theological strictures rather than juridical categories. So why, with time, does the law become more restrictive in what it recognizes as a family?

It is only in 1930 that the juridical concept of the family in the United States explicitly implies either consanguinity or affinity as a necessary component. That is, one is in "a family" only when one is related by marriage, birth, or adoption, as defined by the law. The most recent, 2010 definition is almost identical to the previous one. Otherwise, in the latter two definitions, the term "common" is omitted, so is an indication of the notion of community, replaced by a presumably single "provider" who is connected "by blood" or "marriage" to the other members. The 2010 definition is unique in that a single person is no longer considered a family, though this is arguably implied already in 1930. There are of course economic, political, and social correlations to the emaciation of the family and the increasingly restrictive official definition governing claims of care and generation – via law and inheritance. Here, I will just recount a broad sketch from an economic viewpoint because it will help frame the changing political discourse around kinship.

Rationalizing Time: Labor and Intimacy

Focusing on the past three decades, Wolfgang Streeck recently characterized what he calls a "fundamental restructuring" of the "family and childrearing".[33] Streeck's analysis concentrates on how capitalism has come to permeate and shape just about every aspect of life, becoming a veritable "way of life" rather than a system restricted to the production, provision, and consumption of material goods. The rise of Fordism in the 1920s – the development of the assembly line, the systematization of bodily movement both individual and en-masse – along with centralized state-sanctioned economic authority, mass production and consumption, intensified policing, social and moral conformism, mass media, mass transit, mass incarceration, intensifying urbanism, and so on, saw the development of the "Fordist family", which is reflected in the shift to the 1930 definition above.

Anticipating Michel Foucault's concept of biopolitics, Antonio Gramsci already identifies techniques of control in the interests of productivity and power, as rooted in the most intimate spaces and temporalities of social relation. On the acceleration of productivity ushered in by systematic methods of reorganizing the body in relation to manufacturing, Gramsci writes:

> In America rationalization of work and prohibition are undoubtedly connected. The inquiries conducted by industrialists into workers' private lives

and the inspection services created by some firms to control the "morality" of their workers are necessities of the new methods of work.[34]

This does not stop simply at the level of productivity, rather it reaches into the most intimate spaces of life as a "complex of direct and indirect repression and coercion" that establish monogamy and constancy as the fundamental characteristics of sexual union recognized as legitimate within society as a whole. This includes not just legal definitions, but also religious, psychological, and sociological terms of morality, normality, and social health. Here Gramsci argues that everything down to sexual activity, the way in which sexual relation circumscribes and the methods by which children are educated, or brought into the community as a self or member, divided and identified by class, age, gender, race, language, name, etc. begins to fit into the increasingly vast reach of the rationalization of labor into the domain of morality while beginning to redefine the social:

> It might seem that in this way the sexual function has been mechanized, but in reality we are dealing with the growth of a new form of sexual union .... It seems clear that the new industrialist wants monogamy: it wants the man as a worker not to squander his nervous energies in the disorderly and stimulating pursuit of occasional sexual satisfaction.[35]

The family ethic then develops along the lines of the work ethic as they begin to function in tandem.

Returning to Streeck's analysis, initially, it was seen as a mark of dignity for "the woman of the household" to stay home and take care of the children. But as agency and value become confined to industrial (and other professionalized forms) of labor:

> Morally, entering into paid employment became not just a choice for women but a de facto obligation, taking the place of marriage and child-bearing in the 1950s and 1960s. "Work" became identical with paid work, while not being in paid work – being a Hausfrau or a housewife – became associated with not working at all and increasingly turned into a personal disgrace.[36]

The broad impetus was two-fold and contradictory. On the one hand, with the devaluation of labor (the decline in wages) the household could no longer rely on a single wage. At the same time, a clear aim of feminism, which was only strengthened by women entering the labor force during the First World War, was to get women out from under the thumb of the "bread winner" ("male-provider") who had a monopoly on social power, both within the family and in connecting the family to a broader social and political world. The sense of pride and independence found in being the "provider" – as if care is somehow not "providing" – was increasingly available to women. At the same time, that women appeared to achieve some modicum of independence, the grip of capitalist logic deepened while the communal basis of "the family" further atrophied. The moral imperative of matrimony maintains the economic value it held prior to the increase of flexibility, and thus precarity, of work.[37] It must be acknowledged, as Melinda Cooper points out, that the critique of instrumental reason and the commodification of relations might, if we stop the argument here, easily slip into an anti-feminist, sentimental atavism, ultimately, often blindly, reaffirming the gendered division of labor and naturalize the production of gender.

In a similar vein to Streeck – though in this case clearly feminist – Kathi Week's important book *The Problem with Work* begins with a consideration of the political distribution of the public and private. She identifies two overarching reasons for what she finds as a dearth of attention given to what she calls "the problem of work" – stemming from the fetishization of paid work as a social value in and of itself – from the academic disciplines. The first has to do with the privatization of work. She notes: "we seem to have a hard time grasping the power of relations of both work and family systematically; we often experience and imagine the employment relation – like the marriage relation – not as a social institution but as a unique relationship".[38]

But the privatization of work in liberal capitalist societies, she suggests, is also much more contested and complicated than it seems. She cites John Locke's establishment of the natural rights of humans: "life, liberty and estate (property)" as decisively establishing the private status of work. Insofar as it functions to politically secure and define private property as a legal economic basis, thereby instituting a right, work functions in the interests of the universal. However, ambiguity is introduced as it falls to the domain of the commonwealth or state to protect this right. My "right to work" then ought to be secured under the protective authority of the state, just as liberty and freedom are ostensibly protected by the legislative and juridical order. However, exclusion is not ultimately dictated by the supposed cunning of market forces, but by socially and politically reinforced disparities. Not only work, but also property becomes a privilege, together under the presumptive principles of a supposedly merit-based economy, one which, through structural conditions of debt and poverty punishes the apparent failure of the individual to maintain a sufficiently competitive edge.

With industrialism Weeks notes, things are simplified as wage labor in the factory externalizes production outside of the household, ostensibly moving economic activity in general from the common to the publically privatized. Work in the household becomes invisible within a capitalist economy which has no mechanism to recognize the value of domestic labor, except perhaps indirectly as the need to reproduce labor power, via, for example, the now virtually extinct "family wage".[39] "The effective privatization of work is also a function of the way the labor market individualizes work – never more so than today, with the enormous variety of tasks and schedules that characterize the contemporary employment relation".[40]

According to Weeks, the question is "how to struggle against both labor's misrecognition and devaluation on the one hand, and its metaphysics and moralism on the other hand".[41] We could tweak this question to inquire into the function of the state as the politico-juridical authority that regulates the distribution of vulnerability, which in turn demands or implies the dichotomous private-public spheres. In other words, the ambiguity of the private-public is exacerbated, if not introduced, by the place of work.

* * *

In pre-capitalist society, much of the production of goods and services, for use and exchange, was done in or near the household, the economy being little more than the way in which a community was organized to satisfy the needs of its members, generally in relation to household management (*oikonomeia*). For example, food preparation, ale-brewing, textile, midwifery, healthcare, and the work of taking care of the dead were just some of the kinds of important and well-respected activities and forms of knowledge that originated in and were sustained by the domestic world – which really *produced the household* as such – many of which women had full or partial control over. On taking care of the dead, for example, Georganne Rundblad, writes:

> Some women, up to the late 1800s, were even viewed by their communities to be general caregivers typically performing the laying out of the body at death. These women were what Willie Mae Cartwright, as a Black woman living in the South in the late 19th early 20th centuries, called "shrouding women". In fact, one woman recalled that it was an "old custom ... that female neighbors would wash and lay out the remains, the undertaker being summoned only to take the measure and place the remains in the casket".[42]

> [W]omen in the community were relied on in a "system of mutual aid", especially when a birth threatened to end in fatally. Osterud observed that women "sat up with the mother or cared for the baby themselves so the mother could get some rest. If the child died, they stayed to help the family".[43]

Until the development of the funeral industry and the profession called undertaking, or the newly defined role of the mortician, men were often not allowed to be present around the dead body. Rundblad, following Foucault, points out that this constituted a kind of *local* or *popular* knowledge that, in the course of industrialization, was diminished along with the more restricted – legally defined and economically expressed – enclosure of kinship.[44] The history of these industries was rewritten to exclude acknowledgment of the significance and expertise of women in these roles. Prior to this the efficiency of the domestic world allowed for exchange with other households, which were in many cases, hugely productive communities, again relying on and organized around an organic system of mutual aid rather than the concentration of surplus. After all, they were the loci of generation and subsistence. Reflecting on the broader tactics of survival and resistance to the domination of the laws of accumulation and debt (centered on the home cultivated by women today) Silvia Federici writes:

> The consequences of the globalization of the world economy would certainly have been far more nefarious except for the efforts that millions of women

have made to ensure that their families would be supported, regardless of their value on the capitalist market. Through their subsistence activities, as well as various forms of direct action (from squatting on public land to urban farming) women have helped their communities to avoid total dispossession, to extend budgets, and to add food to the kitchen pots.[45]

Despite the changing form of the family – coercively reinforced by the social sciences via the concept of *nature* – Federici points out that activities of resistance have always persisted underneath the politically, economically, morally, and legally prescribed modes of life, particularly for marginalized and outsider communities. Today it is still the case in general with sustainable food production. Calculated on a global scale, the majority of food is produced by women subsistence farmers.[46] The key point is that in these subsistence communities, food is almost always shared rather than extracted by the global food market and commodified. Federici will take this as a starting point for what she calls the "re-enchantment of the commons", casting intimate forms of material solidarity as *the* initiation for such a project if there is any hope for a shift toward a social model of mutual aid on a mass scale.

Federici gets to the roots of the social-sexual contract in her key study on the body, women, and primitive accumulation, *Caliban and the Witch*. There she notes that the construct of the family to which we can trace our current nuclear household was initiated already with the systematic devaluation of women's labor in Europe in the 15th century. Then groups of male craftworkers organized and agreed to exclude women from the workshops, depriving them of participation and inclusion in the generational transmission of knowledge, and of participation in well-respected work over which they traditionally held authority. This was directly implemented in the "criminalization of women's control over procreation". Through this legal exclusion from bodily autonomy, "the state deprived them of the most fundamental condition for physical and psychological integrity and degraded maternity to the status of forced labor, in addition to confining women to reproductive work in a way unknown in previous societies".[47] With the criminalization of contraception, women were not only deprived of profound forms of knowledge passed down for generations, they were also restricted to the household, socially determined and defined as vessels of reproduction, both of population for the state and of labor power for industry. This was only the beginning of a broader logic that instituted and eventually naturalized the sexual division of labor. Marriage and housekeeping became the "new career" for women, Federici notes. Women were deprived of the means to support themselves. Certain kinds of activity became "men's work". And even when they engaged in productive work approximating the kinds of labor performed in the guilds, for example weaving or sewing, the guilds were often explicitly instructed by city governments to ignore the work done in homes "because it was not real work".[48] With the institution of this new distribution of labor and agency, "the new social sexual contract" working women became the "substitute for the land lost to the enclosures, their most basic means of reproduction, and a communal good anyone could appropriate and use at will".[49]

Extraction and Kinship

On the point of household economy, here I will briefly return to Kathi Weeks. As the division of labor becomes the basis for the distinction between paid and unpaid (or waged and unwaged) work, the intricate web of "mutually constitutive linkages between work and family"[50] becomes almost impossible to untangle. Arguments for the reduction of work hours (as put forth in the *Post Work Manifesto: Wages of Cybernation*, by Stanley Aronowitz[51]) simply fail to take into account the inevitable implication that along with the preservation of the division of labor – the nuclear household – the reduction of waged work hours (or legitimated work) does nothing for the domestic sphere; in which, in general, women will nevertheless attend to the basic demands of household needs. Weeks writes: "The wage system, work processes, work ethics, and modes of worker subjectivity are intimately bound up with kinship forms, household practices, family ethics, and modes of gendered subjectivity".[52]

Indeed, without moving beyond the family-centered model for the demand for shorter hours, we can never really exit the contradiction between the private and public, and the division of labor and gender on which it is predicated.

> This same productivist asceticism, which was designed to encourage work discipline and thrift, has also served to animate the idea of heterosexual marital monogamy. In the nineteenth century, for instance, the white middle-class family was idealized as the form that could redirect sexual appetites and desires toward productive ends.[53]

This ideal was immediately imposed on the households of new immigrant communities, in that it disseminated the gendered division of labor through welfare policy, demands for formal education, work requirements, and at some moments of history religious conversion or repression.[54] Against the catastrophic imperative of infinite growth, Weeks advocates for the universal reduction of labor, which, she suggests, requires a complete rethinking of the work ethic, in what she calls *time movement*. She points out that the latter is deeply bound up with what she calls the *family ethic*, a kind of work-oriented asceticism in which life in general (and we might add, not just human life) is organized around a productivist imperative.

This double ethical bind around which society and the very concept of the responsible, effective, professional individual, its manifestation in the work ethic, and the family ethic has been organized was defined by reformed welfare policy in the United States introduced in 1996 through the Personal Responsibility and Work Opportunity Reconciliation Act. The rationale for the legislation explicitly relied on restrictive definitions of "what counts as work and what counts as family, frequently focus on the poor single mother, often deployed as a racialized figure, for her imagined failure to conform simultaneously to the dominant family model and hegemonic work values"[55] as the reactionary pundits discussed above frame it.

Along similar lines, Arlie Russel Hochschild, as Weeks also notes, makes the argument for shortening the workday, but on the grounds that it will allow for more time with the family. Hochschild's argument holds that a major obstacle to such a reduction is simply that work life in many cases has become more and more like domestic life. This has only contributed to the increasing diminishment of family life. "Work is becoming more like home, and home like work", thus "people tend to prefer more time at work and less time at home".[56] This is particularly the case in the tech industry as described by books such as David Egger's *The Circle.*[57] There, Eggers describes the tactics that shape the work-ethic, and by implication the family-ethic, at tech companies like Google used both to attract new talent in order to integrate the private into the professional, thereby extracting as much time and information from the lives of employees as possible. Not only has technology allowed workers to be on call 24/7; the pressure placed on laborers, particularly in the tech industry, to participate in after-work activities such as live music performances and weekend getaways, while on the other hand, shaming them if they don't take part in recognizing the company not as work but as "family".

This relies on a change in temporality, on the one hand this is no longer *work*, so time is no longer valued according to the wage hour because the qualitative difference between work time and "free time" dissolves. Rather than participation demanded through rules – which would require legal compensation – it is more effectively implemented through social pressure. In Eggers' story, it is because the protagonist wants to spend more time with her ailing mother that she is eventually ostracized by co-workers. These activities are framed as "community building" and appear to be provided by the company gratis, because they "care" about their employees as "a family". A similar trend is the proliferation of share workspaces (perversely dubbed "the sharing" or "gig" economy) in urban centers.[58]

On the window of one of these work share spaces in the hip Berlin neighborhood of Kreuzberg are signs that state: "Welcome to your Family" and "We are community" – on a more diminutive scale, you can discern the Allianz insurance and asset management company logo. The interior design evokes a makeshift, flexible space with open areas unobstructed by partitions, modular furniture, and superbly high ceilings. The language and arrangement evoke a sense of cohabitation, of collective potential, the excitement of shared ideas, where one can let their creativity run free. It is meant to strike you as a hospitable, familiar, and playful space of autonomy far away from the droning office cubicle associated with the corporate world, while still remaining isolated from the rush of competing bodies on the street just outside. Of course, these new spaces project collective appeal as an antidote to the sterility and confinement of the more traditional workplace environment. The force of attraction is precisely in the apparent dissolution of the private and the public, which also characterizes the more precarious forms of labor, namely contract work, which also, of course, increasingly dominates the job market. Now work can be your home, it is your familiar, and your family.

Meanwhile, the work conditions in distribution warehouses like Amazon and big box stores have become so immiserating workers are hardly able to spend time with their loved ones at all, as they struggle to simply afford the basic necessities to survive. The disparity between high-salary and low-wage work is not only expressed in discrepancies in social power expressed in bloated or repressed pay respectively but in the dichotomous ways in which non-work life is systematically diminished.

* * *

In the "gig economy", the so-called shared work spaces perversely borrow from a history of radical commune building which has progressively disappeared from many urban landscapes.[59] With regard to the emergence of alternative political spaces in blighted urban areas, Pierpaolo Mudu notes:

> The reorganization of Fordist production and the transition to models of flexible accumulation based on the widespread use of temporary work contracts and the grey economy brought about a drastic change in the possibility of carrying out political activity in conventional spaces (i.e. workplaces, schools and universities) and in the traditional premises of political parties. The result was a dramatic decrease in political spaces.[60]

Many of the more recent experiments in collective squatting (meaning "occupancy without legal title") can be traced back to the anarchist Provo movement in Amsterdam. In 1966 the collective came up with the *White House Plan*. A working group in the collective created and distributed a list of abandoned houses and painted the doors white. In 1969 the 'Woningbureau (Housing Bureau) de Kraker' was established.[61]

In these collective practices we find recent and contemporary experiments in transformative kinship practices in urban areas. As Hans Pruijt notes: "squatting hinges on a transformational process: unused buildings are transformed into safe, acceptable or comfortable homes, or spaces that are used in other ways and infused with life".[62] For example, in the now fashionable Berlin neighborhood of Mitte, there recently stood one of the most well-known squats of Berlin the *Kunsthaus Tacheles* (1990–2012). The term *tacheles* is Yiddish for frankness. In sheer mass the building was the most impressive on Oranienburgstrasse, now well known for its high-end galleries, haute cuisine, and elite fashion. It was initially occupied just after the wall came down. The collective brought together an international array of radical artists, provided them with a free space to create and experiment with new social arrangements. It was an open space that allowed people to peddle their crafts at the street level, while having its own biergarten/sculpture garden for gatherings, music, events, refuge, and organizing.

On the lower east side of Manhattan a similar, but more enduring, radical communal space, ABC No Rio, provides free access to a dark room, computers, as well as a full screen-printing shop and art gallery, and in the basement, a music venue for weekend matinees usually featuring experimental shows and various performances. Donations could take the form of money or more often by participating in running the space, teaching classes, and so on.[63]

The long-standing Liebig 34 in Samariterkiez, Berlin, an anarcha-queer-feminist living project which formed in 1990 and provided a safe community-building space according to consent-democratic principles was forcibly and violently evicted in 2020. It was seen as such a powerful symbol for leftist political resistance in Berlin that the magazine *Der Spiegel* predicted a civil war would break out in the city when it would finally be uprooted. It took 1500 heavily armed police to evict the 40 occupiers, marking a tragic end to an important radical social experiment in kinship practices in the city. It was justified because of the politically illicit status of the community and the recent purchase of the building by Gijora Padovicz, one of the biggest property speculators in Berlin.

Much like the non-parliamentary leftist Social Centers that emerged in Italy in the 1970s, many of these collectives function as models for a self-enclosed commons and experimental arrangements in intimacy and mutual aid.[64] The point is that this kind of solidarity in these cases is neither commodified nor abstract. The more political examples of these experiments find creative ways to resist the sanctioning force of the city and the economic concept of private property on just about every level through the active, horizontal, and often messy practice of building autonomous community – with national and international networks – within an urban metropolis. It is precisely for the practical rejection of private property that the communities became criminalized and it is why the city resorts to direct violence and militarized police to violently evict them. In these situations the municipal police become security forces enforcing private real estate capital – i.e. sanctioned theft. As long as the city needed people to take over blighted buildings in decaying urban slums, squatting was in a limited way protected by the law. As soon as economic expansion took root again through various forms of policy structured gentrification, squatting suddenly became equal to unsanctioned theft.

The narrowing definition of the family – arguably at times to the complete exclusion of practical kinship – as much as the commodification of spaces that simulates the fluidity of activity organically constructed in grassroots urban cooperatives is instrumental in placing these spaces outside of legitimate community. A profound degree of trust is required for these experiments to function. And much of the work done is spontaneous but also repetitive, even ritualized, and functions to create intricate and in many cases sustainable bonds between the activists.[65] The ages range from infants to elders; children are born and brought up in these communities; food is grown; music and film festivals started; books are written; art, performances, pirate radio stations are created; homeless and otherwise destitute people are fed;[66] artists are given space to work and exhibit; and forms of solidarity develop that provide very real protection within a variously hostile environment – the hostility often comes from the police as security forces for gentrification. It was because these communities were so formidable on an intimate level that it took so much violence to dismantle them. This is not to naively idealize the squatting movement, radical social centers, or the communes and councils that preceded them (in places like Paris in 1871, or Germany in 1918–1919); certainly, there were and are problems, but they serve as models for broader kinship bonds that attempt to function outside of sanctioned enclosures of relationality. Recalling the 19th-century definitions of the family above these reclaimed urban spaces would undoubtedly fit into the legal category of households. But that is another story of police brutality, class struggle, creative resistance, and survival in the face of both urban decay and urban renewal.[67]

* * *

Returning to the previous discussion on economy, along more general lines, Weeks describes Hochschild's argument as centering on the following notion: "Americans live in a culture that devalues the unpaid work of parenting while overvaluing paid work, thus enforcing the relative attractions of work over family".[68] This argument for work–family balance, however, much like the sentimentalist tendency discussed in the introduction and Chapter 1,[69] results in emphasizing the highly restrictive structure of the nuclear family as valuable in and of itself, rather than recognizing it as manufactured by a historical-economic configuration of authority integral to the concentration of power and the distribution of precarity.

Although Hochschild is sensitive to issues surrounding gender-based division of labor and, especially in her earlier work,[70] clearly recognizes it as a key problem to be overcome – calling for parity in household responsibilities – for Weeks, the norms which she claims are "natural" concerning, for example, "intensive parenting" and the structure that approximates the projection of ideal family life, are themselves based on the model of household care shaped by the diminished and anemic nuclear configuration. In essence, Hochschild inevitably privileges the family form, historically constructed around the hetero-patriarchal nuclear model, as an ideal arrangement of social commitment, as something that must now simply be accomplished through equally shared labor by "both parents". While the parts of her argument that idealize – "naturalize, moralize, wax nostalgic about" – this narrow form of kinship may give it a broadly appealing force, they also reproduce a restrictive model of family life "an ideal of family life that is deeply problematic from a feminist perspective, one that has been used as a standard from which to condemn a wide variety of relationship practices and household patterns".[71]

To return to Hochschild's insight that people are spending more time at work and less with the family not because they have to but because they want to, Weeks offers an alternative explanation: "the problem is not that work is that good, that attractive, and that satisfying to the people she interviewed, but rather that family life is really that bad, that there are more fundamental problems with that institution".[72] This, of course, would undercut the broad appeal of Hochschild's argument and expose the fact that rather than being a *haven in a heartless world* the family is "an equally deserving target of reform".[73] For Weeks, following the work of Valerie Lehr, the demand for reduced work hours does not presuppose a solipsistic notion expressed by the cliché "individual liberty", but rather, it would allow us to rethink and build communities outside of the valorizing logic of capitalist "production and accumulation" not to mention consumption and debt. And, rather than simply advocating for an expanded welfare state (which both Weeks and Lehr admit is one possible, though not preferable fix), Weeks' suggestion is to "formulate demands that have the potential to allow greater autonomy from the structures and institutions, including the state, that now presume to dictate so many of our choices".[74]

As we can see from the above reflections, it is clear that the projection of the nuclear monogamous family as an ideal or universal is based on the specious notion that a society in which extreme stratification requires justification, not only in economic terms but through psychological categories, as well as social scientific concepts – i.e. the eternalization of intraspecific aggression within the human body and psyche – simply functions to explain and reflect the current model of society in which conditions of generalized competition and *the virtue of selfishness* are placed at the foundation for life, a generic comportment toward others that fashions enmity as the means for survival. The diminishment of kinship ties and the failure to recognize flexible mutual relations of trust as a necessity shapes the way in which these micro communities are dependent on broader structures of society, ones that precisely undermine the autonomy that develops through intensive cooperation. My argument is not meant to evoke an atavistic nostalgia for archaic communism or preindustrial harmony, but rather, to cite a line of thought from Margaret Mead that in a strange and interesting way evokes Walter Benjamin's concept of history[75]: "There may be human potentialities which date far back in evolutionary time for which new artificially created conditions may find a new use".[76]

The point of discussing the reduction of kinship to its minimal abstract form is to emphasize the ways in which the distribution of vulnerability functions through formal conditions of austerity, at times so extreme, so impossible that the potential to secure a semblance of relational autonomy is entirely precluded as a political concern. As the Goldberg article suggests, along with the diminished legal determination of the family cited above, the nuclear family has become a moral imperative projected onto history, onto biology, as a set of national values, as an eternal truth. The most basic demands for collective life are made entirely dependent on a singular structure and logic which determines care and shapes necessity (by tightly distributing access to its realization); one which demands the persistent augmentation of production, the eternal increase of value at the expense of more immediate substantiality, and one which corresponds to structural conditions which authorize an administered model of the family. The reduction of flexibility in what we could call kin relations broadly considered is key in the substantiation of the nation-state based authority along with the nationalism, capitalism, misogyny, and other exclusions of mutuality that shape it.

Notes

1 Max Horkheimer, Erich Fromm, and Herbert Marcuse, *Studien über Autorität und Familie. Forschungsberichte aus dem Institut für Sozialforshung* (Hannover: Klampen Verlag, 2005) (First published in 1936).

2 Max Horkheimer, "Authority and the Family," in *Critical Theory*, trans. Matthew J. O'Connell and others (New York: Continuum, 1995) 102.

3 Often this is called the Divine Command Theory. Note, for example, William of Ockham, in *Opera politica*, where he argues that it is not the case that humans ought to be good because God is omnibenevolent, not because he is best at adhering to such qualities but because he simply is synonymous with the good. See William of Ockham, *Opera Politica*, edited by H.S. Offler, 4 vols (London: British Academy, 1997) 352. Interestingly in this Ockham agreed with Luther who also subscribed to Divine Command Theory, however, he departed from Luther in that he maintained a general position of fideism.

4 Horkheimer, "Authority and the Family," 103.

5 Ibid., 122.

6 Ibid., 122.

7 Ibid., 123.

8 https://www.latimes.com/opinion/op-ed/la-oe-1027-goldberg-family-structure -20151027-column.html (accessed on 4 February 2019, 14:45).

9 This is the quote of Moynihan in full: "From the wild Irish slums of the 19th century Eastern seaboard, to the riot-torn suburbs of Los Angeles, there is one unmistakable lesson in American history; a community that allows a large number of men to grow up in broken families, dominated by women, never acquiring any stable relationship to male authority, never acquiring any set of rational expectations about the future – that community asks for and gets chaos." Of course, there is an overtly racialized, if not blatantly racist, aspect to quoting Moynihan who is most famous for authoring the Moynihan Reports a.k.a.: *The Negro Family: The Case for National Action*, which, among other things, pathologized the black family in the United States, in particular black mothers, citing the welfare system and social support as the source of ills in poor black communities, as the mechanism preventing them from "advancing economically", etc. Ta-Nahisi Coates and many others cite evidence that the Report was the very source for the failed and also devastating policies of policing and incarceration that has terrorized black communities in the United States since the end of the Jim Crow laws. See Ta-Nehisi Coates, "The Black Family in the Age of Mass Incarceration," *The Atlantic*, 10/2015 (https://www.theatlantic.com/magazine/archive/2015/10/the-black-family-in -the-age-of-mass-incarceration/403246/) See also Michelle Alexander, "The Rebirth of Caste," in *The New Jim Crow Mass Incarceration in the Age of Colorblindness* (New York: The New Press, 2012), 45–47. There she cites both "conservative" and "liberal" politicians who, "appealing to the racism and vulnerability of working class whites" blamed the "drug problems" and crime in black communities on the support received from welfare programs and "broken family life". Hortense Spillers goes perhaps furthest in taking apart the Report. One interesting point she makes is that just as the Report judges the "Negro family" has "no father to speak of, No Name, No Law", to be without father implies to be without "the symbolic law", it blames "the female line" for this, thus reversing the Oedipal structure by naming the mother and daughter as opposing – and even displacing or eliminating – the father. See Hortense J. Spillers, "Mama's Baby, Papa's Maybe: An American Grammar Book," *Diacritics* 17, no. 2, *Culture and Countermemory: The "American" Connection* (Baltimore, MD: Johns Hopkins University Press, Summer, 1987) 65–66.

10 George F. Will, *The Conservative Sensibility* (New York: Hachette Books, 2019).

11 https://www.nytimes.com/2009/12/20/magazine/20george-t.html

12 Reactionary politics always seeks to ground its existence in a false memory of the past. Perhaps most infamously this was expressed in the words of Hitler: "There is no permanent revolution that does not lead to complete anarchy .... There is nothing great on this earth which lasts thousands of years and has come about in decades. The tallest tree has had the longest growth period." Leni Riefenstahl, (dir.) *Triumph of the Will (Triumph des Willens)*, 1935. 26:00 (https://www.dailymotion.com/video/x6ua-

jey). This myth of precedence is rooted, of course, in the idea of genos and the myth of blood as the basis for biological continuity. If this biological continuity is patriarchal then knowledge of the father is needed, and since this knowledge prior to genetic testing could not be secured empirically, it had to be established juridically, this the nuclear family.

13 Sarah Blaffer Hrdy, *Mothers and Others: The Evolutionary Origins of Mutual Understanding* (Cambridge, MA: Harvard University Press, 2009).

14 Ibid., 66.

15 "Women are just as prone as other apes to worry about the well-being of new babies. But what hunter-gatherer mothers do not do postpartum is refuse to let anyone else come near and hold the baby." Ibid., 73.

16 Ibid., 71.

17 As Stephanie Coontz points out in her fascinating history of marriage, "Couples in the Paleolithic world would never have fantasized about running off by themselves to their own little retreat in the forest. No Stone Age lovers would have imagined in their wildest dreams that they could or should be 'everything' to each other. *That way led to death*." Stephanie Coontz, *Marriage, A History* (New York: Penguin, 2005) 38 (my italics). In the chapter titled, "The Invention of Marriage" Coontz critiques both the protective and oppressive theories of marriage showing both to be myths based on 1950's fantasies of "primitive" tribal life. She admits that "no one suggests that prehistoric bands existed in utopian harmony. But social interactions were governed by the overwhelming need to pool and share resources." Ibid., 39.

18 "New and better evidence on how African homo-erectus actually obtained meat, along with more realistic assessments of how rarely even the best contemporary hunters succeed in killing big game (perhaps once or twice a month), challenged the underlying assumptions of the model. Newly available quantitative information on the highly communal way foragers share with the whole group made it clear that the most successful hunter would often get no more for his family than the most hapless did …. Hundreds of thousands of years after homo erectus, men hunting in arid African habitats like those occupied by the !Kung – armed with spears, bows, and poisoned arrows – still provide less than half of the calories for their group." Sarah Blaffer Hrdy, *Mothers and Others*, 148–149.

19 Sarah Blaffer Hrdy, *Mothers and Others*, 150–151.

20 Hrdy cites the *Cuiva* or the *Ache* communities.

21 Sarah Blaffer Hrdy, *Mothers and Others*, 152. See also Stephanie Coontz, *Marriage, a History*, 39–42. Coontz cites 17th-century observations of Native American Indians as well as current aboriginal hunter/gatherer tribes: "on the necessity of sharing and how hunters spend their lives hunting for others just as others spend their lived hinting for them".

22 Sarah Blaffer Hrdy, *Mothers and Others*, 153.

23 Ibid., 153–155.

24 Ibid., 154.

25 In the practice of "partible paternity" for example, it is assumed that the semen of many men all contribute to the conception of the child, thus one is born with "fathers" and one mother. Ibid. 155.

26 David. F. Lancy, *The Anthropology of Childhood: Cherubs, Chattel, Changelings* (Cambridge: Cambridge University Press, 2016) 144, 121.

27 Sarah Blaffer Hrdy, *Mothers and Others*, 7. Also, see Spinoza *Ethics*. Benedict Spinoza, *Ethics*, in *Complete Works*, trans. Samuel Shirley (Indianapolis, IN: Hackett Publishing Company, 2002).

28 Spinoza's conception of the *conatus* indicates striving to preserve existence but also to increase one's power of activity (*Prop. 8, Part III, Prop. 12, Part III*), but the only non-contingent existence is of the immanence of all (*Def. 1, Part I and Def. 6, Part I*). Atomization in this sense occurs only insofar as the substance is perceived inad-

equately. In the adequate perception of the substance, the particular increases its *poten-tia* for action only through increasing its reason and thereby through expanding its range of connections and experiences, of opening up to plurality, broadening ranges of multiplicities, all of which are indefinite rather than delimited (*Prop. 9, Part III*). Moreover, for Spinoza, these multiplicities precisely constitute the individual's possibility of increasing their power of *action*. In other words, much like Peter Kropotkin noted in his observations of the "natural world", cooperation is an attribute that strengthens the lifeworld of a species while competition breaks down collectivity and undermines the conditions for the possibility of sustainable life worlds. Baruch Spinoza, *Ethics* in *Complete Works*, trans. Samuel Shirley (Indianapolis, IN/Cambridge: Hackett Publishing Company Inc., 2002).

29 Sarah Blaffer Hrdy, *Mothers and Others*, 148. See also Chris Knight's "Early Kinship was Matrilineal" in which he asks: "Can a woman really help her baby by taking lovers during pregnancy? The answer seems to be yes. The explanation is probably that additional fathers contribute additional provisions and more protection against infanticide. It is not in a woman's interests to encourage the men in her life engage in contests over biological paternity. From a woman's standpoint, the truth is that her current husband may become injured, die or abandon her. In any event, she may have good reason to switch to a new man. If her new mate cares about not being the father, her existing offspring might suffer infanticide or abuse. Loss of a wanted child is enormously costly to any human mother, making it best not to divulge but precisely to confuse accurate paternity information, taking lovers to distribute illusions among multiple males". Chris Knight "Early Human Kinship Was Matrilineal." In *Early Human Kinship*, edited by N.J. Allen, H. Callan, R. Dunbar and W. James. Oxford: Blackwell, 2008, 76.

30 Sarah Blaffer Hrdy, *Mothers and Others*, 6–7.

31 Ibid., 6–9. See also Michael Tomasello, "Understanding and Sharing Intentions: The Origins of Cultural Cognition," *Behavioral and Brain Sciences* 28, no. 5 (2005): 675–691; 7: 153–156.

32 See "Statistical Definition of 'Family' Unchanged Since 1930," from: https://www.census.gov/newsroom/blogs/random-samplings/2015/01/statistical-definition-of-family-unchanged-since-1930.html (accessed 15 June 2018).

33 Wolfgang Streeck, *How Will Capitalism End? Essays on a Failing System* (New York: Verso Books, 2017).

34 Antonio Gramsci, *The Gramsci Reader*, edited by David Forgacs (New York: NYU Press, 2000) 289–290.

35 Ibid., 292.

36 Wolfgang Streeck, *How Will Capitalism End?* 217.

37 Streeck writes: "The commodification of female labor gave rise to new patterns of child-rearing that reflect the advance of capitalist development. As couples spend more time in employment, they have less time for children. This means they must externalize childcare, either to the market or to the state. Of course, many have no children at all, devoting their time entirely to the exigencies and attractions, as the case maybe, of work and consumption. Typically, children are most numerous among the less educated and the poor, who have few prospects of success outside of the family. While precarious employment postpones childbirth among the middle classes, it has little effect if any on the lower classes. Precarious families, for their part, produce comparatively many children as the number of couples of reproductive age that are married is declining in an era of individualization and growing flexibility of social relations. Contemporary capitalist societies that want more children must therefore prepare for a growing share of them being born to unwed mothers. Unwed mothers, of course, are at high risk of poverty." Ibid., 218.

38 Kathi Weeks, *The Problem with Work: Feminism, Marxism, Antiwork Politics, and Postwork Imaginaries* (Durham, NC and London: Duke University Press, 2011) 3.

39 Karl Marx, *Capital, vol. 1* (New York: Penguin Books, 1990) 275.

40 Kathi Weeks, *The Problem with Work*, 4. The second overarching reason which I will just mention in passing (as it does not directly concern the topic of this thesis here) has to do with the reduction in work-based activism in the United States.

41 Ibid., 13.

42 Georganne Rundblad, "Exhuming Women's Premarket Duties in the Care of the Dead," *Gender and Society* 9, no. 2 (April 1995): 173–192, 175. See also Judith M. Bennett, *Ale, Beer, and Brewsters in England: Women's Work in a Changing World 1300–1600* (Oxford: Oxford University Press, 1999).

43 Rundblad, *Exhuming*. 176.

44 She goes on to note: "This knowledge, what Foucault (1980) would have called "popular" or "local" knowledge, included the proper procedures for laying out the body, a knowledge of the materials that were needed to proceed with laying out, and an understanding of the responsibilities of others, such as the cabinetmaker and the sexton, would be involved in some different aspects of the burial ritual. More importantly, this knowledge allowed these women to approach their task as trained individuals, providing them with the appropriate perspective given the procedures that lay them. As a consequence, social approval was granted to shrouding women to the preparation of the bodies of deceased women." Ibid., 177.

45 Silvia Federici, "The Reproduction of Labour Power in the Global Economy, Marxist Theory and the Unfinished Feminist Revolution."
[https://caringlabor.wordpress.com/2010/10/25/silvia-federici-the-reproduction -of-labour-power-in-the-global-economy-marxist-theory-and-the-unfinished-feminist -revolution/] (accessed 26 December 2018, 10:40 EST)

46 "In sub-Saharan Africa, for example, according to the Food and Agriculture Organization, 'women produce up to 80 percent of all the basic foodstuffs for household consumption and for sale.' Given that the population of sub-Saharan Africa is about three-quarters of a billion people, with a large percentage of them being children, this means that more than a hundred million African women must be subsistence farmers. As the feminist slogan goes: 'women hold up *more* than half the sky.'" However, "not only did colonial officers, missionaries, and later agricultural developers impose commercial crops at the expense of food production, but they excluded African women, who did most of the farming, from the study of modern farming systems and technical assistance. They invariably privileged men with regard to land assignment, even when absent from their homes. Thus, in addition to eroding women's "traditional" rights as participants in communal land systems and independent cultivators, colonialists and developers alike introduced new divisions between women and men. They imposed a new sexual division of labor, based upon women's subordination to men, which, in the colonialists' schemes, included unpaid cooperation with their husbands in the cultivation of cash crops." Silvia Federici, "Women Land Struggles and Globalization," *Revolution Point Zero: Housework, Reproduction and Feminist Struggle*, (Oakland: PM Press, 2012) 127.

47 Silvia Federici, *Caliban and the Witch: Women, the Body and Primitive Accumulation* (Brooklyn: Autonomedia, 2014) 95.

48 Ibid., 94.

49 Ibid., 97.

50 Kathi Weeks, *The Problem with Work*, 163.

51 Stanley Aronowitz, *Post Work Manifesto: Wages of Cybernation* (New York: Routledge, 1998).

52 *Weeks, The Problem with Work*, 163. As Weeks points out, obviously the 8-hour work day implemented after WWII would have simply been impossible had the male breadwinner taken any significant responsibility for domestic tasks.

53 Weeks, *The Problem with Work*, 165.

54 In 2019 the newly elected Coalition Avenir Québec to govern the province of Québec instituted Bill 21 banning the wearing of religious symbolism at work, despite the

prominent display of Christian symbols throughout the province. This bill has been generally recognized to ban the wearing of the Hijab at work and has been challenged by civil liberties groups in the country. See for example, "Quebec law banning hijab at work creates 'politics of fear', say critics", in *The Guardian*, June 17, 2019.

55 Weeks, *The Problem with Work*, 165.

56 Ibid., 156.

57 David Eggers, *The Circle* (New York: Random House, 2013). As one recent article puts it: "A century ago, factory workers were forming unions and going on strike to demand better conditions and a limit on hours. Today, Silicon Valley employees celebrate their own exploitation. "9 to 5 is for the weak" says a popular T-shirt. A venture capitalist named Keith Rabois recently boasted on Twitter that he worked for 18 years while taking less than one week of vacation. Wannabe Zuckerbergs are told that starting a company is like joining the Navy SEALs. For a certain type of person – usually young and male – the hardship is part of the allure." Dan Lyons, "In Silicon Valley 9 to 5 is for Losers," *New York Times*, August, 31, 2017.

58 A similar trend is being realized in the shift from prisons to house arrest. It is touted by conservatives and some liberals as a solution to prison overcrowding and cost. In these cases, the home will become a literal prison. See for example: https://www.motherjones.com/politics/2015/01/house-arrest-surveillance-state-prisons/

One of the leading corporations providing such services brags increased savings for such services: "We hold offenders accountable, assure a maximum level of community protection and save considerable taxpayer dollars from the high cost of incarceration. The costs of jailing an offender vary but can easily approach $70 to $80 per day. In contrast, electronic monitoring equipment averages between $4 and $9 per day – a dramatic savings." See https://housearrest.com

59 "Becoming a "creative city" is increasingly seen as necessary to attract tourists, global investors, and affluent middle and upper classes. Politicians have thus become keen to instrumentalize dynamic local subcultures and harness them as a competitive advantage in the interurban rivalry. In this context, the cultural milieus of artists and other "creatives", subcultural scenes including squats and self-managed social centers, have taken on a new function as they mark urban space as attractive. They charge them with cultural capital, which in the scheme of "creative city" policy then becomes transformed by investors into economic capital." Margit Mayer, "Preface" to *Squatting in Europe: Radical Spaces, Urban Struggles* (Wivenhoe/New York/Port Watson: Minor Compositions/autonomedia, 2013) 4.

60 Pierpaolo Mudu, "Resisting and Challenging Neoliberalism: The Development of Italian Social Centers," in *Squatting in Europe: Radical Spaces and Urban Struggle* (Brooklyn: Autonomedia, 2013) 62.

61 "Kraker's were people who aimed to transform spontaneous squats into long-term housing. But the squatting movement was, and is, by no means a homogenous movement, there are many different approaches and various goals all of which perhaps find common ground in the redistribution of housing and the demand for some semblance of autonomy from the totalizing commodification. Hans Pruijt, "Squatting in Europe," in *Squatting in Europe: Radical Spaces, Urban Struggles* (Brooklyn: Minor Compositions, 2013) 17.

62 Ibid., 19.

63 Like Tacheles, ABC No Rio invited artists from all over the world, many from South American anarchist communities.

64 What must be kept in mind is that these spaces, unlike WeWork, were under constant threat from the police and had to rely only on their own collective resources in order to survive. See: https://www.jacobinmag.com/2014/04/squatters-of-the-lower-east-side/

65 In 1969, the "Woningbureau (Housing Bureau) de Kraker" was established in Amsterdam. Kraker's were people who aimed to transform spontaneous squats into long-term housing. But the squatting movement was, and is, by no means a homog-

enous movement, there are many different approaches and various goals all of which perhaps find common ground in the redistribution of housing and the demand for some semblance of autonomy from the totalizing commodification.

66 http://foodnotbombs.net/new_site/
67 https://www.nytimes.com/1988/08/10/nyregion/class-struggle-erupts-along-avenue-b .html?mtrref=www.google.com&gwh=A6BFF8581E0A93D285B6C7F08FBDEFA3 &gwt=pay
    https://gvshp.org/blog/2015/08/06/the-tompkins-square-park-riots-of-1988/
    http://www.abcnorio.org/about/history/wildner_91.html
    http://www.morusnyc.org/
    https://www.thevillager.com/2015/04/squatters-live-in-kill-city-3/
68 Weeks, *The Problem with Work*, 156.
69 Weeks uses the terms "conservative or neoliberal family values", ibid., 160.
70 See, especially, the research and interviews Arlie Russel Hochschild conducted in *The Second Shift: Working Parents and the Revolution at Home* (New York: Viking, 1989). There she demonstrates how in a household where both parents work, women nevertheless accomplish the majority of household and care work and increasingly bear the burden of tension, stress, and on a moral and social level often carry the responsibility for the failure of the nuclear family.
71 Weeks, *The Problem with Work*, 160.
72 Ibid., 160.
73 Ibid., 160.
74 Ibid., 167. See also Valerie Lehr, *Queer Family Values: Debunking the Myth of the Nuclear Family* (Philadelphia, PA: Temple University Press, 1999). Lehr's basic argument is concerned with critiquing arguments for lesbian and gay marriages that preserve the normative nuclear ideal. Like Weeks, she also argues for shortening the work day in order to allow alternative approaches to community building.
75 "For it is an irretrievable image of the past which threatens to disappear in any present that does not recognize itself as intended in that image." Walter Benjamin, *On the Concept of History*, in Selected Writings, vol. IV, 1938–1940, trans. Edmund Jephcott and others (Cambridge, MA: Harvard University Press, 2006) 391.
76 Quoted in Sarah Blaffer Hrdy, *Mothers and Others*, 143.

Bibliography

Michelle Alexander. "The Rebirth of Caste." In *The New Jim Crow Mass Incarceration in the Age of Colorblindness*. New York: The New Press, 2012.

Stanley Aronowitz. *Post Work Manifesto: Wages of Cybernation*. New York: Routledge, 1998.

Walter Benjamin. "On the Concept of History." In *Selected Writings*, vol. IV, 1938–1940, translated by Edmund Jephcott et al. Cambridge, MA: Harvard University Press, 2006.

Judith M. Bennett. *Ale, Beer, and Brewsters in England: Women's Work in a Changing World 1300–1600*. Oxford: Oxford University Press, 1999.

Ta-Nehisi Coates. "The Black Family in the Age of Mass Incarceration." *The Atlantic*, October 2015. https://www.theatlantic.com/magazine/archive/2015/10/the-black -family-in-the-age-of-mass-incarceration/403246/

Stephanie Coontz. *Marriage, A History*. New York: Penguin, 2005.

David Eggers. *The Circle*. New York: Random House: 2013.

Silvia Federici. *Caliban and the Witch: Women, the Body and Primitive Accumulation*. Brooklyn, NY: Autonomedia, 2014.

Silvia Federici. "The Reproduction of Labour Power in the Global Economy, Marxist Theory and the Unfinished Feminist Revolution." https://caringlabor.wordpress.com

/2010/10/25/silvia-federici-the-reproduction-of-labour-power-in-the-global-economy -marxist-theory-and-the-unfinished-feminist-revolution/ (accessed December, 26, 2018 10:40 EST).

Silvia Federici. "Women Land Struggles and Globalization." *Revolution Point Zero*: *Housework, Reproduction and Feminist Struggle*. Oakland: PM Press, 2012.

Antonio Gramsci. *The Gramsci Reader*. Edited by David Forgacs. New York: New York University Press, 2000.

David Harvey. *New Imperialism*. Oxford: Oxford University Press, 2003.

Arlie Russel Hochschild. conducted in *The Second Shift: Working Parents and the Revolution at Home*. New York: Viking, 1989.

Max Horkheimer. "Authority and the Family." In *Critical Theory*, translated by Matthew J. O'Connell and others. New York: Continuum, 1995.

Max Horkheimer, Erich Fromm, Herbert Marcuse. *Studien über Autorität und Familie. Forschungsberichte aus dem Institut für Sozialforshung*. Hannover: Klampen Verlag, 2005.

Sarah Blaffer Hrdy. *Mothers and Others: The Evolutionary Origins of Mutual Understanding*. Cambridge, MA: Harvard University Press, 2009.

C. Knight "Early Human Kinship Was Matrilineal." In *Early Human Kinship*, edited by N.J. Allen, H. Callan, R. Dunbar and W. James. Oxford: Blackwell, 2008.

David F. Lancy. *The Anthropology of Childhood: Cherubs, Chattel, Changelings*. Cambridge: Cambridge University Press, 2016.

Valerie Lehr. *Queer Family Values: Debunking the Myth of the Nuclear Family*. Philadelphia, PA: Temple University Press, 1999.

Karl Marx. *Capital vol. 1*. New York: Penguin Books, 1990.

Squatting Europe Kollective ed., *Squatting in Europe: Radical Spaces, Urban Struggles*. Wivenhoe/New York/Port Watson: Minor Compositions/Autonomedia, 2013.

William of Ockham. *Opera Politic*, 4 vols. Edited by H.S. Offler. London: British Academy, 1997.

Leni Riefenstahl (dir.). *Triumph of the Will (Triumph des Willens)*, 1935. https://www .dailymotion.com/video/x6uajey

Georgianne Rundblad. "Exhuming Women's Premarket Duties in the Care of the Dead." *Gender and Society* 9, no. 2 (April 1995): 173–192.

Hortense J. Spillers. "Mama's Baby, Papa's Maybe: An American Grammar Book." In *Diacritics* 17, no. 2, *Culture and Countermemory: The "American" Connection*. Baltimore, MD: Johns Hopkins University Press, Summer, 1987.

Baruch Spinoza. *Ethics in Complete Works*. Translated by Samuel Shirley. Indianapolis, IN/Cambridge: Hackett Publishing Company Inc., 2002.

Wolfgang Streeck. *How Will Capitalism End? Essays on a Failing System*. New York: Verso Books, 2017.

Michael Tomasello. "Understanding and sharing intentions: The origins of cultural cognition." *Behavioral and Brain Sciences* 28, no. 5 (Oct 2005): 675–691.

Kathi Weeks. *The Problem with Work: Feminism, Marxism, Antiwork Politics, and Postwork Imaginaries*. Durham, NC and London: Duke University Press, 2011.

George F. Will. *The Conservative Sensibility*. New York: Hachette Books, 2019.

Excursus
Memory, Relation, Death

> Ghosts, it has appeared to me, are more tenaciously alive than the living. They impose laws on us that hold longer than those made by states or ideologists.
>
> Reiner Schürmann, *Origins*[1]

> While the corpse is still in the house, one cannot eat, for it too will want to eat.
>
> Eliot Weinberger, "The Dead"[2]

The following considerations are focused on a somewhat obscure but politically important disagreement between Martin Heidegger and Jean-Paul Sartre. This argument concerns finitude, our relation to embodied ontology, that is, ultimately our relation to death. I am specifically interested in ways that the fact of death, the condition of finitude is, and probably always has been, at the root of kinship as a practice, i.e. intimacy as the relational basis of community. What Thomas Laquer calls the *work of the dead*, which includes mourning rituals and other ways in which communal practices are haunted by the deceased, the practice of memorial makes up the intergenerational narrative substance of kinship ties. The idea is that fundamental to association is the relationship to death, to the dead. It is one important way to memorialize the past, to envision a future, and to enroot hope. In some ways, this section is a bit of a digression, but a necessary one, as the condition of finitude gets to the core of embodied vulnerability which in turn is the condition for relationality. The first few pages consider some ideas concerning the relation between the living, the dead, and community, this is followed by a brief but focused exposition of Heidegger's privatized notion of death. Following this, is an elaboration of Sartre's political critique which then draws out some developments of this idea in the work of Martin Hägglund and others.

The Work of the Dead

Judith Butler notes:

> Over and against the existential concept of finitude that singularizes our relation to death and to life, precariousness underscores our radical

DOI: 10.4324/9781003264644-5

substitutability and anonymity in relation both to certain socially facili-
tated modes of dying and death and to other socially conditioned modes
of persisting and flourishing.[3]

A profusion of historical and literary work on death informs us that the association of kinship with not only the care for the dead but, what I will call,
following Thomas Laquer, *the work of the dead*, is archaic.[4] It's been around
for a while. As Robert Pogue Harrison puts it in the preface to his book *The
Dominion of the Dead*, human beings may have housed their dead long before
housing the living, quoting the iconic urbanist and philosopher of technology
Lewis Mumford: "the city of the dead antedates the city of the living ... is the
forerunner almost the core, of every living city".[5] "Almost the core", the dead
also inhabit the soil, fertilize the earth enriching growth, and harvests but just
as significantly, they have left the built world – speculatively, conceptually,
and materially – dreams, and unfinished projects, ruins all of which could
be understood as the necropolis. Harrison situates the living in the transitory
space and time between the dead and the unborn. Life is understood as a sort
of tightrope or "ligature" between the two dominions. He continues by citing
the three institutions: "religion, matrimony and burial" as created "by those
who came before". In addition, we might consider law, language, and art as
the three mediums through which the transmission of transgenerational continuity is actualized. He continues by making the broad and always suspect
distinction between the non-human and human, defining the former as guided
by "only the law of vitality, but humanity in its distinctive features is through
and through necrocratic".[6]
  We inherit the world of the dead, we mark our kin, communities, cities,
nations, states, and empires with the names of the dead. They litter our streets and
are echoed in our names. The sacred fire burning indefinitely in the hearth is the
animation of the principle of the life of the household and its transgenerational
substance, included acts of sacrifice, stories, craft, local knowledges, and other
household practices. The Roman penates – household gods – refer to a cabinet
or the interior of an altar: "they thought of the house's shelter not so much as a
defense against the elements but as the ancestor's awesome power to protect the
family against misfortune and calamity. A house, in sum was a place where two
realms – one under and the other on the earth – interpenetrate each other".[7] The
act of taking care of the dead is a gesture of care and protection. In the case of
neglect, Hegel famously noted:

> The dead, whose right is violated, knows therefore how to find instruments of
> its vengeance, which are of an actuality and potency equal to the power that
> injures it. These powers are other commonwealths whose altars the dogs or
> birds defiled with the corpse, which has not been raised into unconscious uni-
> versality by its due restoration to the elemental individual, but has remained
> above the earth in the realm of actuality, and now obtains as a force of divine
> law a self-conscious actual universality.[8]

The piety of the family, which Hegel sees as the force of the community, is shattered in the neglect of the dead. To fail to honor the dead – to allow them in Hegel's word to enter "unconscious universality" – is a violation of trust, one which undermines the fundamental bonds – the "substance" – of a community when it neglects the memory of its members. This is the work of the dead, the way the dead continue to hold sway over or haunt the lives of the living.

In his elaborate study, Thomas Laquer describes a two-fold relation to the work of burial. On the one hand, it is the literal task of taking care of the corpse, both preparation and entombment. On the other – arguing against the claim put forth by the ancient Cynic Diogenes, that the body is better off simply exposed as meat for scavengers, and should simply be tossed over the wall of the city – it is a process which carries profound significance for human life and for the basis of relation. It is, Laquer suggests, part of what holds together a common bond, based on the idea that the dead pose a mortal danger to the living. Taking care of the dead is not simply practiced in order to conceal the rotting corpse, to hide the objective fact of death and the inevitable stench of its testimony, the putrefaction from which we recoil. In that case, there would be no way to recognize the Parsee communities that *take care* of their dead by exposing bodies to the sky for their prompt consumption by vultures. In these *Sky Burials*, the dead are laid in *Dakhmas*, constructed Towers of Silence, "believing that dead flesh pollutes fire, water and air – all of which are sacred".[9] These "obligate scavengers" consume the dead as they live symbiotically with these Zoroastrian communities. Thomas Van Dooren sees this as one of many ways to incorporate the dead into life. His broader point is that the separation of life and death is an abstraction, that we must understand as the late Jean-Luc Nancy wrote: "To isolate death from life – not leaving each one intimately woven into the other, with each one intruding upon the other's core [*coeur*] – this is what one must never do".[10] Possibility in both life and death is shaped by this entanglement. "Death understood in this way, positions all organisms ... as parts of a broader multispecies community".[11]

Dwelling, World Forming, and the Ontological Privatization of Death

In his essay "Building, Dwelling, Thinking", Martin Heidegger considers two questions that are of interest regarding the notion of the home or kinship as dwelling, existence, and, as we will see, death. The questions he begins with are: "What is it to dwell? And how does building belong to dwelling"?[12] After tracing the etymological root of the German term *Bauen* (to build) hidden in *Nachbar* (neighbor) as a *Nachgebauer* (near dweller), indicating that the "verbs, buri, büren, beuren, beuron, all signify dwelling, the abode, the place of dwelling", Heidegger notes that here we are given a clue as to the nature of our thinking about building and dwelling. Namely, that *to build* is also already *to dwell*. If we go further, he continues, we soon discover that *bauen* is related (via *buan, bhu,* and *beo*) to the term "*bin*" as in "*ich bin*" and "*du bist*" finally coming to the assertion: "The way in which you are and I am, the manner in which we humans are on the earth, is Buan, dwelling".[13] To say "we are" is to say "we dwell" and vice versa.[14] That is, to construct a community in common – and we might extend this to the activity of constructing kin, i.e. practical kinship – is to exist as human.

Concerning the term *bauen* three points resonate for Heidegger:

1. Building is dwelling.
2. Mortals inhabit the earth through dwelling.
3. *Building as dwelling* opens to building that *takes care of*, or "cultivates growing things and the building that erects buildings".[15]

Furthering his linguistic meditations (via the Gothic *Wunian* meaning peace, to the term for freedom, *Friede* and *das Frye* and finally *fry* to indicate preservation from threat) Heidegger concludes: "*The fundamental character of dwelling is this spring and preserving*".[16] It is here that Heidegger introduces his infamous *geviert* (earth, sky, divinities, mortals).

Thus, humans dwell in their finitude: "They are called mortals because they can die. To die means being capable of death as death. Only man dies, indeed continually, as long as he remains on earth, under the sky, before the divinities".[17] Anticipating death activates dying, the phenomenon of death as such is only, for Heidegger, preempted through consciousness of finitude. Continuing the Abrahamic tradition that demands exemplary status for the human being, Heidegger conceives of these world makers – but, should we say, perhaps more clearly world destroyers? – as a distinct entity from impoverished animals, obscure plants, and rocks that give us nothing except resources which provide security and material for inscription, nourishment, and building.[18] The point here is that, for Heidegger, location is the allowance of space (*Raum*), such that the clearing of a space for settlement is bound within the initiation of "presencing" in relation to *peras* (boundary), which he notes, gives us the concept of *horismos*, or horizon – a key term in Heidegger's earlier considerations of death, particularly in *Sein und Zeit*. However, when it comes to death, Heidegger departs from these more environmental considerations.

For Heidegger, it is through *geworfenheit* – thrownness – that the potentiality of being is disclosed. This is facticity. Facticity is not simply the empirical reality that surrounds and limits us. It includes all of the ways in which we are enrooted in the world (necessity). If facticity is the context of existence, the situation or world in which being is riveted, then Dasein experiences itself as possibility (world-making), openness against this habitat, but also always in terms of it. For Heidegger, the awareness of Being-in-the-world gives rise to anxiety and boredom,[19] which he insists are comportments toward being as Being. For Kierkegaard, this would be considered one step before full-blown existential despair where – through the constant negotiation between necessity and freedom, one becomes at once both more conscious and more despairing – one faces the ordeal of synthetic existence, caught between finitude and the infinite, realized either through infinite faith or infinite resignation.[20]

Key here is that for Heidegger anxiety individualizes Being in its potentiality.

> Here the disclosure and the disclosed are existentially self-same in such a way that in the latter the world has been disclosed as world, and Being-in has been disclosed as a potentiality-for-being which is individualized, pure, and thrown; this makes it plain that with the phenomenon of anxiety a distinctive state-of-mind has become the theme of Interpretation.[21]

We become attuned to our *factical thrownness* through mood or inner feeling. The world reveals itself through thrown projection (*Geworfen entwurf*). I project myself into a world that is cast by the facticity I am propelled by as the project that life becomes. I am anxious or bored most profoundly when faced with the sheer fact of being-there. *Projected being* takes up the given world as the frame of its own potential which in turn individualizes, and that individualization poses a gap between self and world that is, again, felt through mood, and so on.

Projection, for Heidegger, is not a project in the sense of a preconceived plan on what to do, rather, it is already the condition of *Dasein* anticipating itself as *Being-in-the-world* in relation to that in which potentiality is disclosed: "constitutive for Being-in-the-world with regard to the disclosedness of its existentially constitutive state-of-Being by which the factical potentiality-for-Being gets its leeway [*Spielraum:* literally, 'space of play']".[22] In other words, projection is the potentiality that accompanies being in the world, which is already there in the enrootedness of Dasein, and through which Dasein is compelled and activated in its openness, i.e. its disclosure. As Thomas Sheehan puts it: "Facticity [Faktizität] is the early Heidegger term for man's *a priori* thrownness into the ability to give meaning and thus for man's ability to understand this or that thing".[23] Heidegger writes: "Dasein is constantly more than it factually is, supposing that one might want to make an inventory of it as something-at-hand and list the contents of its Being".[24] In other words, *Dasein* always exceeds and precedes the limits of cognition. The significance of Heidegger's term facticity in relation to the dead, and by implication, kinship, or what is taken to intimacy and thus loss, has to do with the way in which death is something "no one can do for me", in that it individualizes Dasein as my unique horizon which gives shape to finitude, to my being-there, to *my death*.

The Necropolis and Kinship

In a compelling and divergent way, this recalls a brief but important set of thoughts on death and relationality in Jean-Paul Sartre's *Being and Nothingness* – under the subtitle: *My Death*. There, Sartre concerns himself with the Heideggerian thought encapsulated by the term being-towards-death, which conceives of death as the horizon of Dasein, that which gives meaning to *my life*, as that which always recedes as I progress. It is the one thing nobody can do for me. Death is intractable. It occludes substitution.

> But in its very essence, death is in every case mine, in so far as it "is" at all … death signifies a peculiar possibility-of-Being in which the very Being of

one's own *Dasein* is an issue. In dying, it is shown that mineness and existence are ontologically constitutive of death.[25]

Again, for Heidegger, Dasein confronts itself as its own possibility as its "own
most potentiality for Being".[26] And through this unique individuation, all other
relations are undone. In other words: "this own-most non-relational possibility
[that is death] is at the same time the uttermost".[27] Insofar as death is already constitutive of thrownness, it expresses facticity.

Resisting this privatized notion of death, Jean-Paul Sartre begins by asking, in
what sense is it that my death is unique? And perhaps more importantly, how is it
that by anticipation, my death gives shape to *my* life as a project, as it is projected
into the world? This unique or "incomparable individuality" that Heidegger confers onto death becomes the individualization of Dasein as such: "it is by projecting itself freely toward its final possibility that the Dasein will attain authentic
existence and wrench itself away from everyday banality in order to attain the
irreplaceable uniqueness of the person."[28] Sartre asks whether death really is the
condition for the determination of my being in this place and time as unique, or
put another way, whether individuality as such expresses death's significance. If
this is *my death*, then it is a distinct event that I can anticipate. But is it really the
case that "the death that will overtake me is *my* death"?[29] The reasoning is in fact
circular. Death is something no one can do for me and thus individuates me – in
that it individualizes Dasein – and it is because I am individuated that I as such
die. Moreover, according to Sartre, to say that death is the only thing no one can
do for me is misleading: "if one considers death the ultimate subjective possibility, the event which concerns only the for-itself, then it is evident that nobody
can die for me".[30] But, Sartre points out, this can be said of all of my embodied
potentialities. Finitude does not just mean that life begins with birth and ends in
death, it means that the conditions of embodiment are limited to a singular position in space and time. In this sense, no one can really love for me either. On
the other hand, Sartre notes, if we look at the phenomenon of death from a more
general perspective, from the point of view of its "function or efficacy" then yes,
others can die for me. For example, in dying for a cause or one's country. This
is the basic structure of sacrifice or martyrdom in which one can give, substitute
or risk one life for an other – i.e. through the ritualized process of transmission
two become interchangeable.[31] From this perspective, there is nothing individual
about my death. For Sartre, death is not the "foundation for the for-itself" rather,
it is simply "an aspect of facticity and of being-for-others".[32] The problem with
anticipating death – or the idea that Dasein comports itself in terms of its own
most possibility as being-towards-death – is that the moment of death for Sartre
is radically absurd. One can drop dead at any instant.[33] How can such radical arbitrariness be thought of as a horizon?

For Sartre, rather than death being mine, it is exactly the moment when my possibilities are given over to others. In other words, "Mortal represents the present
being which I am for the Other; dead represents the future meaning of my actual
for-itself of the other ... death is the always possible annihilation of my possibilities

which is outside my possibilities".[34] Sartre goes on to point out that what makes life meaningful is relation to that which it is not. Life is always engaged with its own future, what Ernst Bloch called the *not-yet-conscious* of utopian thinking.[35]

What I am interested in here though is not so much the dispute between Heidegger and Sartre, or the status of ontological striving, but with Sartre's concept of death as exteriority rather than isolated interiority, as deeply relational, or put another way, that which opens us absolutely to one another. What Heidegger misses here is the fundamentally shared nature of facticity. That death is never simply individuation of *Dasein*, nor is it non-relational, rather it marks the way in which we most radically relate to others. Sartre, and as we will see Martin Hägglund, are right here, *my death* is never mine as such. It is the way in which my projects (the projection of self), are radically open to others. Individuation, as I understand it, is simply a mode of relational continuity. We are born into the *necropolis*, and it is within the city of the dead that we determine the projects that carve us into the world, but these projects are not our own so much as they are a continuation of the projects of the deceased, just as future generations may, or may not, take up and continue, modify and give meaning to the edifices or ruins that shape our lives. If we look to Walter Benjamin's reflections on history, we see this identification of continuity that takes shape or appears in "the time of the now" is an incredibly important political act. In his "Theses on the Philosophy of History", Benjamin critiques the empty, homogenous, formalized time of the historicist. He notes, "no fact that is a cause is for that very reason historical", indeed it only becomes historical "posthumously", that is after death. "A historian who takes this as his point of departure stops telling the sequence of events like the beads of a rosary. Instead, he grasps the constellation which his own era has formed with a definite earlier one".[36]

Mortality, Continuity, Memory

If mortality indicates the condition of being given over to the other, insofar as death marks the limit of my potentiality it also marks the limit of my freedom in relation to others, death then is simply the limit of *situation* for Sartre, but it is not the telos of Dasein:

> Thus death haunts me at the very heart of each of my projects as their inevitable reverse side .... The freedom which is my freedom remains total and infinite. *Death is not an obstacle to my projects; it is only the destiny of these projects elsewhere.*[37]

This is exceedingly important for any consideration of the politics of kinship precisely insofar as it marks the kind of relationality that is responsible for the reproduction of life, understood in a global, entangled, complicated sense – i.e. as a place that encourages the flourishing of life through mutual care, survival, but also habitus and more profoundly *continuity*, what we can call following Elizabeth Freeman, as noted above, *generation*.

Continuing with Sartre:

> It is not impossible (provided one understand this properly) to define a "per-
> son" by his dead – i.e., by the reason of indivualization or of collectivization
> which he has determined in the necropolis, by the roads and pathways which
> he has traced, by the information which he has decided to get for himself, by
> the "roots" which he has put down there.[38]

Again, death then is not *my* possibility but the point at which my possibilities are
transferred elsewhere, and in this sense, it is not the destruction of all projects
but the moment in which the "point of view" of others triumph over the "point of
view which I am toward myself".[39] In this sense, our lives are related not to *our
own* death *per se* (i.e. to my death) but to the necropolis. But here we need to distinguish between two senses of death, or of our relation *to death* and *to the dead*.
Sartre notes that these considerations are a concern with life and its boundary, in
that the interest I take in myself – the *for-itself* – is an interest in which "being is in
question" in that, this self-interest is always projected back onto history and thus
death as that which is always to come, cannot be part of such a consideration.[40]
This is the *negative sense* of death. There is a secondary sense however, in which
"thousands of shimmerings, iridescent relative meanings can come into play upon
this fundamental absurdity of a 'dead' life".[41] Even though my own possibilities are
annihilated, meaning can still emerge from my life in perhaps unexpected ways, in
relation to the ways in which the memory of a life, for example, is preserved or forgotten, or suddenly recuperated or recast generations later. Insofar as death marks
the point at which one is determined by the memory of the living, the life of the
dead "is a life of which the Other makes himself the guardian".[42] Contra Heidegger,
our relationship with the dead is political through and through. We *enact* relation to
the dead. Sartre notes that the dead choose us as we have chosen them:

> This shows us clearly what we hoped to prove; it is that the Other cannot be
> first without any contact with the dead so as to decide subsequently … that
> he will have this or that relation with certain particular dead. In reality, the
> relation with the dead – with all(!) the dead – is an essential structure of the
> fundamental relation which we have called being-for-others. In its upsurge
> into being, the for-itself must assume a position in relation to the dead; his
> initial project organizes them into large anonymous masses or as distinct
> individualities. And for these collective masses as for these individualities
> he determines their removal or their absolute proximity; he unfolds tempo-
> ral distances between them and himself by temporalizing himself just as he
> unfolds spatial distances in terms of his surroundings. While making himself
> known to himself through his end he decides the peculiar importance of the
> extinct collectivities or individualities.[43]

Here is an interesting thought. As we constitute ourselves, our self-consciousness,
our being in the world with others, we have a specific relationship with the dead,

those from whom we have inherited, and continue to adopt and adapt worlds. We become living and generative memorials of the past. It is in this relation to the dead that we can find the ligature between facticity and freedom; it is in that our lives are shaped by our attitudes toward the dead whether it is one of indifference or respect, whether of erasure, critique, or some other form of continuity or catastrophe. Insofar as we are thrown into the world, we are thrown into the world of the dead, and in this "we decide the fate of the dead".[44]

The fantasy of a monadic individual, self-contained creature which becomes, finally a closed case, totally determined and isolated with death is also a relation to the dead. The self is always already cast into a scene, a history and situation that is then taken up or not in one way or another drawing out ligatures between past and future as well as necessity and potentiality. This is the relation to the infinite. To become someone is to relate and to live in relation to the dead; it is the way in which we take responsibility in relation to what has come before, and thus recast as possibility into the future, thereby shaping a history and world. In this sense, the privatized notion of an authentic comportment to Being and thus to death that reigns in Heideggerian metaphysics is critically transformed into a deeply political relation to life as response, obligation, and responsibility. What is important for the considerations here is that Sartre's notion of the necropolis is one which situates the living with respect to a world fecund with the unfinished projects of the dead. It is within this world of ruins that the project taken to be *a life* responds and commits. This is the basis for continuity and community. In a very similar vein, Robert Pogue Harrison suggests that being-towards-death is supplanted by being-towards-the-dead. In other words, even if we go with the Heideggerian understanding of being-towards-death, that shapes the ground from which I choose my projects, I am always already "confronted by my dead". And thus "it makes of my mortality a coffer of legacies consigned to me from my forebears, awaiting retrieval and renewal".[45]

In his recent book on secular faith, Martin Hägglund writes:

> In leading my life, I am not striving for an impossible completion of who I am but for the possible and fragile coherence of who I am trying to be: to hold together and be responsive to the commitments that define who I take myself to be .... Death" he continues, presumably echoing Sartre, "cannot be a meaningful completion of my life.[46]

Hägglund's critique of religion pivots on the idea that theology is always marked by "the subordination of the finite to the eternal".[47] Here he critiques Max Weber's nostalgia for authentically meaningful existence (that experienced by Abraham for example or an "ancient peasant") in which true belief in religious ideas provided a sanctuary from the horror of death. This anchor of eternal meaning allowed mortals to view their lives as important and something to complete, after which there would be some kind of afterlife that appropriately responds by granting eternal love or eternal suffering. This, however, is the negation of death, the repression of finitude. This is why, according to Hägglund, Weber rejected democracy. For Hägglund, endemic to secular life is the idea that death cannot as such be meaningful. It always cuts short our possibilities. But just because life's meaning is not revealed in its *completion* does not mean that it cannot harbor a formidable sense of meaning. For Hägglund, this is precisely the idea of freedom, or, in other words, the possibility of a politics of liberation. He notes, "part of the meaning of what we do is that it can have significance for future generations and make their lives better than ours".[48] It is in this that Hägglund turns to Marx, in particular what he sees as Marx's enduring commitment to a secular understanding of freedom and democracy. In other words, against the atavistic notion that the loss of theological frameworks meant to guide our ethical relations to one another, as well as to make sense of our lives as a story with a beginning, middle, and end – to recall Aristotle's ideal structure of tragic poetry – in order to unify beyond the immediate range of solidarity, Hägglund suggests we find re-enchantment through political struggle for liberation. It is here that the concept of secular faith resonates. Here, he turns to Karl Ove Knausgaard's incredibly frank series of reflections in the series *My Struggle*: "There is a keen awareness in Knausgaard of how we belong to a world that we did not create and depend on others who exceed our control. To own your life is not to free yourself from this dependence".[49] And to become conscious of this – in becoming conscious as such – to return to Kierkegaard, is to deepen the awareness of despair.[50] That, would be the Kierkegaardian meaning of enlightenment. For Hägglund, finitude indicates the fact of dependency on others, in both life and death, it shows that we are relational precisely insofar as we will die. That is, we rely on others not only for the "worlds that open up through family and friends, the projects that shape" us, the "work and political commitments" that we are part of and lend a hand in creating, but also in that "the projects I sustain and that sustain me, can flourish or change in a dynamic way, but they can also break apart, atrophy and die".[51]

Sartre made the same point. Though he holds onto the concept of finitude, he sees death as something that does not particularize us but rather – as noted above – that which marks the extent to which we can be activated in relation to our projects, the continuity of which will be determined by or handed over to future others. Our relation to death is a generational but also a generative relation. This is key for the understanding of kinship. Kinship is never just with the living, nor just with human beings for that matter.

To return to the initial reflections on dwelling and world forming: if the way we dwell significantly determines the way we are, and if taking care of the living and the dead is something which most profoundly defines kinship, then perhaps we can understand kinship, or intimate relational community, not as an apolitical place of household chores, moral asceticism, and the dreadful task of nuclear parenting – often a place of social deprivation and wageless labor – but instead as a potential, and powerful, domain of solidarity and cooperation that secures the possibility for generating continuity and memory, in which we can faithfully take up the projects of those that, in so doing, become the dead that shape our lives. The relation to death then can be understood as that which gives the possibility to perceive and establish *the time of the now*.

Notes

1 Reiner Schürmann, *Origins*, trans. Elizabeth Preston (Chicago, IL: University of Chicago Press, 2016) 5.
2 Eliot Weinberger, "The Dead," in *The Ghosts of Birds: Essays* (New York: New Directions, 2016) 51.
3 Judith Butler, *Frames of War, When Is Life Grievable?* (New York: Verso, 2016) 14.
4 Thomas Laquer, *The Work of the Dead: A Cultural History of Mortal Remains* (Princeton, NJ: Princeton University Press, 2016) 1–10.
5 Robert Pogue Harrison, *The Dominion of the Dead* (Chicago, IL: University of Chicago Press, 2003) 38.
6 Ibid., 38.
7 Ibid., 38–39.
8 G.W.F. Hegel, *The Phenomenology of Spirit*, trans. Michael Inwood (Oxford: Oxford University Press, 2018) 474.
9 Thomas van Dooren, *Flight Ways, Life and Loss at the Edge of Extinction* (New York: Columbia University Press, 2016) 51.
10 Ibid., 48.
11 Ibid., 48.
12 Martin Heidegger, "Building, Dwelling, Thinking," in *Poetry, Language, Thought*, trans. Albert Hoffstadter (New York: Harper Collins, 2001) 143.
13 Ibid., 145.
14 This goes back to the insight Heidegger steps in in his 1929–1930 lectures (Martin Heidegger, *The Fundamental Concepts of Metaphysics: World, Finitude, Solitude*, trans. William McNeill and Nicholas Walker (Indianapolis, IN: Indiana University Press, 1995)) in which he distinguishes humans as world forming (building), from animals as impoverished in world, to rocks and plants which are worldless. See Chapters Five and Six in *The Fundamental Concepts of Metaphysics*.
15 Heidegger, "Building, Dwelling, Thinking", 146.
16 Ibid., 146–147.
17 Ibid., 149.
18 Here, Heidegger does not consider the method of dwelling or the relation between living things and the earth in terms of symbiotic dwelling or entanglements, and so on. Here he is concerned with the human as the site of Dasein.
19 Heidegger actually identifies three types of boredom. Profound boredom is characterized by the absence of "passing time". (Martin Heidegger, *The Fundamental Concepts of Metaphysics: World, Finitude, Solitude*, trans. William McNeill and Nicholas Walker (Indianapolis, IN: Indiana University Press, 1995) 135).
20 See notes above on Kierkegaard's *Sickness unto Death.*
21 Martin Heidegger, *Being and Time*, trans. John McQuarrie and Edward Robinson (New York: Harper Collins, 2008) 188.
22 Ibid., 145.
23 Thomas Sheehan, *Facticity and Ereignis*, edited by Daniel Dahlstrom, *Interpreting Heidegger: New Essays* (Cambridge, UK: Cambridge University Press, 2011) 60.
24 Heidegger, *Being and Time*, 145.
25 Ibid., 240.
26 Ibid., 250.
27 Ibid., 250.
28 Jean-Paul Sartre, *Being and Nothingness* (New York: Simon and Schuster, 1984) 683.
29 Ibid., 683.
30 Ibid., 683.
31 "If to die is to die in order to inspire, to bear witness, for the country, etc., then anybody at all can die in my place – as in the song where lots are to be drawn to see who is to be eaten." Jean-Paul Sartre, *Being and Nothingness*, 684.

32   Sartre, *Being and Nothingness*, 698.
33   "Sudden death undetermined and by definition cannot be waited for at any date; it always, in fact, includes" .... I can die at any moment and so my waiting is deceptive." (698) "Death cannot be awaited unless it is very precisely. Designated as my condemnation to death [execution or terminal illness for example etc.] for it is nothing but the revelation of the absurdity of every expectation, even though it be the expectation of death itself." (685) "To wait for death is to wait for the undetermined and thus it is to render all waiting absurd." (685) This is perhaps best illustrated in Sartre's well-known short story *The Wall* in which Pablo Ibbieta, an anarchist resistance fighter in Spain, is to face a firing squad the next day. His world recedes to the four walls of the room as he contemplates this impending inevitability. It could be said that his life now was precisely and authentically shaped by being-towards-death. He dwells in this miserable condition, only to discover at the end that through sheer chance – an unanticipated absurdity – he escapes this fate. The way that his impending death shaped his life and individuated his *Dasein* turned out to be false. This also recalled David Hume's considerations on suicide, in which he compares the human life to that of an oyster in its significance and fragility. A mere bite from a tsetse fly or minuscule bacterium like *Clostridium botulinum* could immediately end the life of such a seemingly significant, meaningful, and exemplary being.
34   Sartre, *Being and Nothingness*, 687.
35   In an interview with Horst Krüger and Theodor Adorno, Ernst Bloch makes the explicit connection between the anxiety that comes with death and what he called the *not-yet-conscious* of utopian thinking: "death depicts the hardest counter-utopia. Nailing the coffin puts an end to all of our individual series of actions at the very least." Here he compares this with an image by Voltaire in which a survivor of a shipwreck is suddenly told that there is no shore to reach. All striving suddenly appears moot. "Death is completely in the now". Here we find a sense of freedom in the face of the overwhelming knowledge of annihilation. Bloch goes on to distinguish three senses of utopia. The first is social utopia which depicts the "best possible communal conditions" in which people are no longer immiserated. But the other sense which Bloch is more concerned with, has to do with the maintenance of dignity. And the third is, of course, the messianic utopias in which death itself is eliminated. See Ernst Bloch, *The Utopian Function of Art and Literature*, trans. Jack Zipes and Frank Mecklenburg (Cambridge: The MIT Press, 1988) 8–10.
36   This is what leads to Benjamin's notion that the historian who rightfully abandons serial time in this way establishes a glimpse of "the present as the 'time of the now' which is shot through with chips of Messianic time." Walter Benjamin, "Theses on the Philosophy of History," in *Illuminations*, trans. Harry Zohn (New York: Schocken Books, 1969) 263.
37   Sartre, *Being and Nothingness*, 692 (Italics mine).
38   Ibid., 694.
39   Ibid., 691.
40   Or in Sartrean parlance: "This is because the for-itself is the being in whose being *being* is in question; since the for-itself is the being which always lays claim to an 'after', there is no place for death in the being which is for-itself." Ibid., 691.
41   Ibid., 692.
42   Ibid., 692–693.
43   Ibid., 693.
44   Ibid., 694.
45   R.P. Harrison, *The Dominion of the Dead* (Chicago, IL: University of Chicago Press, 2003) 96.
46   Martin Hägglund, *This Life: Secular Faith and Spiritual Freedom* (New York: Pantheon Books, 2019) 18.
47   Ibid., 8. An insight he takes from William James, *The Varieties of Religious Experience*.

48 Ibid., 19.
49 Ibid., 93.
50 "[T]he degree of consciousness potentiates despair." Kierkegaard, *Sickness*, 52.
51 Hägglund, *This Life*, 4.

Bibliography

Walter Benjamin. "Theses on the Philosophy of History." In *Illuminations*. Translated by Harry Zohn. New York: Schocken Books, 1969, p. 1.

Ernst Bloch. *The Utopian Function of Art and Literature*. Translated by Jack Zipes and Frank Mecklenburg. Cambridge: MIT Press, 1988.

Judith Butler. *Frames of War, When Is Life Grievable?* New York: Verso, 2016.

Martin Hägglund. *This Life: Secular Faith and Spiritual Freedom*. New York: Pantheon Books, 2019.

Robert Pogue Harrison. *The Dominion of the Dead*. Chicago, IL: University of Chicago Press, 2003.

G.W.F. Hegel. *The Phenomenology of Spirit*. Translated by Michael Inwood. Oxford: Oxford University Press, 2018.

Martin Heidegger. *Being and Time*. Translated by John McQuarrie and Edward Robinson. New York: Harper Collins, 2008.

Martin Heidegger. "Building, Dwelling, Thinking." In *Poetry, Language, Thought*, translated by Albert Hoffstadter. New York: Harper Collins, 2001.

Martin Heidegger. *The Fundamental Concepts of Metaphysics: World, Finitude, Solitude*. Translated by William McNeill and Nicholas Walker. Indianapolis, IN: Indiana University Press, 1995.

Thomas Laquer. *The Work of the Dead: A Cultural History of Mortal Remains*. Princeton, NJ: Princeton University Press, 2016.

Jean-Paul Sartre. *Being and Nothingness*. New York: Simon and Schuster, 1984.

Thomas Sheehan. "Facticity and Ereignis." In *Interpreting Heidegger: New Essays*, edited by Daniel Dahlstrom. Cambridge: Cambridge University Press, 2011.

Reiner Schürmann. *Origins*. Translated by Elizabeth Preston. Chicago, IL: University of Chicago Press, 2016, p. 5.

Thomas van Dooren. *Flight Ways, Life and Loss at the Edge of Extinction*. New York: Columbia University Press, 2016.

Eliot Weinberger. "The Dead." In *The Ghosts of Birds: Essays*. New York: New Directions, 2016, p. 51.

4 The Political Theology of the Family
Divine, Romantic, Algorithmic

What follows is a consideration of three aspects of the political theology of the family that I call divine, romantic, and algorithmic. They are all related and can be read together as a political theological braid. Though I am not attempting to be exhaustive, here I simply want to draw out some ways in which politics is transmitted theologically and theology is transmitted politically. In one important sense, the theme follows what Kantorowicz called the principle of continuity, that is, what holds association together across broad spans of time. This aspect of political theology plays a role in constituting the sanctioned family, while also being shaped by the way the concept of the relation emerges as a frame of authorization whether it is grounded in practical relation and autonomy – that is knowing and having the resources to survive and thrive collectively and democratically – or in the familial enclosure signified by alienated authority and abstract power. With the term *divine*, I am referring to the idea of divine right but also to a specific kind of transferable sovereignty, which appears in more subtle form in presumably secular society. *Romantic* refers to Freud's theory of Family Romance which describes libidinal transference from the family to the socius. Here, I consider how this transference becomes broadly political by briefly considering the family romance of the French Revolution. The final term *algorithmic* refers to the *algorithmic unconscious*, by which I mean the ways in which the reality principle can be both shaped, and reproduced by the logical force of algorithms, in other words, ways in which algorithmic calculation repeats, supplants, intensifies, or augments existing social relations.

a. *Divine*

All significant concepts of the modern theory of the state are secularized theological concepts not only because of their historical development – in which they were transferred from theology to the theory of the state, whereby, for example, the omnipotent God became the omnipotent lawgiver – but also because of their systematic structure, the recognition of which is necessary for a sociological consideration of these concepts.[1]

At one level, the notion of political theology conveys the expansion of the reach of religious meanings and values into the sphere of political life, the investment of political institutions and actors with the trappings and charisma

DOI: 10.4324/9781003264644-6

of sacred authority. But it thereby also signifies a contraction of the domain of religious life and practices into what eventually became the "private sphere" of citizens. Political theology can thus be seen to function as an operator of secularization the displacement of religion by politics as the central organizing force of sociality and collective identifications but only insofar as this "elevation" of politics above the confessional affiliations and practices of subjects is itself sustained by theological values and concepts.[2]

According to the first definition above, it is not just that the political is ultimately a transvaluation of the theological; it is also that the latter is continuous with or harbored by the former. The political, insofar as it is inherently theological from the standpoint of the modern secular world, or at least for the modern liberal subject, is rejected in favor of the economic, in favor of what appears mechanical, instrumental, industrial, digital, productive, all of which is to say calculable, and therefore verifiable. For Nietzsche, this drive for singular, monocultural, *sovereign* truth is already theological. It is inherent in those qualities of omniscience and omnipotence either possessed by or manifests as the divine. It is also the death drive at the root of European Nihilism ultimately realized in genocide, ontocide, and ecocide. But for Schmitt, it is in the eternal discourse (what the ancient Greeks would have called *logos*) which forecloses the political as predicated on – or perhaps even synonymous with – *the decision*. In other words, the decision is the death of discourse and therefore the beginning of the political for Schmitt. Like the *deus ex machina*, the point of discursive suspension is the sudden entrance of the divine onto the scene of action, whether the language is philosophical or tragic.

The Principle of Continuity

In the second chapter of *The Royal Remains the People's Two Bodies and the Endgames of Sovereignty*, Eric Santner sketches a trajectory following what he grasps as the transition from royal to popular sovereignty in the nation-state following the French Revolution. In reference to Ernst Kantorowicz's *The King's Two Bodies: A Study in Medieval Political Theology*, Santner suggests that the "symbolic structure and dynamics of sovereignty", as an expression of medieval and early modern European forms of power described, do not vanish once the King's two bodies (*the body natural* and *the body politic*) are no longer valid. Instead, he notes, these dynamics *migrate* to a new locus and therefore it "assumes a turbulent and disorienting semiotic density previously concentrated in the 'strange material and physical presence' of the king".[3] The new principle of sovereignty, is that of the People, which is infected by this "relational and multiple power".[4] This field of power, Santner notes, following but also modifying Foucault's concept of biopolitics, has its roots in this double nature of authority. From Kantorowicz, Santner draws the insight that the figure of the King presented a strange and paradoxical element of the flesh, and he claims those biopolitical techniques identified by Foucault as a mark of industrial society and enlightened thought, were already present in the King's body as the exclusive site of political sovereignty.[5] In other words, biopolitics has its precedent in political theology.

Politically, constituting the body politic from the sacralized status of the flesh of the King, i.e. the office of divine right, transferred to the flesh of a People marked a transition in the terms of political legitimation. Santner uses the term *incorporation*, borrowed from psychoanalysis which refers to the desire to ingest the quality of a thing, incorporating its power, and absorbing its authority for its own. This is the quintessential effect of the act of ritual cannibalism. It is what Freud referred to in *Totem and Taboo* as the ingestion of the (power of the) father by the brothers. It also acts as the final moment in the grammar of sacrifice that constitutes association.[6] Here, among other things, *the problem of continuity* as identified in Kantorowicz's work is at issue. Kantorowicz writes:

> What one did was to build up a philosophy according to which a fictitious immortality became transparent through a real mortal man its temporary incarnation, while mortal man became transparent through that new fictitious immortality which, being man-made as immortality always is, was neither that of life eternal in another world nor that of godhead, but that of a very terrestrial political institution.[7]

For Santner, this paradoxical "dimension of the flesh" is incorporated into "the plane of the health, fitness, and wellness of bodies and populations that must, in turn, be obsessively measured and tested".[8] Although I do not disagree entirely with Santner's thesis – yes, of course, the obsession with health, fitness, longevity, and so on, has become a novel site of a particularly modern sacral body – I think the more politically salient point is that the *body of the nation* as constituted by *a People* is dependent on two principles: citizenship and love of the nation-state and the values that attract identity with it. It is the integrity of this adherence that measures political and social health. The nation-state becomes synonymous with a way of life, an economy, a kind of entertainment, language, sport, urban and suburban space, familiar consumer products, slang, and so on, but also and crucially it is ultimately constituted through the legitimation of the use of violence to protect this *flesh* – this flesh evident in the flesh of the *body politic*. Nationalism is corporeal. To belong to a nation-state attains an essential quality which illustrates the distinction between friend and enemy, between "those who are with us and those who are against us".[9] The threat – expressed for example, in white nationalist terrorism, enacted recently in the United States, Germany, Greece, New Zealand, Norway, Canada, and elsewhere – is located in the anxiety of authenticity and the terms of failure, the thought of "being replaced" – a reactive response to the vulnerability of the national flesh – itself associated with the flesh and integrity of the nuclear family – diluted, violated, and corrupted by mass migration. It is a confusion marked by the fear of those who assume the charge of protecting the integrity of the dominant order, of losing a veritably verifiable sacred right.[10] The reason of the nation-state finds its logical end in eliminating contention to its univocity, or on the level of the psyche, incorporating the maxim that singularity is perfection. It is a kind of European Nihilism to refer to Nietzsche's genealogical thought noted above.

Biopolitics and Political Theology

Again, Santner's thesis, which he admits is more of a speculation, suggests the nascent kernel of biopolitics can already be located within the "political theology of kingship". More precisely, before the domination of life by new technologies harnessed under a power characterized as biopolitics, its potential was already fully present in the form of power that it displaced.

First, let's just briefly sketch the basic gesture found in Foucault's theory of biopower. In the first volume of the *History of Sexuality*, Foucault writes,

> "Deduction" has tended to be no longer the major form of power but merely one element among others, working to incite, reinforce, control, monitor, optimize, and organize the forces under it: a power bent on generating forces, making them grow, and ordering them, rather than one dedicated to impeding them, making them submit, or destroying them.[11]

He first explores this transition in a well-known section in the book *Discipline and Punish: Birth of the Prison*, where he opens with the juxtaposition of two scenes excavated from historical archives, each expressing a historical moment in the genealogy of power. These vignettes, separated by about 70 years, are meant to depict some aspects of the transition from *deduction* – expressed in the spectacle of torture of the regicide Damiens in Paris – to the that of *discipline* – depicted in a timetable organizing the hours and days of prisoners,[12] which as he often points out, could just as easily have described the division of time and labor in a monastery, asylum, hospital, or school. For Foucault, this latter expression of power is activated between two poles, not in opposition, but as two primary leveraging forces working in tandem to actualize the ostensibly novel focus on the meticulous categorization and organization of life. These two forces are anatomical and biological, individualizing and specifying. Both are concerned with the disciplined and regulated performance of the body (via the transformation of the "soul") as the most efficient means of control:

1. *Body as a machine*: disciplining, "optimization of its capabilities ... its usefulness and docility"; "integration into systems of efficient and economic controls". This is what Foucault dubs *anatamo-politics* of the human body which he traces back to René Descartes, who conceived of a purely mechanistic body, animated as such, via the pineal gland, the seat of the soul, a divine connection to spirit lacking in all non-human life forms. This was then generalized by the 18th-century French physician Julien Offray de La Mettrie who, dispensing with Descartes' dualism, applied the concept of mechanization to the mind. The idea eventually gained currency in neurological and psychological circles, where the term cognition became associated with the

chemical mechanics of the mind in which the concept of behavior could be materially grounded and thereby tracked and manipulated. This is where Foucault's reverses the old cliché "the soul is imprisoned in the body" which now becomes "the body is the prisoner of the soul".

2. *Biopolitics of population*: Foucault includes records of birth and death, health, psychiatry, measurements of biological processes, longevity, statistics involving "regulatory controls" and mass surveillance. It is through these tactics that populations become organically categorized and thus organized, by gender, race, health, profession, desires, political commitments, and so on.

Again, Foucault suggests that in recognizing the irreversible limits to power presented by death, authority became increasingly concerned with the administration of life, thereby supplanting the ultimate horizon of the expression of sovereignty, previously reaching its apex in the very act of its relinquishment, that is, simply in the right to torture and kill. Yet, the obvious problem emerges, as he notes, with the observation that wars have never been so bloody. The answer, almost self-evident, is that now "they are waged on behalf of the existence of everyone; entire populations are mobilized for the purpose of wholesale slaughter in the name of life necessity: massacres have become vital".[13] As managers of life, protectors of a nation, race, or ethnicity, a way of life, an economic rationale masquerading as patriotism, has become the mantra under which mass slaughter, brutal confinement, systematic impoverishment, but also economic dysfunction, and geopolitical bondage due to a constant state of global war is both regulated, justified, and ultimately viewed as inevitable.

Genocide is the destruction of a *genos*, it specifically targets bonds of kinship, the sites of familiarity with the goal of disabling if not snuffing out a population. The most intimate relations and their perceived security are now tied up with these partitions and massacres. "One might say that the ancient right to take life or let live was replaced by the power to foster life or disallow it".[14] Now, however, it is on behalf of *the people's two bodies* that the power to take life is dialectically entwined with its role in fostering it – the persistence of a community under the banner of a nation-state that not only harbors sacred values but represents a material way of life, the logic of which must be defended.[15] But what is not articulated in Santner's work is that the *biospolitikos*, or the techniques for fostering and administering life, that are presumably generalized through the disciplines (psychology, sociology, anthropology, criminology, etc.), was already present in a more immediate form within the familial – not in terms of epistemic verification, i.e. quantification, statistics, and timetables that function to systematically stratify life, but in terms of immediate relations of care, trust, commitment, and sacrifice. Not only do we find the mechanism of incorporation with the migration of the double body of the King into the body politic of the People, but also the less acknowledged transfer of material practices of care, knowledges, and memory located in the household and local community outsourced to professionalized industry, disciplinary discourses, political authority, economic, educational, and medical institutions and so on.

For Foucault, the symbolic role of *blood relation* – but also "the ability to shed blood" through sacrifice or war in the name of the sovereign, that was so central to the mechanisms of power has been substituted in our time by "themes of health, progeny, race, the future of the species, vitality of the social body" and of course, sex, and the concept of sexuality.[16] But, for now accepting Foucault's thesis – which is at times read as claiming that with the substitution of the old sovereign power, the family as a significant force simply dissolves – it is not that kinship is supplanted, rather, it is that practices of care submit to new mechanisms of control as they become at once reduced and objectified. That is, made visible. It is precisely because the practices of mutual aid and care that sustain communities and provide a semblance of autonomy were based on biological and social necessity, that rationalizing these dynamic and organic relations manifested such a strong force of both seduction and coercion, and ultimately authorization of the nation-state.

"Blood" is already simply one form of this objectification. Concerning the implications of the *techne* of *blood* Foucault writes:

> Racism took shape at this point (racism in its modern, "biologizing", statist form): it was then that a whole politics of settlement (*peuplement*), family, marriage, education, social hierarchization, and property, accompanied by a long series of permanent interventions at the level of the body, conduct, health, and everyday life, received their color and their justification from the mythical concern with protecting the purity of blood and ensuring triumph of the race.[17]

In other words, the grip on substantial relations by the state, expressed at the level of bodily – and therefore relational – intensity also generalizes the determination of interiority and exteriority found in intimate relations sanctioned as *the family*. It is not just the individual or population that is the concern for biopolitical power, but relationality and the possibility of community, countercommunity, and even undercommunity as a resistant and flourishing complex of associations that may remain at the margins of – or entirely outside of, illegible to – the circumscriptions of knowledge and power, monetization, and normalization.

The Familial and Body Politic

We could also say, along similar lines, that power intervenes – or becomes active – at the level of kinship as it attempts to approximate, supplant, mythologize, measure, and preserve the family. Through blood, race, nation, ethnos, all forms of inherited social power, the interdependence that characterizes kinship ties as they respond to ontological vulnerability, traumatic rupture, and so on, becomes the most fecund site of bionational power. The mobilization of a polity under the guise of national security which appears to present a productive counter-tension to neo-liberal globalism, requires the appearance of this coincidence on an explicit level. The realization of terror on the level of genocide, the justification of deliberate targeting and devastation of populations deemed a threat, must be framed in terms of preserving the (false) nostalgia of the home as a haven, immune from the violence which its affluence relies on. The machinations required for the preservation of perpetual violence sustained in the name of the nation-state must become, following the logic of Hannah Arendt's key concept *the banality of evil*, necessary to the smooth functioning of day-to-day life within a hegemonic state. Arendt writes:

> Eichmann needed only to recall the past in order to feel assured that he was not lying and that he was not deceiving himself, for he and the world he lived in had once been in perfect harmony. And that German society of eighty million people had been shielded against reality and factuality by exactly the same means, the same self-deception, lies, and stupidity that had now become ingrained in Eichmann's mentality.[18]

Affluence and relative peace become inextricable from structural poverty and violence.

An analog comes with the expansion of the concept of the King (or paternal authority) from immediate expressions of power – submission achieved through violence – and the concept of the family which is theorized as a sacred site of ethical relationality that, in Hegel's understanding anyhow, becomes an institution integral to the functioning of an ethical and enlightened state. That is, beyond the demands of necessity and affect that kinship responds to, the family as conceived by political authority achieves an idealized form through objectified modes of knowledge concretized within the institutional disciplines, according to which the practices of kinship and obligation are perpetually taken account of. These measures secure and reinforce the authority of *civil society* as it is shaped and sanctioned by the political establishment and vice versa.

In other words, through immediate, affective, and emotional expressions of care and trust, we find something like an infinite resource of nourishment for Foucault's two poles of biopolitics. The first is derived from the demand to take care and be taken care of in terms of a home and all that implies, and the second is the production of a self through language, art, and love. As soon as these aspects of kinship have become generalized, professionalized, and otherwise made available – translated and transmitted – or more precisely, disabled within the economic algorithms of the market and therefore under the auspices of governmental authority, the power of enmity, following the thought of both Foucault and beyond him in the work of Achille Mbembe, who notes, the "contemporary forms of subjugation of life to the power of death (necropolitics) profoundly reconfigure the relations among resistance, sacrifice, and terror", has indeed reached a biological level, but one which does not have to do exclusively with the "body as machine" as it does with the regimentation, division, and commodification of relationality. In this way, the subjugation of life and the distribution of vulnerability become biological.[19] Achille Mbembe claims that the concept of biopolitics, that is power which is concerned primarily with administering life, is inadequate to account for these shifts, that we must also look to topologies of necropolitics.

In other words, biopolitics and necropolitics, as levers of subjugation go hand in hand in a more intricate way than Foucault perhaps anticipated. Mbembe argues that necropolitics and necropower have given rise to a contemporary form of war that maximizes destruction in the production of spaces of the living dead, camps, and enclaves where populations of people dwell in bondage, in a sense, simply waiting to die.[20] The demands for securing the most immediate terms for survival and communal flourishing are both undermined – put at risk – and projected onto the level of the nation-state which in the United States, for example, is often the juridical and violent enforcement of capitalism, under the auspices of economic growth. Beyond the ideological claim that perpetual economic expansion is a general common good for the polity, it becomes a form of national-theological identification, which justifies the administration of sacrifice zones and for which the nationalist is willing to be sacrificed.

This can be seen as a practical analog to Freud's notion of mass psychology. In this situation, a mass is defined by a shared *I-ideal* – e.g. under a charismatic leader who becomes synonymous with a national identity. Through the diminishment of difference within and the multiplication of difference outside, they are constituted *as a group*.[21] The threat conjured in this ideal (as the enemy) corresponds in force to the demand of substantial relations, i.e. necessity. This threat/demand places the family at the root of national sentiment. Santner identifies four distinct characteristics of the double body that are of interest in this regard:

- The connection between "parts and whole within a social formation".
- How the function, as well as the "vitality and flourishing" of a social formation, is understood or inscribed in regimes of knowledge.
- The "organization of temporal succession" which again, Kantorowicz calls *the problem of continuity* resolved by transgenerational (or tertiary) memory in the family and the ontogenetic memory of the nation in relation to the unborn, who are to be proleptically inscribed within those established mnemonic practices.
- The justification and therefore the foundation of legitimacy for a social formation.[22]

These four areas, according to Santner, are all addressed by the peculiar structure of the double body of the King which, as he puts it, gives: "quasi-divine legitimacy, presence, and enduring substance to the governmental authority (to *Herrschaft*) across the succession of generations".[23] Necessary to the integrity of the nation-state we discover a clear and precise legislation that dictates how exactly generation as the persistence of a national polity is constituted – as in Pericles' *epitaphios logos* – projected into the future, and cast into the past through a fabricated history of the dead.

Kantorowicz writes:

> Interesting, however, is the fact that this "incarnation" of the body politic in a kind of flesh not only does away with the human imperfections of the body

natural, but conveys "immortality" to the individual king as King, that is, with regard to his superbody.[24]

Just as the double body of the King allows him to function both on the level of the political subject, like other subjects, and as an "abstract physiological fiction" a "body of immortal flesh" immune to both physical affliction and legal culpability, the double body of the people, rooted in familial relations, allows individuals to be judged according to the law while the national "body of immortal flesh" operates with immunity. In this "migration of the soul", as Santner calls it, is given the quality of immortality, which transcends the law and finitude, that is to say, transferred "from one incarnation to the next".

Again, Kantorowicz:

> What one did was to build up a philosophy according to which a fictitious immortality became transparent through a real mortal man its temporary incarnation, while mortal man became transparent through that new fictitious immortality which, being man-made as immortality always is, was neither that of life eternal in another world nor that of godhead, but that of a very terrestrial political institution.[25]

As Santner points out, this is clearly derived from the two bodies of Christ which follow the structure of incarnation already adopted within the logic of papal succession or what is today called the papal household.[26] The elimination of that which is designated as the enemy of the people allows the threat to appear from a theological source, as does, of course, the threat to the body-familial which in turn is evoked in the institutionalized psycho-theological concept of a "healthy family life". This is ostensibly required for a "healthy society" and maintenance of a healthy economy – the focus of Chapter 3. Here again, we find the doubling of the people as the national body. As noted, the distribution of the conditions for the possibility of flourishing within presumably non-commodified, non-instrumentalized, non-teleological relations is limited to that which functions to produce: i.e. productive individuals who cannot live without it. This is precisely where political theology is most immediately experienced or felt. It is on the level of the intimate that the theological body of the people (nation), possesses the strongest force of persuasion.

Corpus Mysticum

We should keep in mind that Kantorowicz is isolating just one, albeit very complicated, strand of political theology, which he acknowledges he fails to solve, despite publishing over 600 pages on the matter. His hope was to critically contribute to the problem of what Ernst Cassirer called the *myth of the state*, by tracing the "transformations, implications and radiations" of this "single strand".[27] Kantorowicz traces the generation of the notion of two bodies in terms of how such a transposition informs, or produces, political theology through the apparent secularization of the nation-state: "law and justice" displaces "sacrament and altar". Santner writes:

"Kantorowicz argues that at a certain point the idioms and practices of juridical speech come to displace those of liturgical speech as the locus of the performative magic whereby kingship comes to be endowed with its sublime aura".[28]

Kantorowicz writes: "In the Law-centered era ... and in the language of the jurists, the Prince no longer was 'god by grace' or the living image of Grace; he was the living image of justice, and *ex officio* he was the personification of an Idea which likewise was both divine and human".[29] In other words, this "new duality" constitutes a "field of tension" in which human nature and divine Grace are supplanted by the polarity of "Law and Nature" and eventually "Reason and Society".[30] In the section on "Polity-Centered Kingship", Kantorowicz shows that the sheer multitude of mutual counterinfluences between the church and state throughout the middle ages produced intricate hybrids that become almost impossible to untangle. And while Kantorowicz suggests that it is common to make the comparison of the new monarchies to the Church in structure, it was far less common to comment on the ways in which the "late mediaeval and early modern commonwealths" were influenced by and in fact adopted an ecclesiastical organic model, particularly, he writes "by the all-encompassing spiritual prototype of corporational concepts, the *corpus mysticum* of the Church".[31] Kantorowicz briefly plunges into the intriguing history of the term *Corpus Christi*. According to Pauline doctrine, it was designated as the mystical body of the Church only to be changed in 1264 by the Western Church, restricting it to the transubstantiation of the bread (1215) – the host – previously designated as the *corpus mysticum* – a term now, in turn, applying to the body of the Church. This, however, does not last. It is difficult to resist getting too deep into the intricacies here so just a few broad strokes will follow. With the disputation between Papal authority and the authority of the Holy Roman Emperor (the Investiture Struggle which began in the 11th century), emerges the so-called secularization of the Church: "a process which was balanced by an all the more designatedly 'mystical' interpretation even of the administrative body and technical apparatus of the hierarchy".[32] In tandem with the Church's self-designation as the *corpus mysticum* in the middle of the 12th century, the secular authority was identified as the *sacrum imperium* (Holy Roman Empire). In the next two centuries, this organic structure of the Church appears more and more like that of a state, with the pope becoming the embodiment of the "mystical body of Christ" overseeing the Christian polity as a benevolent and charismatic leader.[33] The crucial text for this 12th-century political theology, and theological polity, can be found in Paul's 12th chapter of 1 Corinthians. There we find the following:

> Now there are diversities of gifts, but the same Spirit. And there are differences of administrations, but the same Lord. And there are diversities of operations, but it is the same God which worketh all in all.

Then:

> For as the body is one and hath many members, and all the members of that one body, being many, are of one body: so also is Christ. For by one Spirit we

are baptized into one body, whether we be Jews or Gentiles, whether we be bond or free: and have all been made to drink into one Spirit.[34]

Paul continues to compare the body to a physical human body, naming parts such as feet and hands, ears, and eyes, showing, through a seemingly Aristotelian logic, that they can only be identified as such within an organic telos. What is important to note is the systematic way in which the "diversities of operations" become unified under the divine moral authority of the pope. It is this divine orientation which becomes the ethical compass and guarantor for the body politic, which must be divided and internalized with the so-called secularization of the nation-state, generally understood to arise with the Treaty of Westphalia closing the Thirty Years War. The establishment and maintenance of divine truth became a national rather than transnational interest – recall the reflections on Luther, Calvin, and Kant in Chapter 2. The question of the transference of divine essence to the state becomes both a religious and a psychological issue. On the latter, I will turn to another scene of politico-theological transference through the concept of *family romance*.

b. *Family Romance*

By this it appears that a great family, if it be not part of some Commonwealth, is of itself, as to the rights of sovereignty, a little monarchy.[35]

The Neurotic Family Romance

Freud's concept of *family romance* describes the process of intellectual maturation in children as they transition from the restricted sphere of parental authority and begin to search beyond the family to the broader social world. It is when the sovereignty of the parental unit (and here we are taking for granted the nuclear model which Freud's analysis is tragically predicated on) is questioned and the child turns outward to seek other figures of authority. This provides a model that tells us something about the substitution of one authority for another.

In the family scene, the relation to this "first and only authority" is breached when the child observes and then compares other adults to their own parents. Here, Freud attempts to grasp the initiation of the childhood psyche into social structures extending beyond that of the immediate family. The aim is to understand how authority is transferred from the parents to other people and ultimately describes how the child begins to recognize figures of authority in society. As noted in Chapter 2, Luther and Calvin accomplished this by generalizing the principle of obedience in the fourth commandment, and Hegel, in a different way, articulated this as the necessary dissolution of the family provoked by bourgeois society discussed in Chapter 5. Here, though we find a psychoanalytic version of a similar structure.

Freud envisions this life transition as a confrontation between two or more sets of parents – or households really – within the psyche of the child. When a child notices the superior quality – indicated by greater social power or prestige

– of another adult or set of parents, the child may feel a sense of having been slighted by their own caretakers whose omniscience, omnipotence, and presumable omnibenevolence at this moment begin to erode. Why are they not of better quality? Why can they not afford the same privilege, social prestige, economic clout, and so on? This inspires feelings of resentment, at times outright rejection, which in turn leads to both a skeptical challenge to the authority of the parents and a turn to the broader circle of society for guidance. Sometimes, however, things can go further. In what Freud labels a *neurotic family romance*, the child begins to imagine that they are in fact the offspring of these other socially idealized adults. Their own guardians are then perceived as having denied them their proper place in the superior social or economic category. Consequently, the child is afflicted by ideas of abduction in infancy, displacing the status of their *actual* parents one degree further from that of the mediocre to the contemptable. Later, this phantasy emerges in daydreams which, Freud tells us, "are found to serve as the fulfillment of wishes and as a correction of actual life. They have two principle aims, an erotic and an ambitious one – though an erotic aim is usually concealed behind the latter".[36] Accordingly, it is at this point that the child's imagination becomes focused on the task of achieving liberation from their elders, of "whom he now has a low opinion and of replacing them with others who as a rule are of higher social standing".[37] Freud goes on to describe this ongoing phantasy as the child gains insight into human sexual reproduction and soon intuits the old adage: "*pater semper incertus est* while the mother is *certissitna*".[38] This uncertainty, of course, is at the core of the insecurity of the paternal state discussed in the previous chapters. It is, more deeply, the existential insecurity of the sovereign. It has a multiplying effect. The replacement of the parents is "only an expression of the child's longing for the happy, vanished days when his father seemed to him the noblest and strongest of men and his mother the dearest and loveliest of all women".[39] It is a turn away from the contemporary father and mother, towards authorities that the child suspects, and hopes, maybe their authentic family as they are consumed by nostalgia for what never existed. It also establishes a mechanism of substitution. The desire to be rescued is utopian. And yet this utopian longing is expressed at the point of transition from the reality principle instilled by identification with the parents, to the reality principle found in what is socially authorized as desirable, with regard to, for example, signifiers of social power, e.g. class, race, prestige, and so on. The ego-ideal is no longer primarily informed by the authority of the parents but now follows a model based on the distribution of social power and the attendant distribution of values.

The Political Family Romance

For Lynn Hunt in her book *Family Romance and the French Revolution*, the important point comes with the way in which the *inter* familial, in relation to *intra* familial conflict, links the psyche to the social order, or informs the social subjectivization of the self. By extension, she uses the idea of family romance to refer to "the collective, unconscious images of the familial order that underlie revolutionary politics".[40]

Prior to the French revolution, Hunt argues, the French people – as most European states or polities – experienced politics "as families writ large". This is historically specific to the European aristocratic states, as well as to the transition to what is usually understood as the modern secular nation-state. This model of transference can help us consider the historicity of the family as a political principle that on the level of the psyche is meant to reflect and internalize the idea of the nation, or what might be understood as the familial authority of the state. Rather than replacing the old family with one of a higher social standing, Hunt suggests that the revolutionaries sought to replace the aristocracy "with a different kind of family, one in which the parents were effaced and the children, especially the brothers, acted autonomously".[41] But Hunt goes further in tracking the changing position of the father during this time by analyzing representations of the father figure in literature. Her claim is that a decisive shift can be found beginning in the 1720s. The novels of the subsequent years until the mid-18th century "portrayed a family world in disarray, whether in novels by women in which wives confronted the abuses of husbands or in novels by men in which tyrannical fathers were opposed by rebellious and sacrilegious sons".[42] In the works of Voltaire, Prévost, and Marivaux, she points out, we find a fundamentally tragic depiction of family relations. Later this will change. Closer to, but also during the time of revolution, the family becomes a place of emotional investment and closeness. Here we find the emergence of the bourgeois family drama. Fathers became virtuous, transformed from tyrants into sensitive and caring figures who even withstand abuse from their own children. Examples that Hunt provides are Diderot's *The Father of the Family* (1758), or Baculard d'Arnaud's *Tests of Sentiment*.[43] After this period, family mythology once more changes as the father all but disappears. "Fictional fathers began to be effaced; they were lost, absent, dead, or simply unknown".[44] When they were depicted, they were always ambivalent figures, "much like Louis XVI on the eve of 1789".[45] Hunt collects an array of evidence to suggest that a change took place in the very structures of relations of authority, noting that in novels of the last half of the 18th century, biological fathers recede from view. The few that remain become "new model fathers" that depend on affection and care instead of intractable moral authority.[46]

From a Freudian standpoint, this disappearance simply accentuates or enhances the authority and power of the phallus for "there is no escape from 'the longing of the father'".[47] But Hunt finds this reduction to smack of ahistoricism. What, in that case, cannot be reduced to such a longing? How does this account for changing social relations as well as the changing family? Her thesis is that the transition to the *good father* mortally undermined the possibility for the persistence of absolutist monarchical authority. However, she also points out that this humbling of the father did not lead to raising the status of the mother or daughter. This admission suggests there is some truth to the persistence of the longing for the father in a different, perhaps more cunning form. The father with humility appears truly worthy of his authority, which is now based on some degree of negotiation.

The rules of communication still center on the father, they are simply modified. No real transformation of social power within the household takes place. What is introduced instead is the guilt of the father. The father is the tyrant, and it is his fault. If he is to remain culpable, then he must persist in occupying that position, but now, as penance he must become amenable, to essentially produce a façade of politics. Obedience is mixed with love, and it is through love that he presumably maintains his aura of authentic authority.

Coinciding with this shift is a shift in the view of children, who become innocent and simple, incomplete human beings, development now progressing in formal stages as Jean Piaget later concluded. This leads to the emergence in the mid-18th century of a new genre of literature; namely, books aimed at the child reader. Right around the same time sexual practices became codified through stories that could be translated and transferred to medical analysis and juridical circumscriptions.[48] But we also and already find this idea embedded in Rousseau's political philosophy. For example, in Rousseau's *Social Contract*, we find the following thought:

> You could call the family the prime model of political societies: the ruler corresponds to the father, and the people to the children; and all of them – ruler, people, father, children – because they were born free and equal don't give up their liberty without getting something in return. The whole difference is that in the family the father's care for his children is repaid by his love for them, whereas in the state the ruler's care for the people under him is repaid not by love for them (which he doesn't have!) but by the pleasure of being in charge.[49]

But with the French Revolution, we need to reverse Rousseau's description. It is not the state that follows the model of the family, it is not the state that is the family writ large, but exactly the opposite. The family takes the model of the state as noted in the quote from Thomas Hobbes opening this chapter, *the family is the state writ small*. Doesn't this also, perhaps at the risk of oversimplification, establish the conditions which describe the so-called *America dream* that devolved into the idealization of that catastrophic semi-urban desolation called the suburbs and the corresponding urban ghettos? The head of household "earns" his/her absolutist position, the household is then a reprieve from the state of "war of all against all" that characterizes the economic sphere, that perpetual new frontier in which parcels of private immunity are "rightfully earned" by hard work and ingenuity, the ultimate act of "freedom" – to produce quantifiably verifiable meaning socially and biologically evident in stratification. At the same time, and because of its ideological function, the suburban household becomes a factory reproducing incredibly strong forces of normalization. As a result, the family becomes the site for the justification of economic and social failure. This brings us back to the earlier discussion (Chapter 3) of Patrick Moynahan's report which precisely targets – and racializes – the "failing nuclear family", the tragic absence of the authority figure as the most significant reason for the immiseration of lower social classes. And the outcome of the distribution of vulnerability that characterizes social divisions, with the explicit blessing of traditionalist Abrahamic religious organizations, is uncritically foisted upon the "private sphere". It is this move that allows the rightwing punditry and evangelical capital to shift from the individual to the community, and to shepherd social scientists into their flock. Here, the social sciences are employed in at once reaffirming the "cultural foundations of the state" and justifying the – inevitably racialized, sexualized, and nationalized – production of poverty and lack, and the attendant brutalizing tactics of *correction*.[50]

Returning briefly to Hunt's line of argument, during the revolutionary period, as the focus on children increased, so did their education as well as the "proper role" of the "good mother". Education was not provided by fathers but rather by tutors or mothers. "The novel as it developed in eighteenth century France was inherently antipatriarchal".[51] Hunt suggests that prominent revolutionaries, many of whom were fatherless, cited their mothers as a major influence, with almost no mention of the paternal.[52] The family romance exits the realm of phantasy and becomes historical. This is actualized in the apparent possibility of socioeconomic mobility which in turn is framed as a neutral framework dividing society according to how much each member produces – measured in "earnings". Power is conferred based on the performance of social power. The reward of social power is evidence of a blessed life, which, in turn, substantiates ontological worth and thus in a circular fashion justifies social authority.

Along with these changes, however, we find a parallel shift in the advocates for counterrevolution. As Corey Robin argues in *The Reactionary Mind*, the counterrevolution was not in fact concerned with resuscitating the aristocratic model of domination, but rather sought to find new grounds – *in reaction* to both the revolutionaries but also *in reaction* to the failed aristocracy – for justifying power. Their aim was not only to oppose the egalitarian project of the reformers and revolutionaries, but to destroy their predecessors, those who were responsible for initially losing their grip on authority, for opening up the conditions for the possibility of resistance. This would be done by securing a monopoly of violence in a novel way. The family became a primary focus as it was re-conceptualized by the traditionalists while at the same time projected into the past, framed as an institution – both natural and culturally significant – at risk if not altogether lost or tragically losing. It would become a root for the reinstitution or new rationalized justifications of social domination.

For the reactionaries, the proper order of authority would systematically reinstate the core principle of what was threatened in the revolution, namely a reliable and heritable (i.e. naturalized) form of social stratification, reproduced in the nuclear cells of familial authority. This, as Corey Robin also argues, is a pattern that can be found in all reactionary movements.[53] But the appeal to the family also provides a quasi-democratic basis for the persistence of feudalism. The point is to maintain what Robin calls the *private life of power*. The formula, following John Adams and Edmund Burke, is: "Allow men and women to become democratic citizens of the state; make sure they remain feudal subjects in the family, the factory, and the field".[54] Thus, after drafting the new constitution in 1799, Napoleon famously exclaimed, "what the people want is equality, not liberty".

In 1804, Napoleon instituted the first civic laws to be applied to the whole of France – including conquered territory. In these laws, the family was strictly regulated – which marked a novel shift from Church regulation – including rigid inheritance laws defined by "blood relation" and the introduction of divorce laws, which of course heavily favored the husband.[55] It is this regulation of feudal subjection that shaped the strategy of codification through strict juridical laws determining the family, property, and debt. Without the codification of care and love, and without the authority of the Church to regulate moral life, the sovereign state would weaken if not dissolve, for it would make no claim for the control over the reproduction of social and thus psychic life; therefore, it would hold no stake in creating a committed polity through upbringing, "education" and the cultivation of a conformable, "hard working" population conditioned to know that they are getting "what they deserve" and producing evidence of it in the Manichean division of wealth and poverty. Today, it is not just the state that is organized in relation to the capitalist laws of "economic development", "the Church" too claims to uphold the value of the nuclear family according to "reason" which, the argument goes, God blessed humans with. This reason is entirely organized around a productive and reproductive model of activity as discussed above through the work of Krafft-Ebing.[56]

c. *The Algorithmic Unconscious*

> For the tasks which face the human apparatus of perception at historical turning points cannot be performed solely by optical means – that is, by way of contemplation. They are mastered gradually – taking their cue from tactile reception – through habit.[57]

> "the frantic abolition of all distances brings no nearness; for nearness does not consist in the shortness of distance".[58]

> "The system has its weakest point where it shows its most brutal strength".[59]

The three quotes above capture three ideas that should be kept in mind while considering the following section. The first quote, taken from the second version of Walter Benjamin's *Work of Art in the Age of Technical Reproducibility*, suggests a historical understanding of human perception and apperception. Here, the concern is primarily with the rise of photography and film as well as other forms of mechanical reproducibility, not just the new modes of visual representation they introduce but in that they have inaugurated new ways of feeling, new tactilities. In these historical moments marked by technological shifts, it takes some time for perceptual and thus conceptual acclimation. Here the dissolution of the aura of authenticity, through reproducibility, for example, is not to be lamented but celebrated as the loss of a significant foundation of cult value, i.e. fascism. The idea here suggests a dialectical understanding of technological developments.

The second quote above comes from a relatively late essay by Martin Heidegger, "The Thing" or "Das Ding". Here the concern is with the technological contraction of space. Telecommunications, for example, abolish distance but do not bring close that which is remote to everyday life. This can be understood in the sense that the acceleration of technology does not bring us any closer to grasping our predicament understood socially or politically, or to disclosing the truth of, or authentic comportment to Being for that matter – which was the sense that Heidegger intended. In that sense, technological acceleration is not historically progressive. In fact, it might be precisely the opposite. It might be that with the introduction of new technologies new gaps are introduced, new distances intervene that foreclose an authentic comportment to existence. Gaps in knowledge, relation, politics, intimacy, and so on.

The last quote, from Herbert Marcuse's *Eros and Civilization* notes that what appears strongest in a system is often also the site of its potential failure. The point at which the system exposes its most brutal forms of oppression are the points of insecurity, the moment where it most necessarily represses its own vulnerabilities is the moment when those vulnerabilities are most salient.

The three points briefly: (1) New technologies introduce new modes of perception and correspondingly new concepts. (2) Technological development introduces new forms of estrangement under the auspices of abolishing distance. (3) The expression of systemic violence is also the site of a system's failure.

Technological Stultification

In a chapter titled "Mysteries and Drives from Aufklärung to Psychopower" in *Taking Care of Youth and the Generations*, Bernard Stiegler follows Max Weber's insight informed by the papers of Benjamin Franklin, that this "age of enlightenment" proves instead to be an "age of disenchantment". He notes: "capitalism formed by Calvinistic socialization transforms all beliefs into intrinsically calculable – and thus rationalizable – credit, where 'reason' exclusively means ration and no longer *motive*".[60]

Much like the critical work of Wolfgang Streeck discussed in Chapter 3, Stiegler suggests this logic has become generalized. More alarmingly – through what he calls *psychotechnics* – this rationale has gone so far as to displace not just our faculties of memory, but also the foundations of psychic development shaped through (presumably) authentic relations of care in the family. In the past, these relations were presumably based on the intergenerational transmission of information and intimate bonds, forming what could be called *ancestral continuity*, in which an individual could locate themselves within a trajectory of history and tradition, within a story of belonging. All of this functioned to frame the social demands of mutual care, including of course the transmission of practical skills, theological commitment, cultural values and norms, and knowledge, as well as trust. Stiegler's point is that "modernity" has lost its essential quality of critique as "critical caretaking". The evolving maturity – ushered in by a minority of apparently rationally cultivated leaders – and a critically formed attention responsible for the social legacy of the "scholar before the entire literate world" through the "public use of one's reason" as Kant would have it, has waned. Instead, critique as the act of discerning discrete unities – in the arithmetical or algorithmic sense – critique as "mastery through calculation" has become the dominant technic of the digital enlightenment, or what James Bridle from a quite different angle calls the *new dark age*.

Just as significantly, Stiegler's concerns are rooted in the social effect of electronic media that has had an atrophying effect, and in some ways even replaced many relations, as well as many aspects of everyday life.

> [I]f Aufklärung (adulthood; the affirmation of courage and will against laziness and cowardice) presupposes this psychotechnique of attention formation – that is, writing (and simultaneously reading, of the nootechnics of the book's *hypomn ē maton* is the constitutive condition of a critical public space, a "republic of letters") – then this *pharmakon*, the book, must not take the place of understanding.[61]

While this critique remains broadly within the direction found in the work of 20th-century critical theory, specifically that of Horkheimer, Adorno, and Marcuse, Stiegler is more focused on the dystopian potential (if not inevitability) of technology as such – rather than, for example, the ways in which a specific historical system of power makes use of coercive technics to establish and reproduce its authority technologically. A Ballardian apocalyptic spiral into techno-catastrophe ensues.

Stiegler cites Foucault's analysis of biopolitics through the idea of *Polizeiwissenschaft*, as a distributive outcome of the cunning of power initially implemented in the 19th-century bourgeois state.

> What is characteristic of a police state is its interest in what men do; it is interested in their activity, their "occupation". The objective of the police is therefore control of and responsibility for men's activity insofar as this activity constitutes as a differential element in the development of the state's forces.[62]

Stiegler's critique of technology follows this increasingly foundational and permeating algorithm. He writes

> this newfound calculability must be applied to all objects, very much including objects of desire, which then become increasingly undesirable; eventually they disappear as objects of desire, and along with them a sense of the world's future—if not the world itself.[63]

However, Stiegler continues by identifying two fundamental limits of the framework of "critique-as-calculability". For Stiegler, "rationalization and disenchantment" are the twin operating forces behind capitalism as enlightenment.

The first is identified as the "grammatization process" also dubbed *psychotechnics*. This can simply be understood as the logical outcome of the quantification of human relations what Stiegler calls "hypomnesic attention capture", i.e. technologization of memory. Today it is transformed into electronic data in a vast and interconnected mnemonic apparatus. Recall Marx's analysis of the tendency to the reduction in value as a key outcome of the technological acceleration of exploitation – namely deskilled labor resulting in enormous gains in productivity along with soaring profits, concentrated wealth, and new standards of living.

The second limit emerges from the invention of the figure of the consumer – i.e. consumption as a way of life. In other words, the libidinal drive for overproduction also coincides with the deskilling of consumers – or population in general – giving shape to familial conditions in which just about everything necessary and desirable is left to specialists. Elders do not recall how to do anything anymore, and children are increasingly immersed in a world of technological ersatz care. Meanwhile, parents (we may note the term is derived from *parire* "bring forth, give birth to, produce") find ways to outsource responsibility and knowledge. Stiegler speculates about a third limit in which "care becomes integrated into the value chain" a topic discussed above in Chapter 3.[64]

Here, Stiegler directly identifies his own anxiety within this development as the consequential loss of authentic bonds of care between members of the family. This becomes most readily evident in the so-called generation gap, ostensibly magnified by the acceleration of technological capability, and the attendant illiteracy among the older generations. Adults in the nuclear family are no longer a source of knowledge and increasingly have no idea what their children are even talking about. Their authority, no longer, apparently, based on valuable insight gained from lifelong experience and intergenerational knowledge "passed down", appears more and more as a mere formality. And thus care, usually understood as an activity that implies unique relational and experiential bonds and the dissemination of practices, skills, and stories for survival together producing a thick sense of relational meaning, has been minimized to a troubling point of insignificance. Some aspects of *parenting* and communication between generations have been replaced by screens, others by specialists or institutions such as psychiatrists, influencers, standardized testing instructors, banks, life coaches, celebrities, social workers, bail bonds services, educational institutions, rehabilitation and detention centers, parole officers, lawyers, and brokers. We can recognize Stiegler's general position as a fairly common critique of technology and consumerism.

"The Cradle of the World's Misinformation"

Take Don Delillo's *White Noise*, which presents a kind of anticipatory portrait of this quality of estrangement. It was published in 1985, set in a generic liberal-arts college town aptly dubbed The-College-on-the-Hill. It captures a specific image of a suburban, "white", highly educated, nuclear family through a logic that has only intensified with technological acceleration. The protagonist Jack Gladney is a professor who specializes in Hitler studies – a new field of the liberal arts that he in fact developed. In one scene, just after escaping an airborne toxic event – due to a catastrophic rail accident in an affluent neighborhood – his family arrives at a makeshift shelter in an old high school gymnasium. Heinrich, one of Gladney's sons, finds himself faced with a group of adults disoriented by the rupture of everyday life – after all, these things happen elsewhere, not idyllic liberal-arts college towns – as he meticulously describes the gruesome physiological effects of the toxin Nyodene D. – the lethal ingredient in the menacing gaseous mass. Heinrich then turns to his father, pointing out the woeful ignorance and general helplessness of the mass of adults congealed around him. It is like we have returned to the paleolithic age; he remarks.[65] Illustrating Stiegler's first point, Heinrich comes up with a thought experiment in which they would travel back in time tens of thousands of years. In the face of their daily confidence in the unidirectional progress of civilization, he asks the weary adults what exactly they would do to improve the life conditions of these *stone-agers*? Would they teach them to make a refrigerator? Could they explain how electricity can be generated or even what it is? What from the sophisticated conveniences of their everyday lives could they explain to assist these archaic people improve their rudimentary lot? What would they tell these people, what message from our advanced future could they give them to demonstrate our superiority, our advancement, our futurity?[66]

He asks his father to name one thing he could make. He asks whether he could make a simple match, whether that would even improve conditions, as they certainly had flint. Could his father even identify flint? Would he know what to do with it if he found some? Heinrich continues after his highly educated parent feebly offers that he would tell them to boil their water. His Socratic inquiry advances by asking his father to explain a radio. What is the principle behind the technology of the radio? His father responds that there is no real mystery, a radio works through powerful machines that transmit waves to corresponding receivers that are attuned to remotely capture those waves. Heinrich responds: are they transmitted through air? Do they have wings? Why not just tell them a radio is magic, after all isn't this how it appears to us mysteriously on the shelf stripped from the context of its history, with no explanation of how it was built or on what scientific principles it is designed? Already knowing his father has no answer, he asks him what a nucleotide is. They make up the basic building blocks of life. What good, he asks, is information if it just passes from one computer to another, changing and growing by the second as people progressively pass into obsolescence, as they sink ever deeper into the abyss of consumerist ignorance and conformity.[67] Here, not only does the responsible adult demonstrate a kind of epistemic helplessness with regard to what is going on, both in terms of the toxic event and in terms of everyday technology, but the next generation appears to be more knowledgeable, or at least they seem more aware of their general condition of estrangement illustrated in the generational gap in communication.

But this example also precisely reverses Stiegler's analysis. Rather than the youth helplessly entrapped by the machinations of technologically mediated life, it might simply be that the elders still cling to an antiquated principle of reality, and thereby fail to acknowledge their own helplessness by stubbornly claiming a more authentic comportment to the world – or lamenting the loss of that world. This failure is the reproduction of the divide between (re)action and knowledge expressed in generational terms.

In *White Noise*, the family is characterized as the seat of the world's misinformation. Something in family life, the need to survive within the claustrophobic heat and noise of nuclear existence produces a factual error.[68] The need to survive, not in relation to a complex, plastic, durable, and shifting community of trust, not persistence through resistance to economic immiseration or fascistic systems of isolation, but survival within an anemic, cryptically mediated relation that lacks a sense of purpose or connection beyond that of becoming a micro-machine of desires and repressions, teleologically driven by performance and consumption ... simply striving until things finally fall apart. And they do. Upholding dominant forms of relation and social status through the anxiety of failing one's loved ones is a particularly salient, and often overlooked dynamic. The family functions, Delillo suggests as a hermetically sealed social anemia, galvanized by the ignorance, and confusion of familial solidarity. It is precisely where the attunement to objective reality is weakest that the familial bond appears resilient.[69]

In another scene, Gladney is caught in the grips of depression as he deliberately conceals the fact that he has been fatally poisoned by the cloud. It is just a matter of time before the manufactured poison destroys him from within. Consumed by the thought of his own death, he turns to the only remaining act of satisfaction; shopping for himself and for his family, an act of familial solidarity in the face of an overwhelming world of objects, each attached to a sum measuring its libidinal worth against the time it takes for a living body to afford them – and of course, other living bodies to produce them. The more he purchased the more significant he felt. He found himself immersed in the waters of transcendence; he drifted above these sums as they were at once shed from his body. The amounts returned in the form of ontological credit. He was practically swelling with generosity as he spontaneously announced to his children that they must each choose their Christmas gifts now.[70] The consumerist sublime illustrates Stiegler's second limit of the forces of "rationalization and disenchantment" found in the digital enlightenment (or *dark age*) expressed in the corrosive effects – again, driven by the twin forces of consumerism and technological advancement – have on relations of care and intimacy. Whereas familial relations ought to function to provide physical and emotional resources for survival, important information passed down from generation to generation, and at least some sense of meaning and place, it is also simply always a lie, one which barely and only functions to integrate a child as a functioning member into a social world – which now basically means, a worker, a debtor, and a consumer, a success or a failure, a person perhaps pushed to the margins of survival.[71] But is this really so novel? Do we not already see this in the abstraction of authority peddled by Luther and Calvin and finally Kant as discussed in Chapter 2? Is this a matter of degree or is there something qualitatively distinct here? And what is the nature of this presumably new digital technology inundating our most banal and intimate lives?

Algorithmic Unconscious

Often the term algorithm is assumed to be a novel technological development appearing with the invention of the modern computer, but there is nothing fundamentally new about the concept. What is novel is only the speed at which calculations can be performed and the tasks they are meant to accomplish. The term algorithm is taken from the work of the 9th-century mathematician Muhammad ibn Musa al-Khwarizmi, *Al-kitāb al-mukhtaṣar fī ḥisāb al-ğabr wa'l-muqābala*, the oldest extant text on algebra (also, of course, introducing the term "al-Jabr" [algebra]), but the idea is far more archaic. The mathematician Jean Luc Chabert notes:

> Algorithms are simply a set of step by step instructions, to be carried out quite mechanically, so as to achieve some desired result. Given the discovery of a routine method for deriving a solution to a problem, it is not surprising that the "recipe" was passed on for others to use. Algorithms are not confined to mathematics .... The Babylonians used them for deciding points of law, Latin teachers used them to get the grammar right, and they have been used in all cultures for predicting the future, for deciding medical treatment, or for preparing food. Everybody today uses algorithms of one sort or another, often unconsciously, when following a recipe, using a knitting pattern, or operating household gadgets.[72]

As noted above, the algorithm is simply a set of instructions or a prescriptive series of actions. It is a recipe. It can be performed by a computer within the increasingly fragmented second, actualizing a new dimension of calculation applied to activities such as financial trading, mass surveillance, machine learning which in turn is applied, for example, to chess and Go! as well as translation apps, facial recognition, calculating geophysical processes, population tracking, financial speculation, nuancing systems of authority, precarity, and violence, diagnosing diseases, hacking individuals, corporations or nation-states, influencing, and analyzing metadata and direct data within the vast global surveillance programs conducted by governmental agencies such as the NSA and GCHQ through private firms such as Booz Allen Hamilton and their public facing counterparts Facebook and Google.[73]

One new aspect of the modern algorithm, however, was introduced with the quality of finitude in 1900 during the Second International Congress of Mathematicians in Paris. There it was determined that an algorithm must describe a finite process. In other words, it must be possible to accomplish each step by a determinate set of instructions which can be infinitely repeated. This is key.[74] It is not an ongoing process nor is it open to speculation or spontaneous change. It requires a decision to determine its scope and shape. In this sense, the algorithm is a self-contained process that may terminate with its end or repeat in a prede-termined and indefinite series. As a quantifying technology, it seeks to divide the world infinitely. Division is its telos, its final cause. The drive to make the finite world infinite through the reduction of quality into quantity, the necessary condi-tion for the power of infinite division, is the contradiction at the root of capital.

* * *

Today, the speed of calculation operates at a threshold far below human per-ception and cognition. Whether it is mapping seismic activity, crime prediction according to geophysical and biopolitical terms, or other forms of pattern recogni-tion, the algorithm also reveals something about our own unconscious, or more precisely, the implicit reification of stratification in social and political space and time, e.g. race, gender, class, and desire. This is introduced through the very cali-bration of the calculus, i.e. the determination of terms. The slip here comes with the tendency to interpret the outcome of the machine as neutral, or as objective as the arithmetic used to produce it. There are of course numerous examples of racial, gender, or other biases seemingly produced by digital machines. However, this was already evident in analog technology, in for example the Kodak case in the 1970s, in which film was calibrated according to "natural skin" tones, using the complexion of one white woman used to index "normal skin".[75] While the algorithm can be applied to any calculable problem today, in the digital world it is restricted to the arithmetical process that rises to consciousness only through secondary hermeneutic frames. In other words, the algorithm itself is strictly a for-mal, ultimately binary operation (even if it appears creative), it lacks any dimen-sion of criticality. In his recent work on the *New Dark Age*, James Bridle writes:

> The predictability (or otherwise) of earthquakes and homicides; the racial biases of opaque systems: these are, given enough time and thought, ame-nable to our understanding. They are based on time-worn models, and in the lived experience of the everyday. But what of new models of thought pro-duced by machines – decisions and consequences that we do not understand, because they are produced by cognitive processes utterly unlike our own?[76]

Although the use of the term *thought* to describe these processes is question-able, Bridle points out that the increasing complexity of these models has moved beyond human understanding.[77] The way in which a computer "makes a decision" concerning the next chess move is illegible to human cognition, even as the input and output make perfect sense. This is the point. The machines not only reinforce and distill the reality principle; they are increasingly effective in shaping it. The examples provided above via *White Noise*, seem almost quaint in comparison with the potentially sweeping application of this increasingly opaque technology. They have ostensibly become the systems that underlie the basic activities of eve-ryday life. James Bridle further notes:

> Reliance on computational logics of surveillance to derive truth about the world leaves us in a fundamentally precarious and paradoxical position.

Computational knowledge requires surveillance, because it can only produce its truth from the data available to it directly. In turn, all knowing is reduced to that which is computationally knowable, so all knowing becomes a form of surveillance.[78]

Computational knowledge based on – communicated through – digital binaries become involved in epistemic production, the thing-in-itself in relation to our comportment to everyday life. Some of the most obvious consequences are evident in technologies like Facebook's *Deepface*, utilized, as Bridle notes, not just to identify – which it advertises it can do with 98% accuracy – but also to predict.[79] This kind of proleptic judgment leads to anticipatory action and politics of speculation; it presumes the behaviorist axiom that human life is calculable. Crime prediction, for example, "becomes the justification for stops and searches, tickets and arrests".[80] Paraphrasing Walter Benjamin, Bridle notes: "To train these nascent intelligences on the remnants of prior knowledge is thus to encode such barbarism into our future".[81] In her excellent work on the algorithmic reproduction of structures of racism, Ruha Benjamin defines what she calls the *New Jim Code* as "the employment of new technologies that reflect and reproduce existing inequities but that are promoted and perceived as more objective or progressive than the discriminatory systems of a previous era".[82] Taken to its logical conclusion, the predictive algorithm seeks to destroy the future and foreclose possibility.

Anamnesis and Epiphylogenetic Technics

For Stiegler, the very fabric of the family and therefore society is threatened by what he calls "the destruction of the juvenile psychic apparatus".[83] He worries about the implications of what he calls the proliferation and augmentation of epiphylogenetic technologies presumably leading to the atrophy of care and trust between generations. This is specifically devastating for the "healthy" cohesion of the family.

By *epiphylogenetic*, Stiegler means technological structures that "uniquely inculcates a process of psychic and collective individuation governed by what I have suggested should be formalized as a general organology, in which the psychic apparatus is continuously reconfigured by technical and technological apparatuses and social structures".[84] Here, he suggests that we rethink our understanding of education through a broader organic evolutionary framework of the psychic apparatus as nervous system (he uses the term "cerebral organ") in direct relation to other necessary organs that form a living body as it is intercalated into the *socius* – in this case via "technological configurations". It is through this *tertiary retention* stored in mnemonic organs, that we can properly understand and assess what sort of education is transferred to, or inculcating, adolescent people.[85] Tertiary memory, for Stiegler, conditions intergenerational continuity. It answers the question: how is memory passed down from one generation to another? What are the durational threads?

There is, of course, a vast array of mediums such as oral histories, practices, knowledges, trades and skills, concepts, relations to animals, land, water, language, gatherings, community, theology, politics, music, medicine, the home, mourning, humor, tragedy, and taking care of the living and the dead. This is eventually augmented by technologically reproducible mediums such as books, archives, files, photographs, recordings, analog and digital transmissions and databases or libraries, the internet, school, social media, and other means of inscription, habituation, signaling, spatialization, temporalization, and expression. According to Stiegler, is it precisely the proximity of intergenerational ties, fundamental in providing subsequent generations with access to the reality principle grounded in practical skills and intimate relations, that is under siege by the blind, and impervious drive of technology and consumption. Ancestral transmission "is the very formulation and formalizing of the reality principle in its many forms of knowledge (knowing how to live, knowing what to do, knowing how to think)".[86]

These intergenerational communications function as the object and media for the pleasure principle according to Stiegler. The overarching point of his book on generational care is that surveillance and the reactive targeting of adolescence for what he calls "psychotechnical destruction" has been detrimental to intergenerational communication. He cites, for example, television networks which admit to systematically utilizing "attention-seizing audiovisual mechanisms to bring about … adulthood's regression to childhood".[87] In addition, new laws instituted in France, the United States, and elsewhere undermine the disciplinary role of parents by lowering the age of criminal delinquency, which also allows elders to shirk responsibility or responsiveness.[88] For Stiegler, this degradation ultimately results in the decimation of the progressive trajectory actualizing the universal.[89] It interrupts and corrupts the maturing of civilization, what Kant described as "adulthood as collective individuation". Like Max Weber as discussed above, Stiegler sees the modern enlightenment critically, through the initiation of the development and implementation of *psychotechnology*.

Even though Stiegler attributes something like a *pharmakological* ambivalence to technologies of reproduction, e.g. the book as critical, or the book as a doctrinal substitute for thinking, he clearly situates recent developments characterized as intensely mnemonic and attention-grabbing technologies, as having a fundamentally degrading effect on relation. It is somewhat astonishing, though not altogether surprising, that he never seems to consider or question the nuclear family as a relatively recent social and theologico-political psychotechnology, itself functioning as a formalized tertiary database that in its atrophied nuclear form has also led to erasures of ancestral transmission. Nor does he seem to acknowledge what exactly the data-driven algorithms are in fact telling us about our own quasi-unconscious justifications for social stratification, masked in the technological aura of neutrality supposedly built into the binary structure of digitality. Does the accelerated algorithm introduce something qualitatively new into society, and thereby destructive of the old authentic relations of care, or does it simply reveal fundamental aspects of these presumably authentic relations already contain the very seeds of domination and alienation? Like the stop motion film or time-lapse photography, perhaps something previously imperceptible is now simply being clarified.

While Stiegler's claim is that psychotechnologies have a depriving effect on intimate connections, he fails to recognize that psychotechnology is as ancient as Cleisthenes' political reforms or Pericles' funeral oration or Confucian ethics (as is *I-don't-give-a-fuckism* as a response, for example, the Cynic Diogenes who apparently couldn't care less about the polis or authority or even the oikos [which for him, was a barrel in the city] as such[90]). My point here is to ask, what is it about intergenerational tertiary memory that makes it so sacred? At what point is it – and what in fact is – corrupted? The generational memory he cites as being so influential in childhood development is often already informed by dominant ideas concerning power, economy, gender, obedience, attention, nationalism, and so on. Clearly, our masters are becoming rooted in accelerated and more opaque forms of technological algorithmics, but maybe this also provides a glimpse into the arbitrariness of our masters all along. Perhaps this crisis in memory also opens possibilities to rethink those social arrangements that are meant to protect us from such degradation. Maybe this apparently inevitable trajectory of decay and distraction also has the effect of diminishing the aura of both the family and the state, as well as the interpretive logic that drives algorithmic calculability. While I think an appreciation of intergenerational memory is key in understanding kinship, it is difficult to see this happening within the nuclear family form in a critical or practical way.

Unfortunately, Stiegler's anxiety at the perceived loss of an authentic refuge of care at the hands of a world that outsources memory and intergenerational relation through *epiphylogenetic psychotechnics* simply echoes the sentimentalist school of thought that recognizes the need for social bonds based on care, memory, generation, and mutual obligation – one that presumably transcends economic logic and governmental authority – but fails to question the nuclear form as a sanctioned construct and atrophying enclosure that governance requires in order to maintain a minimal grip on nationalized economic domination. It betrays a kind of despair of necessity.

At times Stiegler's techno-anxiety seems to evoke little more than a reactive nostalgia for the presumably authentic relations apparently flourishing in the pre-data-driven world. It also projects a kind of naïve stupidity onto the younger generations – as if the augmentation of the world by digital technology is not somehow just as much world as the nuclear family itself. In other words, to borrow again from Walter Benjamin, one who grows up with social media is more likely to develop the perceptual unconscious required to critically examine it.[91] The children of the 2020s perceive and interact with the world in a different way than those of the 1960s. Nevertheless, Stiegler's critique is important as it closely examines the need to attend to the very real coercive manipulations inherent in mnemonic technologies. Despite the specialized language he utilizes, he simply fails to go beyond a one-dimensional reaction to them.

* * *

A different and, I think, more critical and comprehensive angle can be found in Silvia Federici's work, which considers the effects of technological saturation in terms of the impoverishment of life, specifically in reducing the possibility for autonomous community building; i.e. forging communal bonds which involve horizontal practices of constancy and endurance. While Stiegler's focus on the technological substitution of memory and the atrophy of care between generations evokes a nostalgia for a functional nuclear family, Federici takes a longer view arguing that "the seduction that technology exerts on us is the effect of the impoverishment – economic, ecological, cultural – that five centuries of capitalism has produced on our lives".[92] Certainly, this has also led to an impoverishment of relations and a profound estrangement from practical skills, but again, this is nothing new. Federici seems more concerned with ecologically and socially sustainable relations and complex biospheres than the loss of middle-class fantasy of familial closeness and properly educated children.

Following the work of Otto Ullrich,[93] Federici points out that the ability of the global economy to distribute the effects of technological acceleration – essentially hiding them – has misled us to the assumption that such advancement and dissemination is far less violent – "on human lives and ecological flourishing" – than it actually is. This follows the oft-cited calculation that projects the generalization of the "American way of life" as requiring five earths.[94] But Federici focusses on a different form of impoverishment – "less visible and equally devastating" – alluded to above in the phrase "wholeness of life". She writes: "I refer here to that complex of needs, desires and capacities that millions of years of evolutionary development in close relation to nature have sedimented in us, which constitute one of the main sources of our resistance to exploitation".[95] Beyond those philosophical positions that frame the human simply as a unique discursively constructed being or in some other way exemplary or outside of nature, Federici is focused on material relational symbiotic needs that have evolved through deep history. Not just the sun, moon, wind, sky, sea, forest, mountains, steppe, wetlands, desert, and the open air (divinities), but the also the need to touch, smell, and feel other bodies (mortals), the brute fact that the "accumulated structure of needs and desires that has been the precondition to our social reproduction"[96] has ultimately become the target of incredibly powerful divisive forces of extraction and control.

In other words, it is not just the capacity to survive but also the ability to achieve an affluent existence outside of the logics of exchange that ground moral, theological, and pragmatic claims for specific forms of sanctioned kinship. Ultimately, the point here is to reconsider relationality and modes of active kinship as a refuge from exploitation, ecological devastation, police and military violence, poverty, and debt:

> The capacity to read the elements, to discover the medical properties of plants and flowers, to gain sustenance from the earth, to live in the woods and forests, to be guided by the stars and wind on the roads and the seas was and remains a source of "autonomy" that has to be destroyed. The development of capitalist industrial technology has been built on that loss and amplified it.[97]

This also evokes the points mentioned above from Delillo's *White Noise* taken in conjunction with the ramifications of embedded social structures that fail to prepare the young generations in practices for sustaining or building autonomous communities, while precisely *disabling* access to the necessities required to persist without the economic-technological apparatuses that are literally wiping life off the face of the earth.[98] Insofar as these effects are hidden from everyday life – while the algorithmic mechanisms of distribution are hidden from consciousness – urgency for creating communes of solidarity that functionally resist such totalization is evidently diminished, at least for those regions where escape is still for the time being possible.

If the "accumulated structure of needs and desires" that have shaped life on an evolutionary scale – measured adherence to social and biological conditions – that have come to shape the possibility of a social world, provide inherent, biological means of resistance, they have also, perhaps, limited the ability to extend care beyond the immediacy of feeling. If so, then it is this perceived limit that is exploited in the crushing demands for survival, the psychological and economic burdens of debt, the moral and political erosion of eternal global war, the threat of incarceration and displacement on various marginalized communities, the increasingly precarious "gig economy", and finally, the effects of stultification within a ruthlessly competitive educational system that functions to inculcate the nascent psyche into catastrophic modes of pedagogical stratification. On this last point, one of the main functions of primary school to tactfully peddle as fact the myth of "ranked intelligence" and the justification of "measures of success" presumably rewarded by social power, by informing children and their caregivers exactly who is "stupid" and who is "smart", who has potential and who does not, which schools are desirable and which are for those who do not have the time, or wherewithal to "care".[99]

By stultification I mean (following Jacques Rancière's *The Ignorant Schoolmaster*[100]), the generalized internalization of inability as well as indifference, so often produced within educational institutions. This is catastrophic psychologically, politically, and socially. And as for those who do not "make the grade" such a logic can only lead to what Stiegler calls *"I don't-Give-A-Fuck-ism"*. Something, I imagine that Stiegler identifies as symptomatic of his own upbringing and his eventual five-year stint in prison for armed robbery. Perhaps it is in childhood that the tools for creating the means for communal autonomy can be initiated, even if it is simply in encouraging the confidence, curiosity, and play required for imagining transformation, and for envisioning other possible worlds, ones that for example supplant competition with cooperation. But, again, Stiegler's nostalgia undermines the very concern expressed in his work by lamenting the loss of a social institution cultivated through a coerced, anemic, monocultural normativity. Perhaps we can take some direction from Herbert Marcuse when he writes in his seminal *Eros and Civilization*: "[I]n the administered society, the biological necessity does not immediately issue in action; organization demands counter-organization. Today the fight for life, the fight for Eros, is the *political* fight".[101]

Notes

1   Carl Schmitt, *Political Theology: Four Chapters on the Concept of Sovereignty*, trans. George Schwab (Chicago, IL and London: University of Chicago Press, 2006) 36.

2   Eric Santner, *The Royal Remains the People's Two Bodies and the Endgames of Sovereignty* (Chicago, IL and London: University of Chicago Press, 2007) xii.

3   Ibid., 33–34.

4   Ibid., 10.

5   "the complex symbolic structures and dynamics of sovereignty described by Kantorowicz in the context of medieval and early modern European monarchies do not simply disappear from the space of politics once the body of the king is no longer available as the primary incarnation of the principle and functions of sovereignty; rather, these structures and dynamics along with their attendant paradoxes and impasses 'migrate' into a new location that thereby assumes a turbulent and disorienting semiotic density previously concentrated in the 'strange material and physical presence' of the king." Ibid., 33.

6   See Henri Herbert and Marcel Mauss, *Sacrifice: Its Nature and Its Functions*, trans. W.D. Halls (Chicago: University of Chicago Press, 1964) 10.

7   Ernst Kantorowicz, *The King's Two Bodies* (Princeton, NJ: Princeton University Press, 2016) 437.

8   Santner, *The Royal Remains*, 34.

9   Key to the definition of the concept of the political for Schmitt.

10 As Santner points out, the body politic never quite abandons the lineage to a "Christ centered kingship". Santner, *The Royal Remains*, 36.

11 Michel Foucault, *The Michel Foucault Reader* (New York: Pantheon, 1984) 259.

12 Michel Foucault, *Discipline and Punish*, trans. Alan Sheridan (New York: Random House, 1978) 3–7.

13 Michel Foucault, *The History of Sexuality, vol. 1,* trans. Robert Hurley (New York: Vintage Books, 1990) 260.

14 Ibid., 261. Achille Mbembe in an almost dialectic manner excavates exactly this point (using Foucault's notion of biopolitics and sovereignty [the right to take life and let life]) to analyze the ways in which death has in fact operated as a primary pole in biopolitical distribution of space, to create landscapes of death: from the plantation, to the concentration, work and refugee camps, prisons, Bedouin communities in the West Bank investigated in the important work of Eyal Weizman's "Forensic Architects" and so on. See Eyal Weizman, *Forensic Architecture* (New York: Zone Books, 2017) also forensic-architecture.org. These topologies of death he calls *necropolitics* in an essay of that name. See Achille Mbembe, "Necropolitics," trans. Libby Meintjes in *Public Culture*, 1 January 2003; 15, no.1: 11–40.

15 Santner writes: The authority and legitimacy of the state, which at a formal-legal level represents each citizen for all other citizens, was itself now seen to be "rooted" in the soil of a particular territory and in the linguistic and cultural resources linked to it. To be enjoyed in the full and complex sense of that word, membership in the polity required a form of "naturalization" that could, however, no longer be secured by reference to the pompous body of the king and the dynamics of his representational corporeality; the passage from early modern subject to modern citizen was thus supplemented, from the beginning, by the qualification of national identity. Santner, *The Royal Remains*, 51.

16 Foucault, *History of Sexuality, vol. 1*, 147.

17 Ibid., 149.

18 Arendt continues: These lies changed from year to year, and they frequently contradicted each other; moreover, they were not necessarily the same for the various branches of the Party hierarchy or the people at large. But the practice of self-deception had become so common, almost a moral prerequisite for survival, that even now,

eighteen years after the collapse of the Nazi regime, when most of the specific content of its lies has been forgotten, it is sometimes difficult not to believe that mendacity has become an integral part of the German national character. Hannah Arendt, *Eichmann in Jerusalem: A Report on the Banality of Evil* (New York: Penguin, 1992) 52.

19 In his essay *Necropolitics*, Mbembe also considers topologies from the plantation to the colony to the refugee camp, the blurring of lines between resistance and suicide, sacrifice and redemption, martyrdom, and freedom. Achille Mbembe, "Necropolitics," trans. Libby Meintjes in *Public Culture*, 1 January 2003; 15, no. 1: 11–40.

20 In his essay *Necropolitics*, Mbembe also considers topologies from the plantation to the colony to the refugee camp, the blurring of lines between resistance and suicide, sacrifice and redemption, and martyrdom and freedom. Achille Mbembe, "Necropolitics," trans. Libby Meintjes in *Public Culture*, 1 January 2003; 15, no. 1: 11–40.

21 Freud notes in his conclusion: "Both conditions, hypnosis and mass formation, are hereditary deposits from the phylogenesis of the human libido – hypnosis as susceptibility, the mass moreover as direct survival. Replacing direct sexual tendencies by goal-inhibited ones furthers in both of them the separation of 'I' from 'I'-ideal on which a start has already been made in the case of being in love." Sigmund Freud, *Mass Psychology and other writings*, trans. J.A. Underwood (New York: Penguin Books, 2004) 98–99.

22 Santner, *The Royal Remains the People's Two Bodies*, 34.

23 Ibid., 34–35.

24 Kantorowicz, *The King's Two Bodies*, 13–14.

25 Ibid., 437.

26 However, Kantorowicz does not claim that the structure found in the King's Two Bodies is simply an invention of Christiandom. In the epilogue, he considers the possibility that this idea may be found in antiquity. One example is Plutarch's account of Alexander the Great who apparently "distinguished between a friend of Alexander and a friend of the king." Here he remarks on many other highly compelling pre-Christian examples. Ibid., 497–498.

27 Ernst Kantorowicz, *The King's Two Bodies*, xxxv.

28 Eric Santner, *The Royal Remains the People's Two Bodies*, 36.

29 Ernst Kantorowicz, *The King's Two Bodies*, 140.

30 Ibid. 141–142.

31 Ibid. 193–194.

32 Ibid., 197.

33 Ibid., 203–206.

34 *The Bible*, King James Version (New York: Penguin Books, 2006).

35 Thomas Hobbes, *Leviathan or the Matter, Forme, & Power of a Common-Wealth Ecclesiasticall and Civill* (London: Andrew Crooke, at the Green Dragon in St. Pauls Church-yard, 1651) Chapter XVII.

36 Sigmund Freud, *On Sexuality – Three Essays on the Theory of Sexuality and Other Works*, trans. James Strachey in *The Penguin Freud Library*, edited by Angela Richards, et al., 222–23.

37 Ibid., 222–23.

38 i.e. unlike the mother, "the father's identity is always in question". Again, in the *Leviathan*, the point is made that genetic continuity through the father is only certain through monogamy, which is instituted by the commonwealth.

39 Lynn Hunt, *Family Romance and the French Revolution* (Berkeley, CA: University of California Press, 1992) xii.

40 Ibid., xiii.

41 Ibid., xiv. Referencing Fredric Jameson's book *The Political Unconscious*, she aligns this phrase with his claim that, "'the structure of the psyche is historical, and has a history.'"

42 Hunt, *Family Romance*, 23.
43 Ibid., 23–24.
44 Ibid., 23.
45 Ibid., 23.
46 Ibid., 25.
47 Ibid., 27.
48 It might also be pointed out that the source for much of the early children's literature came from folktales. Thus, the vast endeavor at collecting and standardizing oral history that for example the Brothers Grimm undertook, was not just a social and pedagogical project it was also a national project.
49 Jean-Jacques Rousseau, *The Social Contract* (New York: Penguin, 1968) 2.
50 Judith Butler makes a parallel point in discussing the role of psychoanalysts in France in justifying the separation of children in immigrant families by the state in order to "reforge kinship ties in certain ways". She cites the work of Michel Schneider who in offering his opinions on cultural affairs has publicly maintained that the state must step in to take the place of the absent father, not through welfare benefits (itself conceived as a maternal deformation of the state), but through the imposition of law, discipline, and uncompromising modes of punishment and imprisonment. In his view, this is the only way to secure the cultural foundations of citizenship, that is, the cultural foundations that are required for the exercise of a certain conception of freedom. Thus, the state policies that create extreme class differentials, pervasive racism in employment practices, efforts to separate families in order to save children from Islamic formations, and efforts to sequester the *banlieues* as intensified sites of racialized poverty, are exonerated and effaced through such explanations." Judith Butler, "Secular Politics, Torture and Secular Time," in *Frames of War, When Is Life Grievable?* (New York: Verso, 2016) 115.
51 Hunt, *Family Romance*, 28.
52 Hunt lists: "Danton, Barnave, Condorcet, Marat, Barbaroux, Saint Just and Larevellière-Lépeaux." Hunt, *Family Romance*, 28. Pierre Trahard, *Le Sensibilité réveolutionaire*, 1789–1794 (Geneva, 1967) 35–36.
53 Corey Robin, *The Reactionary Mind* (New York: Oxford University Press, 2018), see Chapter 1 "The Private Life of Power".
54 Ibid., 14.
55 Just after the Louisiana Purchase, Thomas Jefferson followed suit. https://www.napoleon-series.org/research/government/code/book3/c_title05.html#chapter1 (accessed 13 March 2019).
56 For example "The Manhattan Declaration" which was a manifesto penned on 20 October 2009 primarily by the far-right Catholic professor Robert George and signed by over 150 religious leaders from Evangelical, Protestant, and Catholic traditions. The three heading topics are Life, Marriage, and Religious Liberty. For just a brief example of the argument, it notes:

>   Some who enter into same-sex and polyamorous relationships no doubt regard their unions as truly marital. They fail to understand, however, that marriage is made possible by the sexual complementarity of man and woman, and that the comprehensive, multi-level sharing of life that marriage is includes bodily unity of the sort that unites husband and wife biologically as one. (https://www.manhattandeclaration.org/)

57 Walter Benjamin, *The Work of Art in the Age of Its Technological Reproducibility: Second Version*, trans. Edmund Jephcott, Rodney Livingstone, Howard Eiland, and Others (Cambridge, MA: The Belknap Press of Harvard University Press, 2008) 40.
58 Martin Heidegger, "The Thing," trans. Albert Hofstadter in *Poetry, Language, Thought* (New York: Harper and Row Publishers, 1967) 153.

59 Hebert Marcuse, *Eros and Civilization: A Philosophical Inquiry into Freud* (Boston, MA: Beacon Press, 1966) xxiv.

60 Bernard Stiegler, *Taking Care of Youth and the Generations*, trans. Stephan Barker (Stanford, CA: Stanford University Press, 2010) 46.

61 Stiegler, *Taking Care*, 21.

62 Foucault identifies three objectives of the police. Population control, necessities of life and health, activity (non-idle populations,) and finally circulation, specifically infrastructure. Michel Foucault, *Security, Territory, Population, Lectures at the College de France, 1977–1978*, trans. Graham Burchell (New York: Picador, 2007) 323–325.

63 Stiegler, *Taking Care*, 47.

64 Ibid., 48.

65 Don Delillo, *White Noise* (New York: Penguin Books, 1985) 141.

66 Ibid., 142.

67 Ibid., 141–142.

68 Ibid., 81.

69 Ibid., 82. This of course acquires an entirely new dimension with the new phenomenon of "snowplow parenting" in extremely privileged households, recently discussed in the *New York Times* in relation to the "college bribery scandals". In those cases, parents create a total bubble around their children well into their young adulthood. [https://www.nytimes.com/2019/03/16/style/snowplow-parenting-scandal.html]

70 *Delillo, White Noise*, 84.

71 For example, our beloved New York City boasts at least 63,839 homeless people, with 15,492 people in homeless families and 22,938 homeless children (see www.coalitionforthehomeless.org/). But in the same year according to the New York City comptroller "NYC economy surges in Q4 2018." (https://comptroller.nyc.gov/reports/new-york-city-quarterly-economic-update/)

72 Jean Luc Chabert, *From the Pebble to the Microchip*, edited by Jean Luc Chabert (Berlin, Heidelberg, New York: Springer Verlag, 1994) 1.

73 The two organizations work in tandem to create a near total global listening/tracking system. "Global mass surveillance relies on political secrecy and technological opacity, and the two feed upon one another." See Bridle, *New Dark Age*, 177–180.

74 Jean Luc Chabert, *From the Pebble to the Microchip*, edited by Jean Luc Chabert (Berlin, Heidelberg, New York: Springer Verlag, 1994), 2.

75 See James Bridle, *The New Dark Age* (Brooklyn: Verso Books, 2019) 143–144.

76 Ibid., 146.

77 Referring to the evolution of Google Translate, which in 2006 switched to a model of statistical inference and in 2016 made another hugely important shift, Bridle notes: "the Translate system started using a neural network developed by Google Brain, and its abilities suddenly improved exponentially." The network basically constructed a model of the world. "In this new architecture, words are encoded by their distance from one another in a mesh of meaning – a mesh only a computer could comprehend." This creates a complexity with a "thousand dimensions of vectors". Ibid., 148.

78 Ibid., 185. Which is why, James Bridle notes, Jean Luc Godard refused to use Kodak in his work in Mozambique. Ibid., 143.

79 Ibid., 142.

80 Ibid., 146.

81 Bridle, *New Dark Age*, 144. The Benjaminian thought comes from his *Theses on the Philosophy of History*: "There is no document of civilization that is not at the same time a document of barbarism." In *Walter Benjamin: Selected Writings, Volume 4: 1938–1940* (Cambridge, MA: Harvard University Press, 2006).

82 Ruha Benjamin also notes: "the New Jim Code wherein tech advancement, posed as a solution, conjures a prior racial regime." Ruha Benjamin, *Race after Technology, Abolitionist Tools for the New Jim Code* (Medford: Polity Press, 2019) 5, 98.

83 *Bridle, New Dark Age*, 140.
84 Stiegler, *Taking Care*, 7.
85 Ibid., 7.
86 Ibid., 7.
87 Ibid., 16.
88 It "simultaneously means questioning the status of adults as well, finally relieving adults of the very responsibility that gives them their status as adults." Stiegler, *Taking Care*, 1.
89 This was, of course, before the veritable explosion of research and targeted manipulation by data mining firms such as Cambridge Analytica, which for example, harvested millions of people's Facebook profiles and platforms such as Nationbuilder. Nevermind, Google, Twitter, Instagram, Facebook, etc., the ways in which they permeate not just "private" and social life but shape our very subjectivities through the symbolical binary algorithm.
90 Stiegler uses this phrase (*je-m'en-foutisme*) to indicate general lack of care, irresponsible, short-sighted attitudes.
91 "If one considers the dangerous tensions which technology and its consequences have engendered in the masses at large – tendencies which at critical stages take on a psychotic character – one also has to recognize that this same technologization [*Technisierung*] has created the possibility of psychic immunization against such mass psychoses. It does so by means of certain films in which the forced development of sadistic fantasies or masochistic delusions can prevent their natural and dangerous maturation in the masses." Walter Benjamin, *The Work of Art in the Age of Its Technological Reproducibility: Second Version*, trans. Edmund Jephcott, Rodney Livingstone, Howard Eiland, and Others (Cambridge, MA: The Belknap Press of Harvard University Press, 2008) 38.
92 Silvia Federici, *Re-Enchanting the Commons: Feminism and the Politics of the Commons (Kairos)* (Oakland, CA: PM Press, 2018) 189–190.
93 See Otto Ullrich, "Technology," in *The Development Dictionary: A Guide to Knowledge as Power*, edited by Wolfgang Sachs (London: Zed Books, 1993) 281.
94 (http://css.umich.edu/factsheets/us-environmental-footprint-factsheet)
    This is often followed by technophilic, *misoterran* dreams of colonizing Mars and other planets.
95 Federici, *Re-Enchanting*, 190.
96 Ibid., 190.
97 Ibid., 191
98 On an analysis on the substitution of the performance principle for the reality principle see of course Herbert Marcuse's *Eros and Civilization*. There he writes: "The performance principle, which is that of an acquisitive and antagonistic society in the process of constant expansion, presupposes a long development during which domination has been increasingly rationalized: control over social labor now reproduces society on an enlarged scale and under improving conditions." Herbert Marcuse, *Eros and Civilization* (Boston, MA: Beacon Press, 1974) 41.
99 Stephen Jay Gould's *The Mismeasure of Man* is probably one of the best texts I have come across, from a scientific point of view, that critiques the idea of biological determinism ideologically reinforced by, and rooted in, the technique of "intelligence ranking" through statistics, IQ tests, head measurements, specious theories of hereditary IQ, performance in educational institutions and so on. As stated in his introduction: "*The Mismeasure of Man* treats one particular form of quantified claim about the ranking of human groups: the argument that intelligence can be meaningfully abstracted as a single number capable of ranking all people on a linear scale of intrinsic and unalterable mental worth." Stephen Jay Gould, *The Mismeasure of Man* (New York: W. W. Norton and Co., 1996) 20. Just as compelling is Paulo Freire's critique of the "banking method of education" in his well-known and excellent work *Pedagogy*

of the Oppressed. Freire writes: "In the banking concept of education, knowledge is a gift bestowed by those who consider themselves knowledgeable upon those whom they consider to know nothing." This amounts to a projection of complete ignorance onto the students and sets the tone for a strict hierarchical order in terms of possession and controlled transmission in relation to obedience, behavior and conformism. The student is treated as a container for knowledge while the teacher's task is to fill it – like a bank – justifying the existence of the master regardless of the effectivity of teaching, or of what exactly is being taught. Knowledge is treated as currency to be deposited into the brains of students. Freire outlines the ways in which pedagogy has been structurally informed by oppression and thus indoctrinates children into oppressive systems instilled in broader society. (Paulo Freire, "The Banking Concept of Education," in *Pedagogies of the Oppressed* (New York: Continuum, 2005) 72–75.

100   In his book *The Ignorant School Master: Five Lessons on Intellectual Emancipation*, trans. Kristin Ross (Stanford, CA: Stanford University Press, 1991), Jacques Rancière recounts the story of Jacques Jacotot a reputable school teacher in Belgium who was presented with an unprecedented problem – in his experience at least – when a group of Flemish students requested him as a French instructor. The problem was that he knew no Flemish and they knew no French. What he realized countered everything he assumed about the process of learning. He found a series of bilingual editions of a journal and assigned the students various projects but due to the communication gap he was never able to resort to the old pedagogical method of instruction – i.e. the transmission of information from the knowledgeable to the ignorant. He realized that as long as the traditional teacher student (master slave) relation was upheld this transference can never fully occur, the gap is held open by the pedagogical structure. Moreover, he realized that pedagogy was not primarily about such a transmission. It is the concept of "understanding" that becomes an obstacle to learning. Specifically, the idea that the student "does not understand unless he is explained to" manufactures a cryptic and ultimately frustrating mystification of learning. "The child who recites under the threat of the rod obeys the rod and that's all: he will apply his intelligence to something else. But the child who is explained to will devote his intelligence to the work of grieving: to understanding, that is to say, to understanding that he doesn't understand unless he is explained to." (8) Jacotot did not have the knowledge to teach the students the corresponding grammar, he could not explain the "flexations and roots of the French language", he simply encouraged them, and suggesting various paths to accomplish their task. He encouraged rather than reprimanded them, he left intact their will and confidence to learn French from the translations, "necessity has constrained him to leave his intelligence out of the picture …. And, in one fell swoop, he had suppressed the imaginary distance that is the principle for all pedagogical stultification … Without thinking about it he had made them discover this thing that he discovered with them: that all sentences, and consequently all intelligences that produce them are of the same nature." (9) There is no other intelligence at work, no "false bottom" or secret knowledge or cryptic equipment of thinking only privy to those with a formal education. Just as all the students learned their mother tongue, through mistakes, misunderstandings, association and immersion, "blindly figuring out riddles" and so on, they are able to learn this unknown tongue. Their teacher did not address them as an examiner, as a master explicator who possessed something the students lacked, but rather "under the sign of equality" (11). It was only their desire and confidence that allowed them to take up the challenge themselves. And it was only curiosity and will that Jacotot could encourage. In other words, nothing was transmitted. For Rancière "beneath the pedagogical relation of ignorance to science, the more fundamental philosophical elation of stultification to emancipation must be recognized" (14). here we have the difference between the stultifying schoolmaster and the emancipating one, the "learned master or the ignorant one" (14). Later in the book Rancière considers this in relation to those who come from a situation of impov-

erishment an ignorance. In these cases, the ignorant parent may encourage their children to learn. Emancipation for Rancière means learning to be equal within unequal society (133).

101 See 'Political Preface 1966' in Herbert Marcuse, *Eros and Civilization* (Boston, MA: Beacon Press, 1974) xxv.

Bibliography

Hannah Arendt. *Eichmann in Jerusalem: A Report on the Banality of Evil.* New York: Penguin, 1992.

Ruha Benjamin. *Race After Technology, Abolitionist Tools for the New Jim Code.* Medford, OR: Polity Press, 2019.

Walter Benjamin. *Selected Writings, Volume 4: 1938–1940.* Cambridge, MA: Harvard University Press, 2006.

Walter Benjamin. *The Work of Art in the Age of its Technological Reproducibility: Second Version.* Translated by Edmund Jephcott, Rodney Livingstone, Howard Eiland, et al. Cambridge, MA: The Belknap Press of Harvard University Press, 2008.

James Bridle. *The New Dark Age.* Brooklyn, NY: Verso Books, 2019.

Judith Butler. "Secular Politics, Torture and Secular Time." In *Frames of War, When Is Life Grievable?* New York: Verso, 2016.

Jean Luc Chabert. *From the Pebble to the Microchip.* Edited by Jean Luc Chabert. Berlin, Heidelberg, and New York: Springer Verlag, 1994.

Don Delillo. *White Noise.* New York: Penguin Books, 1985.

Silvia Federici. *Re-Enchanting the Commons: Feminism and the Politics of the Commons (Kairos).* Oakland, CA: PM Press, 2018.

Michel Foucault. *Discipline and Punish.* Translated by Alan Sheridan. New York: Random House, 1978.

Michel Foucault. *Security, Territory, Population, Lectures at the College de France, 1977–1978.* Translated by Graham Burchell. New York: Picador, 2007.

Michel Foucault. *The Michel Foucault Reader.* New York: Pantheon, 1984.

Michel Foucault. *The History of Sexuality, vol. 1.* Translated by Robert Hurley. New York: Vintage Books, 1990.

Paulo Freire. "The Banking Concept of Education." In *Pedagogies of the Oppressed.* New York: Continuum, 2005.

Sigmund Freud. *Mass Psychology and Other Writings.* Translated by J.A. Underwood. New York: Penguin Books, 2004.

Sigmund Freud. "On Sexuality." In *Three Essays on the Theory of Sexuality and Other Works*, translated by James Strachey in *The Penguin Freud Library*, edited by Angela Richards, et al., 2000.

Stephen Jay Gould. *The Mismeasure of Man.* New York: W. W. Norton and Co., 1996.

Martin Heidegger. "The Thing." In *Poetry, Language, Thought*, Translated by Albert Hofstadter. New York: Harper and Row Publishers, 1967.

Henri Herbert and Marcel Mauss. *Sacrifice: Its Nature and its Functions.* Translated by W. D. Halls. Chicago, IL: University of Chicago Press, 1964.

Thomas Hobbes. *Leviathan or the Matter, Forme, & Power of a Common-Wealth Ecclesiasticall and Civill.* London: Andrew Crooke, at the Green Dragon in St. Pauls Church-yard, 1651.

Lynn Hunt. *Family Romance and the French Revolution*. Berkeley, CA: University of California Press, 1992.

Ernst Kantorowicz. *The King's Two Bodies*. Princeton, NJ: Princeton University Press, 2016.

Herbert Marcuse. *Eros and Civilization*. Boston, MA: Beacon Press, 1974.

Achille Mbembe. "Necropolitics." *Public Culture* 15, no. 1 (1 January 2003): 11–40. trans. Libby Meintjes.

Jacques Rancière. *The Ignorant School Master: Five Lessons on Intellectual Emancipation*. Translated by Kristin Ross. Stanford, CA: Stanford University Press, 1991.

Corey Robin. *The Reactionary Mind*. New York: Oxford University Press, 2018.

Jean-Jacques Rousseau. *The Social Contract*. New York: Penguin, 1968.

Eric Santner. *The Royal Remains the People's Two Bodies and the Endgames of Sovereignty*. Chicago, IL and London: University of Chicago Press, 2007.

Carl Schmitt. *Political Theology: Four Chapters on the Concept of Sovereignty*, trans. George Schwab. Chicago, IL and London: University of Chicsago Press, 2006.

Bernard Stiegler. *Taking Care of Youth and the Generations*, translated by Stephan Barker. Stanford, CA: Stanford University Press, 2010.

The Bible, King James Version. New York: Penguin Books, 2006.

Otto Ullrich, "Technology." In *The Development Dictionary: A Guide to Knowledge as Power*, edited by Wolfgang Sachs. London: Zed Books, 1993.

5 Extraction, Intimacy, and Kinship

The age for which the ground fails to come hangs in the abyss.[1]

Capital keeps us constantly on the move, separating us from our countries, farms, gardens, homes and workplaces, because this guarantees cheap wages, communal disorganization and maximum vulnerability in front of the law, the courts, the police.[2]

It is not enough that the conditions of labor are concentrated at one pole of society in the shape of capital, while at the other pole are grouped masses of men who have nothing to sell but their labor-power. Nor is it enough that they are compelled to sell themselves voluntarily. The advance of capitalist production develops a working class which by education, tradition and habit looks upon the requirements of that mode of production as self-evident natural laws. The organization of the capitalist process of production, once it is fully developed, breaks down all resistance.[3]

The production of communal disarray and extreme precariousness as Silvia Federici notes in the second quote above, is concomitant to the categorical demand for growth. The imperative is paradoxically justified by the claim that expansion is required in order to end disorganization and vulnerability. As Marx already noted, the process of production endemic to capitalism instead functions to systematically erode conditions for the possibility of solidarity and resistance. Once forms of communal autonomy and the local knowledges they co-sustain are diminished, the system of capital stands as the ultimate anchor for the reality principle. To oppose its logic is to oppose reality. To imagine the end of capitalism is to imagine the end of the world, to echo Slavoj Žižek and Mark Fisher. Today, as systems and institutions fall into perpetual crisis on all fronts, the ultimate foundation in violence and isolation is ever more evident. In response, forms of collective resistance might take on organizational configurations other than the customary structure of leadership – more horizontal than vertical – through practices that generate new threads of solidarity, valuing rather than diminishing, or repressing difference.

Here I want to return to a theme partially developed in the previous sections; i.e. eudaemonia is most fundamentally satisfied in relations of trust and care that are fostered in kinship practices that respond to (or facilitate) common access to material, social, and spiritual necessities. Today, a politics of

DOI: 10.4324/9781003264644-7

emancipation must acknowledge both the necessary demands and limits of the universal or any singular concept of sovereignty. Here I would like to consider the possibility that collectives or communities can flourish without categorically determining the modes of life that generate webs of sustainable and flourishing relations. These determinations often take the form of enclosures which are used to channel relationality into modes of isolation that disable practices of kinship. More specifically, I will begin by critically examining the position of the family within the Hegelian bourgeois state, as an example of the political containment of intimacy and the associated contradictions, which can be grasped in the instrumentalization of poverty and the privatization of kinship. From there, I will turn to Rosa Luxemburg's theory of accumulation and consider indigenous political ontologies based on non-proprietary forms of relation.

Division of the State and the Familial Enclosure of Kinship

The state is cast as the political actualization of freedom in Hegel's late political philosophy. Two challenges Hegel faces – and I think fails to overcome – are the contradiction that love presents to the *modus vivendi* of the state, and the contradiction that the structural presence of poverty presents to the enlightened state – again, the modern political configuration which presumably actualizes freedom. These two issues are connected. The following thoughts are neither meant to be exhaustive nor expansive but simply intended to focus on the place of the family in political life, as Hegel frames it, to show how the family becomes an institution for the confinement of the principle (what he calls the family principle) of ethics.

For Hegel the family has a specifically ethical function in politics – an ethical function predicated on adherence to the sanctioned form of kinship (the family), which constitutes one-third of the tripartite division of the modern political state: the family, civil society, and the state. I will draw out a few consequences and contradictions of framing the family as the first ethical root of the state, to consider how relationality becomes enclosed and utilized as a force of authorization, ultimately instrumentalized by formal political authority. This is done by enrooting kinship in the political concept of private property. I will then move on to consider original accumulation and extraction through settler-colonial violence that enacted and continues to enact the destruction of kinship practices in indigenous communities.

Hapticality and the Monstrosity of Love

Hegel writes, "the earth, the firm solid ground, is a precondition of the principle of family life, so is the sea the natural element for industry, whose relations with the external world it enlivens".[4] The necessary condition for the family then is territoriality as well as possession, which is endemic to the structure of the nuclear household, while industry – at the time increasingly mercantilist – looks outward for global trade and colonial expansion. But here Hegel does not explicitly elaborate on what makes the family fundamentally distinct, what exactly is to be understood by the family principle (*Familienprinzip* or *Prinzip des Familienlebens*). However, with closer examination, we might get a clue as to what it is about the family that could serve as a foundation for such a relation in Hegel's system. Property and possession may be necessary prerequisites but they are not unique to the family, even though from an individual standpoint, it is the locus where these concepts might be initiated, e.g. children as the property of parents. One obvious place to check is ethical action (*die Sittlichkeit*). If there is such a thing as a fundamental ethical composure to the world, for Hegel this would be the name for it. In his *Lectures on Natural Right and Political Science* of 1817–1818, Hegel claims *Sittlichkeit* is "absolute foundation". He also admits that it is constituted by feeling and indeterminacy.[5] That is, it is a matter of sensation (*Empfindung*) and potentiality.

In the *Elements of the Philosophy of Right*, Hegel describes the underlying principle of agonism found in the obligation to *Sittlichkeit*; one that is unique to the relations found in the family, and one which the state is meant to contain without reducing or sublating them within economic, contractual, political, or even religious terms. In the *Zusatz* to the first paragraph in Section 1 under *The Family*, we find the following:

> Love means in general the consciousness of my unity with another, so that I am not isolated in my own life [*für mich*], but gain my self-consciousness only through the renunciation of my independent existence [*meines Fürsichseins*] and through knowing myself as the unity of myself with another and of the other with me [*durch das Mich-Wissen, als der Einheit meiner mit dem anderen und des anderen mit mir*]. But love is a feeling [*Empfindung*], that is, ethical life in its natural form. In the state, it is no longer present. There, one is conscious of unity as law; there, the content must be rational, and I must know it.[6]

Die Empfindung (sensation) is the "natural form" of ethics for Hegel. It is being conscious of myself through the "renunciation of my independent existence" and thus it is consciousness of my unity with an other – or we might add others – that is evoked through such feeling. But it is not rational, it cannot be subsumed under the categories of knowledge, and it is not legislated, so it cannot be exhausted or regulated by the law or right. *Die Empfindung* is absent in the state: when I am in the family, I am not in the state. Sensation is haptic. In this case we can say that the natural form of ethics for Hegel is indeterminate haptic relationality, or again what Fred Moten and Stephano Harney call hapticality: "the capacity to feel though others, for others to feel through you, for you to feel them feeling you".[7]

Hegel continues:

> Love is therefore the most *monstrous* contradiction [*der ungeheuerste Widerspruch*]; the understanding cannot resolve it, because there is nothing

more intractable than this punctiliousness of the self-consciousness which is negated and which I ought nevertheless to possess as affirmative. Love is both the production and the resolution of the contradiction.[8]

This monstrosity indicates a radical gap between hapticity, which is intimate, immediate association, the source of *Sittlichkeit* on one side and the mechanism of the state, which requires it even as, or because it is irreducible to its logic, i.e. excluded. In this sense the family is external to the state. Love introduces contradiction into the ethical core of the state, and that is the point. Ethical unity is not only based on absolute contradiction, a double movement of renunciation and possession, which is simultaneous and reflexive in the other, it is also always a matter of the *sensation* [*die Empfindung*] of finding myself in another.

In addition:

> The first moment in love is that I do not wish to be an independent person in my own right [*für mich*] and that, if I were, I would feel deficient and incomplete. The second moment is that I find myself in another person, that I gain recognition in this person [*daß ich in ihr gelt*], who in turn gains recognition in me. [9]

But this kind of recognition is not a matter of cognition. It is not again a matter of knowledge, it is not conceptual. For kinship to become a matter of knowledge, it must be subsumed under the category of *the family* and as such inscribed in the law of the state. But, as noted, with epistemic authorization, love as such disappears. The family in the bourgeois state then becomes a machine for the perpetual production and dissolution of the place of sanctioned feeling, or the political enclosure of haptic relationality. The family produces "free individuals", economic subjects to inhabit and compete within the set of rules that constitute civil society. This is "the abstract moment of determinate individuality [*Einzelheit*]", but the moral imperative (*das Sollen*) for the modern subject is to algorithmically reproduce *the family*, which begins again with love which is both cast out and embalmed within the family of the state.

For Hegel ethics is an activity, "which embraces the entire existence of the blood relation" which "does not concern the citizen for he [the citizen] does not belong to the family".[10] In other words, as noted, the family conceived through the myth of blood is internal to the organic state but irreducible to the political relation. It functions as the immediate ethical foundation for the state as it contains but does not destroy the monstrosity of love. It is an internal exclusion, and thus adopts the mirror image of the sovereign. The ethical act "has as its object and content this specific individual belonging to the family, takes him as a universal being, divested of his sensuous, particular reality".[11]

Hegel's Family: The Political Circumscription of Intimacy

According to David Ciavatta's reading of Hegel's late political philosophy, to grasp what it means to be in a family "involves uncovering basic and indispensable ways in which the human self is – in the very act of maintaining the familial sphere – thoroughly embroiled in responding to such ontological concerns". For example, it has to do with "what it is to be a self, with what it means to be in relation to others, with how the individual self stands in relation to the all-encompassing 'spirit' that gives meaning and purpose to all things".[12] The family, for Hegel, is not merely the set of relations which prepares individuals for life in civil society. The family is in no way derivative, or even, for that matter, "primitive", nor can it be reduced to the enlightenment rational/irrational dyad. Rather, the family is a substantial moment or experience of social cohesion, neither simply nor solely predicated on the social form sanctioned by the state. It is for this reason, according to Hegel, why Antigone's resistance indirectly destroys the state.[13]

Ciavatta's analysis of feeling, in Hegel, focuses on the permeable nature of the self. He claims that, for Hegel, the significance of the family is

> rooted most essentially in an original and distinctive experience of mutual recognition, an experience that answers above all to existential needs that are constitutive of us in our ongoing project of affirming and maintaining our identities as selves in the face of a natural world that is indifferent to us.[14]

Ciavatta distances Hegel from the position, often attributed to his work, that reproduction and the sexual division of labor is the primary quality establishing the family as the ethical root of society.[15] He also extends Hegel's concept of recognition by claiming that the family provides a unique relation of intimate or immediate familiarity not found in any other social activity.[16] It is one that precedes social relation but also, significantly, sets the stage for all future relations, as an initial and initiating anchor of apprehension, rather than recognition. Put in slightly different terms, the family informs those first relations that satisfy the universal and necessary conditions for the possibility of forming intimate relations in life.

Ciavatta does not imply that intimate familiarity supplants the primacy of the dialectic of lordship and bondage, which is so often cited as a model for political struggles of domination, submission, authorization, consciousness of death, and recognition. While the relation of master/slave articulates crucial aspects of embodiment in the face of the other, for Ciavatta the meaning of "being in a family" has to do with "overcoming the alienation and estrangement that we experience in the face of nature – whether nature in the form of our own bodies and desires, or in the form of the given, external world generally".[17] In other words, the ontological significance of *being in a family* has to do with what we do once we have gained some grasp on self-consciousness, that is to say, psychic division. What then does it mean to be a self in relation to other selves and how does one confront or negotiate factical indifference, including embodiment? Moreover, how is this related to the "generation of a meaningful and coherent experiential world"?[18]

Intersubjective recognition, according to Ciavatta, is bound up with and informed by familial relation. It is from a primary and necessary coexistence with others in the home that from a position of belonging, the self is practically informed about the world: "for she is able to experience the external world, through her family member's eyes, not simply as an alien – as in the case of the slave before his master – but as fundamentally inclusive of her, as having her own particular identity and agency already ingrained in this texture".[19] Again, for Hegel, the family is "the immediate substantiality of spirit which has as its determination the spirits feeling [*Empfindung*] of its own unity, which is love".[20] In other words, the family is the foundation according to which belonging, care, and a sense of self are haptically conveyed. These aspects of relationality presuppose recognition, that foundation of Hegelian political psychology.

What Ciavatta points out though, and this is important for the considerations here, is that for Hegel, the intimacy that characterizes familial non-reflective and immediate relations, is also unconscious and therefore underlies the conditions for the possibility of recognition. But it is immediacy in the context of being with others, and thus appears as the preconscious foundation of community. In other words, the familial is a more advanced stage of non-mediated being, one which is immediate in relation to an already constituted society and state – that is, in relation to two other spheres of sociality that operate in terms of formal recognition (economic and political). It comes prior to – and thus withstands – reflection or deliberation, but it is not simply surpassed in either the instrumental relations of civic society or the political life of the state. It is the persistence of immediacy felt in the sense of familiarity.

Although reflecting on familial dynamics is possible and may lead to one dissolving, altering, adopting, etc. familial bonds, the family provides that "background element entrenched in a community's way of life".[21] One's comportment toward the world is initially shaped by the familiar, the condition of familiarity, by the first intimate relations regardless of whether they coincide with or diverge from societal norms and regardless of whether from a psychological perspective the familial leads to "tragic failures of recognition" or provides the conditions for a "healthy" entrance into the broader socius. Language, etiquette, even the internalization of the social or political status of a family, ideas of class, race, and gender, and corresponding associative temporalities and spatial relations, rituals, habits, ways of communicating in relation to events, activities, objects, animals, authority, memory, sexuality, geographies, and relations within and outside of the home, all provide aspects of immediate familiarity irreducible to reflection in that they are simply given, or a better term might be, lived. The familiar is a necessary aspect of psychic life. It establishes comportment for social apperception.

While it is entirely accurate to recognize the family as a distinct relation in this arrangement, Ciavatta seems to overlook or downplay, the restrictive relation to the state and civil society, which in Hegel formulates a symbiotic system between the three spheres of social-political-economic life. It is this that gives the state the organic structure to determine the sanctioned form of the familial used to justify the sovereign authority of the state that not only determines the "proper" shape that relations of care and familiarity must take but also dictates the ways in which power and authority are transmitted transgenerationally. Ciavatta fails to recognize the importance of kinship in terms of resisting the coercive structure of the modern state and the atomistic economic rationale it relies on. This, in a way, is the very distinction attributed to it by Hegel. Because of this, the family is taken to be a singular moment in life. It is an ossified structure that overdetermines social apperception, and in a way saves the state and economy from their own instrumental logic. This is why Hegel is critical of the social contract. In other words, it seems clear why the other two spheres of political life require love; however, it is uncertain why love requires their existence.

The Incommensurable within the Three-fold Composition of the State

Hegel establishes "family capital [*Gut*]" as "an indestructible stem", "independent of contingencies and time" (independent of wage labor, that is), as that which is held in common for the "care of the whole".[22] In other words, here he establishes a structure whereby the internal ethical community called "the family" functions as a collective association wherein "the true relationship is one of common ownership: where spouses may not own particular property as particular individuals"[23] – that is preserved in opposition to the economic sphere; a contradiction that is not resolved so much as it is perpetually suspended by the tripartite composition of the state.

This conflict itself expresses the ethical relation from the standpoint of the political edifice. It must be maintained but also remain contingent on the eternal preservation of the distinction between three domains: private (family), public (civil society), and political (state).

> The patriotic disposition acquires its specifically determined *content* from the various aspects of the organism of the state .... Hence these different aspects are the *various powers* of the state with their functions and spheres of action, by means of which the universal continually engenders itself, and engenders itself in a necessary way. Throughout this process the universal maintains its identity, since it is itself the presupposition of its own production. *This organism is the political constitution.*[24]

The form the political organism takes is reflected in and a reflection of its content, that is, what it produces and reproduces. The family principle produces ethical relations; civil society (estates and corporation) produces self-determined individuals habituated (second nature) as a comportment of trust towards the state. This is the definition of patriotism for Hegel.[25]

Of course, the family not only reproduces ethical relations, but it also reproduces the polity and establishes the "right of inheritance", for Hegel.[26] Whereas Cicero considered kinship proximity to indicate the measure of relational authentication in a privileged structure radiating outward from the immediate family, for Hegel it is in the relation of love between the monogamous couple in the context of sexual reproduction that establishes the ethical root of the state. In section 238 of the

Elements, Hegel explains that the sphere of civil society undermines the substantiality of the family by ripping the individual out of the familiar. This "alienates the members of the family from one another, and recognizes them as self-sufficient persons".[27] Here, Hegel identifies two aspects of education (*Bildung*): providing means and skills in order to "earn a living" – in order to become an economic subject – and in conditioning the self to become a "self-sufficient subject" also providing security in case the individual is unable to participate in civil society. From this standpoint, the family becomes contingent and subordinate to this process; its aim, to manufacture productive individuals. Civil society substitutes the substantiality of the family with its own autochthonous foundation, transforming what Hegel calls immediacy, required for both survival and sociality, into a community obligated to sustain the economic sphere, in turn, guaranteed and protected by the state.

In other words, the logic of the market adopts the guise of a paternal figure replacing the father of the family:

> The individual becomes a son of civil society.... Thus, if a human being is to be a member of civil society, he has rights and claims in relation to it, just as he had in relation to his family. Civil society must protect its members and defend their rights, just as the individual [*der Einzelne*] owes a duty to the rights of civil society.[28]

And yet, a few paragraphs earlier, Hegel claims that however malicious the police become (in terms of "surveillance, suspicion, inquiry and accountability"), there is no objective limit to their power. "[M]ore precise determinations will depend on custom, the spirit of the rest of the constitution, prevailing conditions, current emergencies, etc.".[29] The universal right of security – for persons and property – must be guaranteed, but insofar as this involves guaranteeing personal welfare (and thus contingent interests), subjective considerations come into play. Potentially, anything can provide ground for suspicion and certainly, the prevention of a violation of the economic order is imperative to the state's paternally oriented organic cohesion.

* * *

As noted, the justification of the three spheres of political and social life (family, civil society, state) is in the organic knot held fast by a paradoxical relation of mutual negation. Love in the family negates the law of the state, generalized egoism/self-determination in civil society is rendered abstract from the point of view of the state, and civil society extracts the individual from the familial as the family in turn dissolves. All the while the overarching state provides the generic logic that frames the relations in the other spheres, grounding them in necessity and freedom. Herbert Marcuse points out:

> The civil community appears, only to disappear at once in a "spectacle of excess, misery, and physical and social corruption". ... The family not only has its "external reality" in property, but also the existence of its "substantial personality".[30]

For Hegel, then, what saves the modern bourgeois state from the reign of selfishness is the ethical root of the family, which confines and encloses the intractable presence of love. The ethical idea dissolves in order to "achieve self-sufficient reality" which ultimately returns to the family, or more precisely, the constitution of a new family, which then also dissolves; individual self-determination realized in "the stage of difference".[31] The overarching stabilizing principle, that which protects society from barbarism, is found in the state, but ethical immunization is located in the family, while modern freedom is realized in civil society.

> Only in and through the family is property transformed from the "arbitrary expression of a particular need" to a "permanent and secure asset", and the "selfishness of greed" is transformed into something ethical, into labor and care for a common possession.[32]

* * *

The system that places the state before ethical relationality, anterior to embodied necessity, prior to the vulnerability it secures and distributes, confers onto it the aura of necessity, appearing both external and decisive as the constituting authority. Moreover, it functions as the "immanent end" of the two other spheres as it represents the universal principle towards which they appear to tend.[33] Real (non-abstract) freedom for Hegel consists of the coincidence of particular interests, characterizing the family and civil society, and the universal interests of the state (never mind incidents of collision between the family and civil society. In those cases, like Athena in Aeschylus' *Eumenides* it will be the state, *deus ex machina*, that institutes harmony.)

There is no room for the incommensurable in Hegel's political philosophy, and the state itself never submits to the negations of history. Instead, its organic composition takes the place of the movement of spirit, as the procedural elimination of remnants and ruins: women and others structurally repressed and exploited through racialization and normative orders of sexuality, poverty, and the displaced; refugees, first nations, those rendered queer, insane, criminal, but also anything that falls under the category of nature, ecosystems, and worlds that remain outside of the three spheres of political activity, these are the dregs of history and the pariahs of the state. These are the perennial targets of reactionary fantasies for the re-enchantment of the state.

* * *

As Eric Weil and Joanna Hodge both read it, Marx's reversal of Hegel's movement of spirit, which grounds the political in social relations rather than in the movement of the idea, is already present in Hegel's earlier work, but disappears as soon as the state becomes the sovereign principle of universal spirit, no longer, as such, submitting to the negating movement of history. Lawrence Krader points out that by foreclosing negation or critique, Hegel's machine of the enlightened state falls into the contradiction of the "non-actuality of the immanent", and the "non-potentiality of the external".[34] Joanna Hodge, on the other hand, points out that Marx employs the "concept of negativity developed in the *Phenomenology* to the fundamental structures elaborated in the *Philosophy of Right*".[35] In his "Critique of Hegel's Doctrine of the State", Marx writes:

> Precisely because "subordination" and "dependence" are external relationships, running counter to autonomous existence and limiting it, the relationship of the "family" and "civil society" to the state is one of "external necessity", a necessity which effects the internal essence of a thing .... With this subordination and dependence Hegel has further developed a one side of the divided identity, namely the aspect of estrangement within the unity".[36]

So what if the family no longer secures relational intimacy, or no longer tolerates love or haptic relationality, and what happens when the enlightened nation-state is no longer a stable or stabilizing principle? In these cases, the contradictions of the political institutions reach the extremities of crisis. The three spheres no longer hang together.

Infinitude's Despair: The Limits of Accumulation

Returning to the theme that opened this chapter, that is, the diminishment of conditions for solidarity, resistance, and autonomy within the logic of capitalism, I will attempt to develop the relation between the intractable ethical core of Hegel's political state, *feeling* or *sense* [*die Empfindung*] ("the moment I find myself in another") or haptic relationality, and the theme of extraction or what Marx called original accumulation. As noted at the beginning, I will begin with an examination of Rosa Luxemburg's modification of Marx's concept.

In part three of *The Accumulation of Capital*, Rosa Luxemburg critiques an overarching assumption that situates the political-economic system of capitalism – the capitalist mode of production – as both universal and exhaustive of all economic relations. Specifically, Luxemburg takes issue with Marx's thesis that all members within capitalist society fall under the categories of capitalist or producer, and that the system of capitalism can be grasped apart from non-capitalist forms of production, the forms of life which Luxemburg will stress, within which the drive for expansion finds nourishment.

Commenting on Marx's diagram of enlarged (or expanded) reproduction found in volume 2 of *Capital*, Luxemburg writes, "all 'third persons' of capitalist society – civil servants, the liberal professions, the clergy, etc. – must, as consumers, be counted within these two classes, and preferably within the capitalist class."[37] While Luxemburg admits that Marx's schematic, if taken precisely as that – as a formal explanation of accumulation within the logic of capital – does illustrate a specific economic dynamic unique to capitalism, she also insists that in practice, things are much more complicated. It should be noted that Jackie Wang, among others, points out that in other places, Marx of course "writes about a complex cast of characters that cannot be reduced solely to capitalists and workers ... so these models should not be taken as empirical descriptions of reality)."[38] Nevertheless, the point here is that Luxemburg focuses on and begins to theorize this gap in the abstract model through considerations that anticipate a broader understanding of the mechanism of accumulation by dispossession. One aspect of this can be found in the drive for totalization (that is the transformation of *all value* into quantified value[39]) characterizing the calculus required for surplus value, the very principle at the root of capital. In order to avoid the problem of overproduction, or underproduction, a flexible source of labor is of course needed. However, a more formal problem emerges when the imperative of infinite growth is actualized in a finite world – in other words, the drive to perpetually expand within an already generalized logic of commodification, ultimately leads to stagnation, crisis, or cannibalization.[40] The logic of capital presupposes infinite expansion. It produces unending and insatiable desire and need as it progressively informs the changing technological shape of the metabolic relation between human production and "nature". Here I am not so much interested in explicating the nuances of disagreement within Marxian theory, but rather directly considering Luxemburg's structural point in relation to the family both *official* and *practical*, as discussed in Chapter 1, to view how such a logic that, as Jackie Wang points out, functions through both homogenization and differentiation, might apply to the relation between kinship and the state, bodies and value, and hapticality and system.[41]

In Chapter 26 of the first volume of *Capital* on the "Secret of Primitive Accumulation", Marx turns to the problem of the origin of capitalism. He notes that capitalist economy functions along an ever-expanding cycle in which the translation of use value (production) to exchange value (wage and price [required for the extraction of surplus value]) produces a commodity, determined by the "calculation of the labor time socially necessary to produce it".[42] In other words, the surplus value extracted through wage labor, itself presupposes the value extracted. This operation is predicated on the division of society into two primary classes: those that own and thus control "the means of production and subsistence" and those that own only their labor power, that is, the activity sold on the market according to time or piece, required to produce value. The question Marx is concerned with, is how these two classes – marked by extreme wealth and extreme desperation – come about, and, therefore, how the machine of capitalism is jump-started. According to Marx, the sundering of society into such extreme poles of social power, and lack thereof, does not happen gradually. It is generated through a systematic process of massive theft, whether via war, revolution, colonization, or some other major catastrophe, e.g., ecological or economic. The global system of extraction of "natural" resources, "the destruction of communal cultures",[43] slavery (particularly in the southern United States which initially provided cotton for the English textile industry[44]), poverty, debt, gentrification, or some other forces of expropriation are all concrete examples of this act of theft. The concentration of social power through the rapid and total appropriation of access to necessity ("resources") is required for the initiation of the dichotomous machine of surplus. All of this to create conditions in which people "finally had nothing to sell but their skin".[45]

Marx takes this to be the economic equivalent of the theological concept of original sin. He continues with the following key point:

The process, which therefore creates the capital-relation can be nothing other than the process which divorces the worker from the ownership of the conditions of his own labor ... so-called primitive accumulation, therefore, is nothing else than the historical process of divorcing the producer from the means of production.[46]

That is, in alienating practices, relations and systems of communal sustainability already in place. The violence of the state is actualized as a tool for stratification and dispossession, and it persists in reproducing the conditions for the acceleration of capital accumulation, which in turn functions to both concentrate and centralize social power.[47] For Luxemburg, this is an unending process endemic to the survival of capital:

> The more ruthlessly capital sets about the destruction of noncapitalist strata at home and in the outside world, the more it lowers the standard of living for the workers as a whole, the greater also is the change in the day-to-day history of capital. It becomes a string of political and social disasters and convulsions, and under these conditions, punctuated by periodical economic catastrophes or crises, accumulation can go no longer.[48]

The site for extraction, internal to the nation-state, ultimately becomes relations of intimacy and conditions of survival. Here, we find systems of extraction in the form of healthcare, education, dwelling, transportation, childcare, and so on. All of these are necessities for families, for the survival of even the most minimal forms of relation. The division of the private and the public not only reinforces differences in the interests of extraction, for example in the nuclear family, the reduction of kinship ties, ligatures of trust, but also in terms of gender, race, and citizenship. Luce Irigaray suggests, following Marx and Engels, that social stratification can be traced back to an initial gendered division of labor which remains at the root of other forms of social domination. She writes:

> To be sure, the means of production have evolved, new techniques have been developed, but it does seem that as soon as the father-man was assured of his reproductive power and had marked his products with his name, that is, from the very origin of private property and the patriarchal family, social exploitation occurred.

The control over reproduction – both biological and of labor power – is maintained in its translation to exchange value which validates the symbolic order

> without any compensation in kind going to them for that "work". For such compensation would imply a double system of exchange, that is, a shattering of the monopolization of the proper name (and of what it signifies as appropriative power) by father-men.[49]

The nuclear family finds its original site of justification here and it can be directly connected to the reproduction of conditions of poverty. This is the underlying justification for the political theological ban on the right to abortion. It has more to do with the control over (re)production by men, the maintenance of the patriarchal symbolic order and the preservation of the gendered division of labor, as the root of other forms of social stratification rather than the confused notion of the beginning of life. Briefly, I will return to Hegel's composite state not just to show that he was already aware of the problem of poverty as a second intractable contradiction but to grasp the justification for social domination through the division of (as well as the opposition of which seems to be the case in popular discourse today) the family, civil society, and the state. This will allow us to excavate the proprietary logic that shapes the nuclear family as a site for extraction.

Municipal Plunder and the Systematic Erosion of Communal Autonomy

Prior to Marx it was Hegel who identified the dialectical problem of accumulation and poverty as a modern political dilemma. If the poor are supported without the "mediation of work", their existence contradicts the principal structure – in which a civil society (*bürgerliche Gesellschaft* or bourgeois society, the second ethical root of the state) is preserved along with the family (again, the first ethical root of the state). In civil society, each individual has the opportunity to achieve honor and self-sufficiency. However, in the case of full employment (i.e. allowing the poor to work in order to achieve a sense of "self-sufficiency"), the problem encountered is that of overproduction. Hegel concludes: "this shows that, despite an excess of wealth, civil society is not wealthy enough – i.e. its own distinct resources are not sufficient – to prevent an excess of poverty and the formation of a rabble".[50]

The solution found in England, accordingly, is to simply allow the poor to beg directly from the public, thus allowing them to maintain a sense of self-determination while keeping productivity within the range of profitability. But ultimately, poverty was identified as *the* perplexing problem in a modern economy.[51] The only solution, according to Hegel, which is clearly unsatisfying, to say the least, is to let the police handle it. Frank Ruda points out that the rabble presents a double contradiction to Hegel's enlightened state. "[In] poverty there is an inadequate relation between the concept (free will) and reality (poverty)".[52] A life of poverty is a life directed solely by necessity as opposed to freedom. In the enlightened state, which is meant to actualize universal freedom, the involuntary bondage of some otherwise rational individuals contradicts the composite order of the whole. This conflict results from the general contradiction of a society in which everyone must fend for themselves ("subsist by means of their own labor") when in actuality no one could survive alone, nor could they even, according to Hegel, establish or reestablish the minimal conditions for the possibility of actualizing self-consciousness.[53]

Even as Hegel seems to admit the clear inadequacy here, the irony in his suggestion is that the police in capitalist society primarily function to protect and often directly or indirectly control investment and property (e.g. today in policies such as broken windows, stop-and-frisk, various methods of targeting the poor and communities of color, the enforcement of arbitrary drug laws, immigration, and border security, etc.). The role of the police is not, of course, to eliminate poverty but to suppress the symptoms of poverty – to enforce the distribution of power – that threaten the otherwise peaceful cohesion – security – of the economy and state.[54] The task is to keep the poor in a state of impoverishment where access to necessities is limited by the demands of miserable working conditions and poverty wages. It is to maintain the general condition of survival as the primary activity of everyday life.

But the police do not just enforce the distribution of space and authority, they also function as agents of indirect and direct extraction from poor communities. To cite a recent and particularly egregious example of direct extraction, discussed in Jackie Wang's *Carceral Capitalism*, a Justice Department investigation following the Ferguson Uprising in August 2014 revealed that beyond the normalized abuse at the hands of the police systematically "killing and harassing residents", "the city was also using the police and the courts to generate revenue to balance the municipal budget".[55] The investigation ultimately revealed the existence of a system of municipal plunder. Taking into account the sanctioned ways that police are used to fill the coffers of city and county governments in the United States, e.g. arrest and ticket quotas, as well as the general function of the police to protect property and "protect and serve" the principles of social stratification in the enforcement of the uneven and often apartheid distribution of space, we find that this form of extraction from impoverished and minoritized communities is in fact embedded in the juridical system. This is also institutionalized in forced prison labor, which in the United States, according to the Federal prison industries program (UNICOR) indentures over 17,000 inmates each making between 23 cents and $1.15 per hour, pulls in half a billion dollars in profit every year.[56]

It is no wonder, notes the Bordertown Violence Working Group, "that mass incarceration is a defining feature of settler colonialism today or that the abolition of the prison and its camp guards, the police, is central to decolonization".[57] This open war on the poor, and poor families, was recognized by Marx as a fundamental part of the structure of governance in relation to the perpetuation of a surplus population and the attendant extraction of surplus value as a guaranteed source of economic funding. This is complemented by a regime of morality that justifies the brutal exploitation of what becomes a new class within the polity branded as immoral, subhuman, and so on. Already in the 19th century, Marx noted:

> Anyone wandering about and begging is declared a rogue and a vagabond. Justices of the peace in Petty Sessions are authorized to have them publicly whipped and to imprison them for six months for the first offense, and two years for the second .... Incorrigible and dangerous rogues are to be branded with an R on the left shoulder[58]

This, of course, becomes racialized as the authority of the social sciences in conjunction with the juridical order – beginning with the invention of the category *criminal* – begins to replace the institution of slavery with the carceral system, in what Michelle Alexander calls the New Jim Crow as a conservative reaction to emancipation.[59]

This fits very well into the genesis of the ideological framework motivating the reactionary tendency to blame poverty on the dissolution of the sacred nuclear family, as discussed in Chapter 3 concerning the Moynihan Report, and the specious claims of George Will, Jonah Goldberg, and others. Rather than being branded, the social life of the marginalized is structurally shaped by ghettoization and incarceration, lack of adequate healthcare, or access to childcare and education, or healthy food. These become institutional norms that no longer even show up as a contradiction within the nation-state. They are generally accepted, even expected as a necessary sacrifice for affluence.

These practices contribute to maintaining a general state of social and biological desperation that undermines the basic demands that sustain community, much less organized resistance, revolt, or autonomy. The population that lacks labor must be monitored, confined, controlled. This is the basic function of the category "criminal" and the vast industry of mass incarceration and detention centers which may soon be augmented by expanding house arrest. In the last case, the household will also become an extension of the carceral system, further diminishing the potential power of flexible relational practices. Insofar as unemployment is institutionally necessary to provide a flexible source of labor for the functioning of capital, so are the destitute whose existence serves as a justification for the police, and by extension the police state, which again maintains naturalized structures of social difference.

The Persistence of Accumulation: Capital's Other

Here, we get a glimpse into the roots of the critique found in the work of Rosa Luxemburg when she notes:

> nothing forces us to assume that there is not a fraction of the constant and variable capital which is also realized out of the capitalist realm. Accordingly, the expansion of production as well as the replacement in kind of the materials consumed in production may be undertaken by means of products from the non-capitalist sphere.[60]

This is expressed much later, of course, by David Harvey in his discussion of "accumulation by dispossession". For now, we can just use a shorthand definition from *The New Imperialism*: "we might say that capitalism necessarily and always creates its own 'other'. ... The idea that some sort of 'outside' is necessary for the stabilization of capitalism therefore has relevance".[61] Similarly, in paragraph 246 of the *Grundlinien*, Hegel writes:

> This inner dialectic of [capitalist] society drives it ... to go beyond its own confines and look for consumers, and hence the means it requires for

subsistence [*Subsistenz*], in other nations [*Völkern*] which lack those means of which it has a surplus or which generally lag behind it is creativity, etc.[62]

Two sections later, Hegel explicitly identifies this relation as one of colonization,

> whether sporadic or systematic – to which fully developed civil society is driven, and by which it provides part of its population with a return to the *family principle* in a new country, and itself with a new market and sphere of industrial activity.[63]

By sporadic colonization is meant mass immigration, while systematic indicates state-organized colonization – i.e. settler colonialism. It is this dialectic that Luxemburg identifies as the "struggle against the natural economy".[64] By natural economy, Luxemburg means those forms of activity and relation that do not rely on the logic of capitalist accumulation, whether it is the communist peasant or indigenous community, the autonomous commune, the "feudal corvée farm", or the soviet or council democracy (as opposed to parliamentary or representative democracy) or other broad forms of political practices that drew from or articulated modes of kinship. She writes: "Each new colonial expansion is accompanied, as a matter of course, by a relentless battle of capital against the social and economic ties of the natives, who are also forcibly robbed of their means of production and labor power".[65]

Luxemburg's point is that by observing the ways in which settler colonialism and extraction have functioned to accelerate accumulation, it not only becomes clear, as Marx already pointed out, that the system of capital is underwritten by the monopoly on violence assumed by the colonial state, which looks outward for expansion of power internationally through the extraction of cheap and easy resources – including a population of laborers and consumers – but that this process is not limited to the initiation of capitalism as a total economic system. "The process of accumulation, elastic and spasmodic as it is, requires inevitably free access to ever new areas of raw materials in case of need, both when imports from old sources fail or when social demand suddenly increases".[66] It must be grasped as an ongoing two-fold movement that accompanies the perpetual accumulation of capital, and it fundamentally relies on the power and authorizing force of the sovereign state to shape, sustain, and justify these forms of extraction. The mechanism of catastrophic growth simultaneously peers inward for new ways of wresting value from within the not-yet commodified social and biological practices.

* * *

> Force is the only solution open to capital; the accumulation of capital seen as a historical process, employs force as a permanent weapon, not only at its genesis but further on down to the present day ... The method of violence then is in the immediate consequence of the clash between capitalism and the organization of natural economy which would restrict accumulation.[67]

This is a key point for Luxemburg. It is the persistence of systematized violence underlying everyday economic rationality applied to modes of relation that do not comport or immediately comply with the formula for extraction, that is employed to break down both autonomy and resistance. Many examples can be found in the struggles against fossil fuel industry expansion which has intensified and after 2016, also known as "the year of the water protector" has reached a new level of militancy.[68] Just recently, the oil giant Enbridge reportedly spent $2 million to hire Minnesota State Police to protect its pipeline (known as the Black Snake to the indigenous communities) construction through Ojibwe territory.[69] The off-duty police were hired to attack and disperse water protectors with rubber bullets, skunk spray, and other presumably "less than lethal" weapons. Tara Houske, an Ojibwe lawyer, noted:

> The level of force being used, partnered with the very close range that law enforcement was facing us, led to some pretty serious injuries … It was really an extreme level of force, partnered with a really punitive and oppressive style of jailing".[70]

This is, by far, not the first time municipal police have been used to directly enforce the economic interests of extractive industries. Extractive industries rely on police protection and legal protection in the courts as well as government subsidies to engage in systematic plunder of what are dubbed "natural resources" but which indigenous communities take as kin, that is as sacred, with inherent dignity irreducible to systems of exchange and coercion.

It is important to recognize that in indigenous cosmologies, kinship is not limited to human relations, much less the nuclear model still peddled by some "social scientists". Kinship is an onto-political relation. It is a way of life and a social comportment to life as such. The river which will inevitably be poisoned by the pipeline is considered kin, intercalated in a vast and complex life-world that is fundamental to the existence of the communities that live within and alongside.[71] There is no juridical or contractual category that exists to recognize the sacred integrity of the non-human and, therefore, non-proprietary concept of kinship. Indigenous political ontology inherently resists the quantifiable division assumed by capital. Such an ontology presents an offense to western metaphysics. It presents a monstrous contradiction – to borrow from Hegel – to the colonial nation-state and, therefore, cannot be broken down by systems of exchange, nor enclosed by political institutions. This is, precisely, why a two-pronged strategy of violence and criminalization are employed to dismantle the resistance enrooted in kinship practices of indigenous communities.

The systematic brutality built into the very structure of the economic-legal order of the nation-state is expressed through both techniques of isolation that target support networks that as such rely on the interconnection of a broad range of synthetic kinship relations, and by the legal configuration of the family according to the logic of commodification, that is, according to the nuclear ideal which guarantees the prerequisite transmission of private property according to individual ownership. The result is a system of generalized atrophy of relationality. Practices of mutual aid are hampered as they fail to fit into the nuclear standard, neither recognized politically, socially, or economically. Much has been written on the devastating effects of re-education programs and the enforcement of nuclear family configurations on communities that conceive of kin and property otherwise.[72] In these final pages, I will consider a few examples and then briefly indicate some approaches to a politics of kinship as resistance.

Settler State Techne and Disincorporation: Property and Kin

According to the American Indian resistance collective *The Red Nation*, the scam of settler colonialism is rooted in the fantasy of private property, and it consists of four components.[73] In the first, we are confronted by the cast of characters beginning with the settler hero: "Christian, white, male, head-of-household". In contrast to the exceptional visibility of this heroic figure, the Indian is invisible, without subjectivity, lacking inner life, without productive skills, without education. The second is the scene at the center of which we find the lands where the native dwells. They are framed as uninhabited, unused, as wastelands ripe for extraction. The "specialty of the settler" is private property, the dissemination and distribution of which is cast as a dramatic scene of enlightenment, taming the wild, inscribing the universal grid of private worlds upon the vast and presumably empty landscape, rendering it fungible, and therefore legible to the colonialist. This is the *plot*, the third element of the scam. It is a logic that must take in the entire earth. On the one hand, the scene must be specific. The hero actualizes a universal, totalitarian project often under the names of "freedom" and "liberty". The foe, however, is not a typical enemy. Much like Cicero's pirates discussed in Chapter 2, the foe here is non-human, and the non-human remains outside of the category of civilization, and prior to the concept of human, an obstacle to progress much like the "overburden" that must be "cleared" for fossil fuel extraction in the Alberta tar sands. What makes the foe non-human is the presumption of ignorance, ignorance of the concept of private property. However, it is not ignorance on the part of the foe, but refusal. The political ontology of the Native American Indian cannot admit the category because the former is based on the recognition of the intricate connectivity of life in which humans play only a minor role. In this way, indigenous, non-human-centric kinship disincorporates the body of the nuclear family by activating relations without the principle of private property. And this marks the fourth element. The scam comes to an end.

One of the main contradictions in the fantasy is what the authors call the hero problem. The question is how to produce what Giorgio Agamben calls bare life, the point at which no degree of association, sympathy, or identification is possible. The foe must either be invisible or cast as a categorical threat to the "human", to the principle of civilization, the recognition of property, the recognition of the state and the body politic, i.e. the enemy of all. But a third possibility emerges where the first two are no longer tenable. That is a sympathetic comportment to the foe expressed in the myth of the noble savage. Here the foe suffers from alcoholism, laziness, lack of proper knowledge and manners, and is plagued by the chronic inability to acclimate to progressive society.[74] It is this last illustration of the enemy that substantiates and justifies the systematic abduction of children, their internment in re-education camps quaintly called "boarding schools" following the pioneering model of the Carlisle Indian Industrial School established in 1879 in Pennsylvania. Its founder, Richard Henry Pratt, popularized the motto: "kill the Indian save the man". This motto served as the guiding principle for the new institutions spreading throughout North America. These were veritable factories for the systematic destruction of kinship practices. Not only was intimate relationality deracinated in these brutal experiments – which naturally began with the interdiction on indigenous languages, dances, and other key rituals which, in turn, became important modes of resistance – but the very basis for political subjectivation was eviscerated. These were institutions designed to produce isolation through violent repression. In actuality, they were nothing more than labs of torture justified by the specious development of onto-political pedagogical sciences. As discussed through the work of Elaine Scarry in Chapter 1, it was here, on the bodies of indigenous people that the state made its sovereignty known, destroying consciousness of anything except pain in an attempt to rebuild the subject in the guise of a "rational westerner". This marked the extreme distillation of the logic of the settler state that goes as deep as the systematic destruction of the conditions for the possibility of non-proprietary kinship practices still active today. It is justified by the rationalization of capitalist expansion in tandem with technological acceleration seeping into the pores of psychic and social life, its ultimate *telos* realized in genocide, ontocide, ecocide, and eventually extinction.

Approaching a Politics of Intimacy

This brings us back to the previous considerations. That is the relationship between extraction – dispossession – and inscrutable modes of solidarity. The more "the family" is projected into the past and utilized as a gauge for social and psychic health, the more real histories of alternative forms of relating are repressed or denied, and the less likely it might be to recover the past. Much like the sentiment expressed by Margaret Mead, discussed in Chapter 3, with regard to resistance to such practices, Nick Estes writes (in reference to indigenous forms of resistance):

> By drawing upon earlier struggles and incorporating elements of them into their own experience, each generation continues to build dynamic and vital traditions of resistance. Such collective experiences build over time and are grounded in specific Indigenous territories and nations.[75]

In their revolutionary exposition *Red Nation Rising: From Bordertown Violence to Native American Liberation*, the members of the Bordertown Violence Working Group note: "Native kinship relations are still alive and strong, if not always in practice, then in the imagination of Native revolutionaries seeking to end the exploitation, extraction, and dispossession of Native life that drives the moral economy of bordertowns".[76] What constitutes images, memories, and practices of kinship? "Personal dignity, equality, freedom and autonomy, fraternity, matriarchy, and the absence of poverty".[77] Exactly those practices and relations that so astonished and impressed Lewis Henry Morgan when he observed the Haudenosaunee communities – despite, of course, his reflexive use of these observations in perpetuating the settler colonial narrative.

> Mni Wiconi, "water is life", relates to Wotakuye, or "being a good relative". Indigenous resistance to the trespass of settlers, pipelines, and dams is part of being a good relative to the water, land, and animals, not to mention the human world.[78]

As Estes notes further, this goes directly against another form of relation which seeks to draw profit from the land and life – the quintessential expression of necropolitics. Not only must we look to the practices and relations of indigenous pasts and present, that practiced a non-humanistic form of kinship, one that sought to nourish the land and life, as Silvia Federici reminds us, we find "a conception of people's relation to property and the land that still nourishes our imagination" but also we must not just acknowledge new forms of communal and collective living that both borrow from pasts and auger new forms of life for the future, the imperative must be to radically change the dominant political ontology, to recast kinship, for example, as a foundation for communes and autonomous zones, food and medical production, and distribution of many kinds and degrees, as frames of resistance and association that found ways to recast political life, to generate new ground beyond the ruins of the near future, as we continue, for now to "hang in the abyss".

Notes

1 Martin Heidegger, "What Are Poets For?," in *Poetry, Language Thought*, trans, Albert Hofstadter (New York: Harper Perennial, 2001).
2 Silvia Federici, *Re-enchanting the World Feminism and the Politics of the Commons* (Oakland, CA: PM Press, 2019) 29.
3 Karl Marx, *Capital vol. 1* (New York: Penguin Books, 1990) 899.
4 Hegel, *Elements of the Philosophy of Right*, trans. H.B. Nisbet (New York: Cambridge University Press, 2014) 247.
5 G.W.F. Hegel, "Natural Right and Political Science," Heidelberg, 1817–1818, in *Lectures on Natural Right and Political Philosophy, The First Philosophy of Right*, trans. J. Michael Stewart and Peter C. Hodgson (Oxford: Oxford Un. Press) 17, 134.
6 Hegel, *Elements*, 158, I changed just one word in Wood's translation. I substituted *immense*, which he uses to translate *ungeheuer* to *monstrous*. Also, Hegel follows this with the comment that the law intervenes only with the dissolution of the family, this has to do with the child growing up and entering the world of economy, inheritance and the marriage of the next generation. He also identifies the three aspects that complete the family.

   a) Marriage as the immediate shape of the concept of the family.
   b) Externality through property and possession as well as household management.
   c) Upbringing and "the dissolution of the family". (Ibid., 159–160).

7 "Hapticality, the capacity to feel though others, for others to feel through you, for you to feel them feeling you, this feel of the shipped is not regulated, at least not successfully, by a state, a religion, a people, an empire, a piece of land, a totem." Stephano Harney and Fred Moten, *The Undercommons: Fugitive Planning and Black Study* (Brooklyn: Minor Compositions, 2013) 98.

8 Hegel, *Elements*, 158, also see 159–160.

9 Hegel, *Elements*, 158, I changed just one word in Wood's translation. I substituted *immense*, which he uses to translate *ungeheuer* (which is simply wrong), to *monstrous*. Also, Hegel follows this with the comment that the law intervenes only with the dissolution of the family, this has to do with the child growing up and entering the world of economy, inheritance and the marriage of the next generation. He also identifies the three aspects that complete the family.

d) Marriage as the immediate shape of the concept of the family.
e) Externality through property and possession as well as household management.
f) Upbringing and "the dissolution of the family". (Ibid., 159–160).

10 Ibid., 263.

11 Ibid., 263.

12 David Ciavatta, *Spirit, the Family, and the Unconscious in Hegel's Philosophy* (Albany, NY: SUNY Press, 2010) 3.

13 But the ethical consciousness is more complete, its guilt more pure, if it knows beforehand the law and the power it confronts, if it takes them to be violence and wrong, to be an ethical contingency, and, like Antigone, knowingly commits the crime. The accomplished deed reverses its view; the very accomplishment declares that what is ethical must be actual; for the actuality of the purpose is the purpose of acting. Acting immediately declares the unity of actuality and substance, it declares that actuality is not contingent for the essence, but that, in union with the essence, it is not granted to any right that is not true right. Hegel, *Phenomenology*, 470.

14 Ciavatta, *Spirit*, 2.

15 "The sexual contract is a repressed dimension of contract theory. An integral part of the rational choice of the familiar, original agreement." More specifically, in Hegel's apparent critique of the contractarian notion of marriage, she rightly notes: "Hegel rejects the keystone of contract theory, the idea of the individual as owner. He also rejects the contractarian idea of social life as nothing but contract all the way down. On these issues, he is the most profound critic of contract. However, Hegel's arguments are fatally compromised by his acceptance of the sexual contract. In order to incorporate women into civil society while excluding them, Hegel re-enacts the contradictions in Kant's theories." Carol Pateman, *The Sexual Contract* (Stanford, CA: Stanford University Press, 1988) ix and 173.

16 Ciavatta, *Spirit*, 2.

17 Ibid., 5.

18 Ibid., 5.

19 Ibid., 5.

20 Hegel, *Elements*, 158.

21 Ciavatte, *Spirit*, 6.

22 Hegel, "Natural Right and Political Science," 83.

23 Ibid., 83.

24 G.W.F. Hegel, *Outlines of the Philosophy of Right*, trans, Stephen Houlgate (Oxford: Oxford University Press, 2011) 269 (italics mine).

25 "[P]atriotism ... is that disposition which, in the normal conditions and circumstances of life, habitually knows that the community is the substantial basis and end." Hegel, *Elements*, 268. And in *the addition* to that same paragraph, it is noted: "They

trust that the state will continue to exist [*bestehen*] and that particular interests can be fulfilled within it alone; but habit blinds us to the basis of our entire existence [*Existenz*]."

26 Hegel, "Natural Right and Political Science," see 84.

27 Hegel, *Elements*, 238.

28 Ibid., 238.

29 Ibid., 234.

30 Herbert Marcuse, *Reason and Revolution: Hegel and the Rise of Social Theory* (Amherst: Humanity Books, 1999), 203–204. "But all these features of the family are only realized in that the center around which all features of the family are grouped in Hegel: in the specific relationship between *family* and *property*. The family not only has its 'external reality' in property, but also the existence of its 'substantial personality'. Only in and through the family is property transformed from the 'arbitrary expression of a particular need' to a 'permanent and secure asset', and the 'selfishness of greed' is transformed into something ethical, into labor and care for a common possession." Ibid., 62.

31 The family disintegrates in a natural manner and essentially through the principle of personality, into a plurality of families whose relation to one another is in general that of self-sufficient concrete persons and is consequently of an external kind. In other words, the moments, which are bound together in the unity of the family as the ethical idea, which is still in its concept, must be released from the concept to achieve self-sufficient reality. This is the stage of difference. Hegel, *Elements of the Philosophy of Right*, 219.

32 Marcuse, *Reason and Revolution*, 203–204. But all these features of the family are only realized in that the center around which all features of the family are grouped in Hegel: in the specific relationship between *family* and *property*. The family not only has its "external reality" in property, but also the existence of its "substantial personality". Only in and through the family is property transformed from the "arbitrary expression of a particular need" to a "permanent and secure asset", and the "selfishness of greed" is transformed into something ethical, into labor and care for a common possession. Ibid., 62.

33 Hegel, *Elements*, 261.

34 Lawrence Krader puts it nicely: Because the state was not made the dependent of society by Hegel in this connection, he did not interpose the dialectic of contradiction of interest and counterposition of forces into the structure of society and the atate; Hegel fell therefore into the contradiction of the non-actuality of the immanent, and the non-potentiality of the external. The contradiction is not overcome because no transition between them was indicated by Hegel. (Lawrence Krader (ed.), "Introduction," in *The Ethnological Notebooks of Karl Marx* (Assen, NL: Van) 65.

35 Joanna Hodge, "Queering Hegel," in *Hegel's Philosophy and Feminist Thought*, edited by K. Hutchings and T. Pulkkinen (New York: Palgrave, 2010) 49–50 and footnote 17. Eric Weil, *Hegel and the State*, trans. Mark A Cohen (Baltimore, MD: Johns Hopkins University Press, 1998) 120.

36 Karl Marx, "Critique of Hegel's Doctrine of the State," in *Early Writings*, trans. Rodney Livingston and Gregor Benton (London: Penguin, 1992) 59–60.

37 Rosa Luxemburg, *The Accumulation of Capital* (New York: Routledge, 2003) 328.

38 Jackie Wang, *Carceral Capitalism* (Cambridge: Semiotext(e)) 100.

39 Karl Marx, *Capital, vol. 1*, 125–131.

40 Luxemburg, *Accumulation*, 349.

41 However, if we are open to the claims of such thinkers as Rosa Luxemburg and David Harvey, that capitalism has a dual character, then it becomes possible to analyze how these two axes – one that homogenizes, the other that differentiates – operate simultaneously. If the exploitation axis is characterized by the homogenizing wage relation (insofar as it produces worker-subjects who have nothing to sell but their labor-power),

then the axis of expropriation relies on a logic of differentiation that reproduces racialized (as well as gendered) subjects. Jackie Wang, *Carceral Capitalism* (Los Angeles, CA: Semiotext(e), 2018) 101.

42 Karl Marx, *Capital vol. 1*, 293.

43 A fascinating and excellent analysis of the control and destruction of women's communal activities and of women's bodies can be found in Silvia Federici, *Caliban and the Witch: Women, the Body and Primitive Accumulation* (Brooklyn: Autonomedia, 2014).

44 Luxemburg, *Accumulation*, 343.

45 Marx, *Capital vol. 1*, 873.

46 Ibid., 874.

47 Concentration meaning increasing production/exploitation and centralization having to do with redistributing wealth to the top mainly through debt, taxes and rent increases. The latter is often associated with the recent shift from industrial to finance capitalism. See Marx, *Capital, vol. 1*, 779.

48 Luxemburg, *Accumulation*, 447.

49 Luce Irigaray, *The Sex Which is not One* (Ithaca, NY: Cornell University Press, 1985), 17.

50 Hegel, *Elements*, 245.

51 As Allen Wood explains: "Hegel holds that poverty and the rabble mentality are systematic products of civil society, but he does not pretend that civil society has any remedy for the ills it creates." Allen Wood, "Introduction," *Elements* xxi.

52 Frank Ruda, *Hegel's Rabble* (New York: Bloomsbury, 2011) 114.

53 Ibid., 114.

54 As Jacques Rancière notes: "the police is the regime of identity and the calculus of identities, the symbolic constitution of a society as a set of defined and identifiable groups." The police, in other words, is opposed to the political, understood as the act of political subjectivation, the manifestation of a "we". Resistance to distributive enforcement is activated, for Rancière, through disincorporation, i.e. through the rejection of the aesthetic distribution of identities that predicates the state. A political configuration in which the structure of authority is incontrovertibly upheld by wealth, implied in its monopoly on violence, the problem of poverty – i.e. the necessity of poverty – marks a point of contradiction. *A Politics of Aesthetic Indetermination: An Interview with Frank Ruda & Jan Voelker* 25.

55 See Jackie Wang, *Carceral Capitalism* (Los Angeles, CA: Semiotext(e), 2018) 14–15. Another example from the infamous police department of Ferguson where Black households were strapped by "fines, fees, citations, tickets, and arrests to such an extent that the revenues were the town's second leading source of revenue, accounting for 'the equivalent of more than 81 percent of the police salaries before overtime.'" Failure to pay led to immediate arrest, with 16,000 outstanding arrest warrants, mostly for misdemeanors. These fines paid for one-third of the city's municipal budget! See "Black Lives Matter: A Movement Not a Moment" in Keeanga-Yamahtt Taylor, *From #Black Lives Matter to Black Liberation* (Chicago, IL: Haymarket Books, 2016) 155.

56 Katherine Stevenson, "Profiting off of Prison Labor," Businessreview.berkeley.edu

57 Nick Estes, Melanie K. Yazzie, Jennifer Nez Denetdale, and David Correia, *Red Nation Rising: From Bordertown Violence to Native Liberation* (Oakland, CA: PM Press, 2021), 113.

58 Marx, *Capital, vol. 1*, 898.

59 The 13th amendment states: "Neither slavery not involuntary servitude, except as a punishment for a crime hereof the party shall have been duly convicted, shall exist within the United States, or any place subject to their jurisdiction." See also Michelle Alexander, *The New Jim Crow: Mass Incarceration in the Age of Colorblindness* (New York: The New Press, 2012) 1–19.

60 Luxemburg, *Accumulation*, 339.

61 Also, he notes: "Any social formation or territory that is brought or inserts itself into the logic of capitalist development must undergo wide-ranging structural, institutional, and legal changes of the sort that Marx describes under the rubric of primitive accumulation. The collapse of the Soviet Union posed exactly this problem. The result was a savage episode of primitive accumulation under the heading of 'shock therapy' as advised by the capitalist powers and international institutions." David Harvey, *New Imperialism* (Oxford: Oxford University Press, 2003) 141–143 and 153.

62 Hegel, *Elements*, 246.

63 Ibid., 248.

64 Luxemburg, *Accumulation*, 348.

65 Ibid., 350.

66 Ibid., 338.

67 Ibid., 351.

68 The Red Nation points out that the 2016 Standing Rock resistance was just one of a "constellation of Indigenous-led uprisings across North America and the UD-occupied Pacific: Dooda Desert Rock (2006), Unist'ot'en Camp (2010), Keystone XL (2011), Idle No More (2012), Trans Mountain (2013), Enbridge Line 3 (2014), Protect Mauna Kea (2014), Sve Oak Flat (2015), Nihilaal Bee Iiná (2015), Bayou Bridge (2017), O'odham Anti-Border Collective (2019), Kumeyaay Defense Against the Wall (2020), and 1492 Land Back Line (2020), among many more." (The Red Nation, *The Red Deal*, 7).

69 https://www.theguardian.com/us-news/2021/jun/04/minnesota-pipeline-line-3-sexual-women-violence. Just to note this is only one of the series of recent Indigenous initiated uprisings in North America.

70 https://www.vice.com/en/article/4avp3w/an-oil-company-paid-police-dollar2-million-to-defend-its-pipeline-from-protests (accessed 26 August 2021).

71 "Over the last 200 years, the US military has waged relentless war on the Oceti Sakowin as much as it has on their kinship relations, such as Pte Oyate (the buffalo nation) and Mni Sose (the Missouri River). What happened at Standing Rock was the most recent iteration of an Indian War that never ends." Estes, *Our History*, 10.

72 For example, in 1889, the United States government violated the 1868 Fort Laramie Treaty by breaking up the Sioux Nation and enforcing private property laws. See *Standing Rock Syllabus*, timeline page 10. Also see E. Tuck and K.W. Lang, "Decolonization Is not a Metaphor," *Decolonization: Indigeneity, Education & Society* 1, no. 1 (2012). The authors note: "For the settlers, Indigenous peoples are in the way and, in the destruction of Indigenous peoples, Indigenous communities, and over time and through law and policy, Indigenous peoples' claims to land under settler regimes, land is recast as property and as a resource. Indigenous peoples must be erased, must be made into ghosts. At the same time, settler colonialism involves the subjugation and forced labor of chattel slaves, whose bodies and lives become the property, and who are kept landless." Ibid., 6. It should also be noted that the determination of private property according to individual ownership necessarily leads to the atrophy of communal property as lack of heirs, along with individual debt, often leads to land ceded to the state or bank and then the market. This has been an ongoing problem endemic to forcing the concept of privatization on indigenous communes.

73 Estes, Yazzie, Denetdale, Correia, *Red Nation Rising*, 97–99.

74 Ibid., 98.

75 Nick Estes, *Our History is the Future: Standing Rock versus the Dakota Access Pipeline, and the Long Tradition of Indigenous Resistance* (Brooklyn: Verso, 2019) 21. The Margaret Mead quote was: "There may be human potentialities which date far back in evolutionary time for which new artificially created conditions may find a new use. Quoted in Sarah Blaffer Hrdy, *Mothers and Others: The Evolutionary Origins of Mutual Understanding* (Cambridge, MA: Harvard University Press, 2009) 143.

76 Estes, Yazzie, Denetdale, Correia. *Red Nation Rising*, 117.

77 Ibid., 117.
78 Estes, *Our History*, 21.

Bibliography

David Ciavatta. *Spirit, the Family, and the Unconscious in Hegel's Philosophy*. Albany, NY: SUNY Press, 2010.

Nick Estes. *Our History is the Future: Standing Rock Versus the Dakota Access Pipeline, and the Long Tradition of Indigenous Resistance*. Brooklyn, NY: Verso, 2019.

Nick Estes, Melanie K. Yazzie, Jennifer Nez Denetdale, David Correia. *Red Nation Rising: From Bordertown Violence to Native Liberation*. Oakland, CA: PM Press, 2021.

Silvia Federici. *Caliban and the Witch: Women, the Body and Primitive Accumulation*. Brooklyn, NY: Autonomedia, 2014.

Silvia Federici. *Re-enchanting the World Feminism and the Politics of the Commons*. Oakland, CA: PM Press, 2019.

David Harvey. *New Imperialism*. Oxford: Oxford University Press, 2003.

G.W.F. Hegel. *Elements of the Philosophy of Right*. Translated by H.B. Nisbet. New York: Cambridge University Press, 2014.

G.W.F. Hegel. "Natural Right and Political Science." Heidelberg, 1817–1818. In *Lectures on Natural Right and Political Philosophy, The First Philosophy of Right*, translated by J. Michael Stewart and Peter C. Hodgson. Oxford: Oxford University Press, 2012.

G.W.F. Hegel. *Outlines of the Philosophy of Right*. Translated by Stephen Houlgate. Oxford: Oxford University Press, 2011.

Martin Heidegger. "What are Poets For?" In *Poetry, Language Thought*, translated by Albert Hofstadter. New York: Harper Perennial, 2001.

Joanna Hodge. "Queering Hegel." In *Hegel's Philosophy and Feminist Thought*, edited by Hutchings, K. and Pulkkinen, Tuija. New York: Palgrave, 2010.

Sarah Blaffer Hrdy. "Mothers and Others." *The Evolutionary Origins of Mutual Understanding*. Cambridge, MA: Harvard University Press, 2009.

https://www.theguardian.com/us-news/2021/jun/04/minnesota-pipeline-line-3-sexual-women-violence

https://www.vice.com/en/article/4avp3w/an-oil-company-paid-police-dollar2-million-to-defend-its-pipeline-from-protests

Luce Irigaray. *The Sex Which is Not One*. Ithaca, NY: Cornell University Press, 1985.

Lawrence Krader. "Introduction." In *The Ethnological Notebooks of Karl Marx*. Assen, the Netherlands: Van.

Rosa Luxemburg. *The Accumulation of Capital*. New York: Routledge, 2003.

Herbert Marcuse. *Reason and Revolution: Hegel and the Rise of Social Theory*. Amherst: Humanity Books, 1999.

Karl Marx. *Capital vol. 1*. New York: Penguin Books, 1990.

Karl Marx. "Critique of Hegel's doctrine of the state." In *Early Writings*. London: Penguin, 1992.

John G. Neihardt. *Black Elk Speaks*. Lincoln and London: University of Nebraska Press, 1979.

Carol Pateman. *The Sexual Contract*. Stanford, CA: Stanford University Press, 1988.

Frank Ruda. *Hegel's Rabble*. New York: Bloomsbury, 2011.

Keeanga-Yamahtt Taylor. *From #Black Lives Matter to Black Liberation*. Chicago, IL: Haymarket Books, 2016.

E. Tuck and K. W. Lang. "Decolonization is not a metaphor." *Decolonization: Indigeneity, Education & Society* 1, no. 1 (2012): 1–40.

Jackie Wang. *Carceral Capitalism.* Los Angeles, CA: Semiotext(e), 2018.

Eric Weil. *Hegel and the State.* Translated by Mark A. Cohen. Baltimore, MD: Johns Hopkins University Press, 1998.

https://www.theguardian.com/us-news/2021/jun/04/minnesota-pipeline-line-3-sexual -women-violence

https://www.vice.com/en/article/4avp3w/an-oil-company-paid-police-dollar2-million-to -defend-its-pipeline-from-protests

Index

Note: Page numbers with "n" indicates the end notes in the text.